On the Road to Lost Fathers: Jack Kerouac in a Lacanian Perspective

NEW AMERICANISTS IN POLAND

Edited by Tomasz Basiuk

Volume 10

Tomasz Sawczuk

On the Road to Lost Fathers: Jack Kerouac in a Lacanian Perspective

PETER LANG

Bibliographic Information published by the Deutsche Nationalbibliothek
The Deutsche Nationalbibliothek lists this publication
in the Deutsche Nationalbibliografie; detailed bibliographic
data is available in the internet at http://dnb.d-nb.de.

This publication was financially supported
by the University of Białystok

ISSN 2191-2254
ISBN 978-3-631-77347-5 (Print)
E-ISBN 978-3-631-78681-9 (E-PDF)
E-ISBN 978-3-631-78682-6 (EPUB)
E-ISBN 978-3-631-78683-3 (MOBI)
DOI 10.3726/b15487

Peter Lang – Berlin · Bern · Bruxelles · New York ·
Oxford · Warszawa · Wien

This publication has been peer reviewed.

www.peterlang.com

For my daughter, Oliwia

Contents

Acknowledgments

This book would not have happened were it not for a number of people whose knowledge, kindness, patience, and support were of immense value and helped me to bring the project to a successful close. I would like to express my deepest gratitude to my supervisor, Professor Zbigniew Maszewski, whose continuous guidance and a careful critical eye were kindly shared with me all along the process of writing. I remain grateful to Professor Marek Paryż and Professor Jacek Gutorow for their valuable suggestions and insightful reviews of my doctoral thesis, which became the basis for this book. I owe many thanks to people who, for many years now, have been to me true mentors in the field of Beat studies: Professor A. Robert Lee, who has been always there to lend me a hand with his expert knowledge and Andrzej Pietrasz, with whom countless hours have been spent discussing the Beats. The book would not be possible without the scholarship received from the Clifford and Mary Corbridge Trust of Robinson College in the University of Cambridge. It truly boosted my research efforts and allowed me to consult my ideas with Dr. Michael Hrebeniak, whom I would also like to thank. Finally, I wish to thank my family: my wife Monika, my parents, my mother-in-law and my brother. I owe so much to their love, encouragement and ongoing support.

This publication has received financial support from the Polish Ministry of Science and Higher Education under subsidy granted to the Faculty of Philology, University of Bialystok for R&D and related tasks aimed at development of young scientists and PhD students.

Parts of Chapter 5 appeared in "Painting a Friend, Un-painting the World: on Some Aspects of Visuality in Jack Kerouac's Visions of Cody" in Z. Maszewski, W. Łaszkiewicz, and T. Sawczuk (eds.), *Visuality and Vision in American Literature* (Białystok: Białystok University Press, 2014) and portions of Chapter 7 were published as "Longing for What (Never) Was: Jack Kerouac and the Nostalgic Subject in a Lacanian Perspective" in Z. Maszewski, W. Łaszkiewicz and J. Partyka (eds.), *Nostalgia in North-American Literature and Culture* (Cambridge: CSP, 2016).

List of Abbreviations

Jack Kerouac

BOD	Kerouac, Jack. *Book of Dreams*. San Francisco: City Lights Books, 2001. Print.
BS	Kerouac, Jack. *Big Sur*. London: Harper Perennial, 2006. Print.
DA	Kerouac, Jack. *Desolation Angels*. London: Granada, 1982. Print.
DC	Kerouac, Jack. *Dear Carolyn: Letters to Carolyn Cassady*. Eds. Arthur W. Knight and Kit Knight. California, PA: A. and K. Knight, 1983. Print.
EOSP	Kerouac, Jack. "Essentials of Spontaneous Prose." *The Center for Programs in Contemporary Writing*. The University of Pennsylvania, n.d. Web. 5 Apr 2012.
KLW	Kerouac, Jack. *Kerouac's Last Word: Jack Kerouac in Escapade*. Ed. Tom Clark. Sudbury, Mass: Water Row Press, 1986. Print.
OTR	Kerouac, Jack. *On the Road*. London: Penguin Books, 1998. Print.
OTR: OS	Kerouac, Jack, *On the Road: The Original Scroll*. New York: Viking, 2007. Print.
SIP	Kerouac, Jack. *Satori in Paris and Pic: Two Novels*. New York: Grove Press, 1988. Print.
SL1	Kerouac, Jack. *Selected Letters, 1940–1956*. Ed. Ann Charters. New York: Viking, 1995. Print.
SL2	Kerouac, Jack. *Selected Letters, 1957–1969*. Ed. Ann Charters. New York: Viking, 1999. Print.
T	Kerouac, Jack. *Tristessa*. New York: Penguin Books, 1992. Print.
TS	Kerouac Jack, *The Subterraneans*. New York: Grove Press, 2007. Print.
TTATC	Kerouac, Jack. *The Town and the City*. London: Penguin books, 2000. Print.
VOC	Kerouac Jack, *Visions of Cody*. London: Flamingo/HarperCollins, 1995. Print.
VOD	Kerouac Jack, *Vanity of Duluoz*. London: Paladin, 1990. Print.
VOG	Kerouac, Jack. *Visions of Gerard*. New York: McGraw-Hill, 1976. Print.
WW	Kerouac, Jack. *Windblown World: The Journals of Jack Kerouac, 1947–1954*. Ed. Douglas Brinkley. New York: Viking, 2004. Print.

Jacques Lacan

E: AS Lacan, Jacques. *Écrits: A Selection.* Trans. Alan Sheridan. London: Routledge, 2005. Print.

Écrits Lacan, Jacques. *Écrits: The First Complete Edition in English.* Trans. Bruce Fink. New York: W.W. Norton & Co, 2006. Print.

S I Lacan, Jacques, *The Seminar of Jacques Lacan: Book I.* Ed. Jacques-Alain Miller. Trans. John Forrester. New York, N.Y: W.W. Norton, 1991. Print.

S II Lacan, Jacques. *The Seminar of Jacques Lacan: Book II: the Ego in Freud's Theory and in the Technique of Psychoanalysis, 1954–1955.* Ed. Jacques-Alain Miller. Trans. John Forrester. New York: Norton, 1988. Print.

S III Lacan, Jacques. *The Seminar of Jacques Lacan: Book III: the Psychoses, 1955–1956.* Ed. Jacques-Alain Miller. Trans. Russell Grigg. London: Routledge, 1993. Print.

S V Lacan, Jacques. *The Seminar of Jacques Lacan Book V: The Formations of the Unconscious 1957–1958*, unpublished translation by Cormac Gallagher.

S VII Lacan, Jacques. *The Seminar of Jacques Lacan, Book VII.* Ed. Jacques-Alain Miller. Trans. Dennis Porter. New York, N.Y: W.W. Norton, 1997. Print.

S X Lacan, Jacques. *The Seminar of Jacques Lacan Book X: Anxiety 1962–1963*, unpublished translation by Cormac Gallagher.

S XI Lacan, Jacques. *The Seminar of Jacques Lacan Book XI: The Four Fundamental Concepts of Psychoanalysis.* Ed. Jacques-Alain Miller. Trans. Alan Sheridan. New York, N.Y: Norton and Company, 1998. Print.

S XIV Lacan, Jacques. *The Seminar of Jacques Lacan Book XIV: The Logic of Fantasy, 1966–1967*, unpublished translation by Cormac Gallagher.

S XVII Lacan, Jacques. *The Seminar of Jacques Lacan Book XVII: The Other Side of Psychoanalysis 1969–1970.* Ed. Jacques-Alain Miller. Trans. Russell Grigg. New York: Norton, 2007. Print.

S XX Lacan, Jacques. *The Seminar of Jacques Lacan Book XX: On Feminine Sexuality, The Limits of Love and Knowledge: Encore 1972–1973.* Ed. Jacques-Alain Miller. Trans. Bruce Fink. New York: Norton, 1999. Print.

S XXII Lacan, Jacques. *The Seminar of Jacques Lacan: Seminar XXII, R. S. I., 1974 - 1975*, unpublished translation by Cormac Gallagher.

Introduction

The book is a modest attempt to bring close the apparently incompatible worlds of the Beat Generation writer, Jack Kerouac, and the French psychoanalyst, Jacques Lacan, with a view to finding points of convergence between the standpoints which at first glance could be easily recognized as mutually exclusive. The unemotional, baroque, gnomic, elitist, and anti-metaphysical works of Lacan offer surprisingly much when confronted with the passionate, sentimental, democratic, and spiritual poetics of Kerouac. What is perhaps accountable for diminishing the cultural as well as geographical distance between the two figures, and their respective milieux, is their prime focus on the problem of language; both Kerouac and Lacan perceived it as the carrier of one's unconscious as well as a means supporting one's coming to terms with traumatic experiences. Both were highly distrustful as regards the shape of American institutional psychoanalysis. Finally, a rapprochement between the French Freud and the Beat writer seems all the more invited in the surge of critical strategies currently recognized in the fields of the Beat studies and Lacanian literary criticism. These areas have acknowledged, respectively, the necessity of breaking the confines of the American context and the need to reverse the process of elucidating literary works with psychoanalysis. It is here that I would like to locate my attempt to offer a comprehensive insight into the correspondences between Kerouac, his body of work, and (Lacanian) psychoanalysis as well as to investigate if Kerouac's textual strategies might be revealing for Lacanian criticism.

While, as I indicate in Chapter Three, various scholars have produced Lacanian readings of William S. Burroughs, Gary Snyder, as well as other established American writers, Jack Kerouac has been somehow missing in the picture.[1] The existing body of Kerouac studies already includes the use of psychoanalytic theories, yet it is as much beneficial as problematic. A number of critics have found psychoanalysis to be valuable in understanding and interpreting the American

1 The possibly only Lacanian remarks made by a scholar to comment on Kerouac's works were Michael Hrebeniak's passing comment on Kerouac's active method of creation being a superimposition of modernist methods of triggering the unconscious understood as Lacanian signifying chains (see Hrebeniak 163) as well as Thomas R. Bierowski's brief mention of Lacan on the occasion of investigating into the confessional style of Leo Percepied from *The Subterraneans* (see Bierowski 108).

writer's works, somehow revealing the potential locked within.[2] On the other hand, having adopted classical Freudian way of psychoanalytic interpretation, many scholars fell into the trap of providing a now longtime-discredited psychobiography, which seemed alluring inasmuch as Kerouac performed what is now often termed as life-writing, yet which ended up a forceful and harmful application of already-preconceived psychoanalytic matrix onto the person of the author. Such is the case of a major Freudian psychoanalytic study of Jack Kerouac's oeuvre, which is James T. Jones's *Jack Kerouac's Duluoz Legend: The Mythic Form of an Autobiographical Fiction* (1999). Notwithstanding its comprehensive, often-insightful and groundbreaking character, the study, as many critics pointed out, is clearly problematic and controversial. In the most general view, Jones's thesis revolves around the idea that creating the Duluoz Legend, a unified collection of several novels covering the writer's entire life, was a means allowing Kerouac to sublimate his Oedipal longings. As posited by the scholar, the death of two father figures, his older brother Gerard and his father Leo, engendered Kerouac's incestuous desire for his mother, which resulted in guilt and the need to rework it in the form of as much autobiographical as mythical fiction. The subsequent installments of the Duluoz Legend present, in Jones's eyes, various modes of coping with and recapitulating the Oedipus complex. Ordering Kerouac's works according to the years they cover, Jones begins his argument with *Visions of Gerard* and *Dr. Sax*, positing that the former depicts the brother rivalry for their mother while the latter, with the mythical descriptions of flood destroying the city and the mythical snake being slayed, stands for the retreat of Kerouac's father and hints at the writer achieving sexual maturity, which involves Oedipal longings. Moving further, the scholar discusses *The Town and the City* together with *Vanity of Duluoz*, which mostly cover the same time period and, with their heavy focus on the figures of father and brother, might be an inversion of Kerouac's love for his mother (Jones, *The Mythic Form* 82). Next, *Pic*, *On the Road*, and *Visions of Cody* constitute a triptych of inevitability of fate, which boils down to repetitions of Oedipal motifs and Kerouac, the son, becoming Kerouac, the father. Dealing further with *Maggie Cassidy*, *The Subterraneans* and *Tristessa*, Jones draws one's attention to the Oedipal triangles which seem to be *modus operandi* of each of these works. Chapter Six is a discussion of *The Dharma*

2 Some critics have openly called for a psychoanalytic criticism for Kerouac's works; see Stefano Maffina's *The Role of Jack Kerouac's Identity in the Development of his Poetics*, where the scholar refers to the psychoanalytic charge of *On the Road*, *Big Sur*, and *Book of Dreams*, 59–62.

Bums and *Desolation Angels*, which, in Jones's opinion, show finding temporary solace in Buddhism, yet eventually, are the sign of Kerouac finally accepting his Oedipal curse and the necessity of being a companion for his mother. *Book of Dreams* is consequently read as the atonement of Oedipal sins, and finally, *Big Sur* and *Satori in Paris* are meant to be an honest, Catholic act of confession, which absolves the writer's sins and torments. What is striking about Jones's work and has been disapproved of are its simplistic attempts of oedipalizing and psychoanalyzing the writer by drawing on his fiction. Autobiographical as Kerouac's oeuvre undoubtedly is, it puts one at risk of merging fact and fiction, which Jones is believed to have practiced and which has remained unclear to some of the scholars.[3]

Other Freudian commentators on Kerouac include Regina Weinreich, who devotes a short passage of her *The Spontaneous Poetics of Jack Kerouac: A Study of the Fiction* (1987) to point to the relation between Sal Paradise and Dean Moriarty from *On the Road* as a displaced one between a son and a father, or two brothers (Weinreich 38). Brendon Nicholls sees Kerouac's project of the Duluoz Legend as founded on a certain longing for a "brown/ black female body" (Nicholls 524–549), which is ultimately correlated to racially mythicized and fetishized figures of the mother and motherland. Nicholls opens up for Freudian terminology, mainly the notion of castration, to elucidate the fetishism prompted by the charm of racial difference, as believed by him, originating in one of Kerouac's early experiences. Another important contribution (the more important inasmuch as it was published in *Psychoanalytic Review*) is that of Gladys Foxe offering a psychoanalytic insight into the creation of *On the Road* and seeing the novel as the aftermath of Kerouac's war trauma. Foxe's article is by no means a rigorous reading of the novel, but rather a set of loose reflections, yet it remains significant as it inquires the ways *On the Road* could be meaningful and telling for the psychoanalytic clinic (57). Kerouac's most famous novel was also viewed through the prism of Freud's theory of the uncanny so as to prove its textual performativity of whiteness (Trudeau 149–168). Finally, Kerouac's prose has been the subject of Jungian literary criticism, which is the case of James T. Jones and his essay on the image of "the Shrouded Stranger" appearing in both Kerouac's and Ginsberg's works. The scholar suggests that the Beat writers' inclusion of the shadow figure into their literary work was a sign of their attempts at

---

3 Here, I draw on Robert Holton's review of the book (see Holton, 499–501) and on my private correspondence with prof. A. Robert Lee.

blending their private demons into the collective archetype and, by doing so, retaining psychic and social stability (Jones, "Sharing a Shadow" 223–241).

Having looked at the above-mentioned studies, all of them being undoubtedly valuable and insightful yet somehow a mosaic treatment of the subject matter, it thus appears that Kerouac's oeuvre calls for a comprehensive psychoanalytic reading. To stop at this, however, would be not enough and, in the first place, one must call for a *different* psychoanalytic reading; the one which, in the spirit of modern psychoanalytic criticism, would consider the following needs. First, it would need to withdraw its claims for a psychobiography in order to redirect and invest its theories in the literature itself with a carefully balanced referencing to the writer's life. As the second point, it should be capable of such looking at a literary text so that it would be revealing for the theory itself. As arguably the most pertinent and developed form of psychoanalytic literary criticism up to date, the Lacanian body of work fits perfectly well to serve such tasks, the more interesting a challenge as it has never been put in a constellation with Kerouac. What is more, Kerouac studies strongly invite a thorough Lacanian reading since the key themes of lack, loss, trauma, self-estrangement, and the intricacies of literary works arisen thereof, remain in close bond with the very root of the Lacanian thought. In addition, as this book will hopefully prove, Lacan is not only a silent partner to the American writer's works, but also to his substantial criticism voiced at the shape of institutional psychoanalysis that emerged in the middle of the twentieth-century America. Therefore, the following Lacanian reading of Kerouac is threefold, offering a fresh insight into the writer's literary oeuvre, his non-fiction writings, and the culture of the twentieth-century United States.

Chapter One, "The Development of Psychoanalysis in the United States," aims at investigating into the major events of and the rationale behind the development of psychoanalytic thought on the American soil (including the place of Lacan) in order to furnish the cultural background for and have a better understanding of Jack Kerouac's personal approach to psychoanalysis, which shall be the focus of Chapter Four. Kerouac, as well as other Beat writers, could not have evaded the immense influence of psychoanalytic thought. As it is argued by Burnham, "[b]y the mid-twentieth century, Freud's ideas had become a conspicuous – indeed, unavoidable – part of the American cultural landscape" ("Introduction" 3). Elizabeth Lunbeck adds that, regardless of all the controversies and perturbations it underwent, psychoanalysis in America

> has arguably enjoyed the greatest purchase, the most far-reaching cultural influence, the most powerful institutional instantiations – its bleak pessimism and patently un-American severity notwithstanding. (2012, 209)

As a powerful and wide-ranging medium of cultural influence, psychoanalysis accompanied America throughout the entire twentieth century. John Burnham notices that

> the story of Freud and American culture becomes completely intertwined with almost all of the major intellectual and cultural changes that occurred from the 1920s and 1930s to the 1970s and 1980s and after. To become mainstream at any time was a remarkable achievement for propagators of psychoanalytic thinking. ("Conclusion" 251)

As I will indicate in the introductory chapter, psychoanalysis did exceptionally well among American modernist intellectuals, first and foremost, Lionel Trilling, who happened to teach Kerouac at Columbia University. I will also draw particular attention to ego-psychology, a development in psychoanalysis which became nothing short of religion in the American clinic from the 1940s to the 1960s and which earned the enmity of Jacques Lacan.

Chapter Two, "Fundamental Lacanian Concepts," discusses key terms in Lacanian thought. Among many other notions, this part investigates Lacan's ideas on subjectivity, his theory of three registers, and his understanding of desire. By doing so, a theoretical apparatus is established in order to offer a close reading of and gain a fresh insight into Jack Kerouac's oeuvre through the prism of Lacanian thought, which is further offered in the three final chapters of the book.

Chapter Three, "Literary Studies and American Literature: Lacanian Perspectives," first briefly delves into the historical controversies of applying psychoanalysis to literary studies in order to further explore the practicality of Lacanian theory therein. A frequent object of critique itself, Lacanian criticism might be said to have stood the test of both time and a critical challenge, as evidenced by a plethora of contemporary literary and cultural scholars deploying its theoretical background. The chapter proposes a number of scholarly and critical perspectives on approaching literature with Lacan and reflects on a much sought after reversal in the process which anticipates approaching Lacan with literature. What follows is a comprehensive outline of the Lacanian influence on the Anglophone academe as well as an overview of studies tackling the American literary works with the Lacanian body of work. Finally, the chapter provides insight into a number of critical works employing (Lacanian) psychoanalysis in studying Beat Generation literature.

Both his works and personal comments display Jack Kerouac's multifaceted attitude to psychoanalytic thought, the more puzzling as often changing. In Chapter Four, "Jack Kerouac and Psychoanalysis in America: Direct Encounters," I hope to elucidate all the intricacies of the American writer's stance towards psychoanalysis. As Freud's work never signified one, coherent body of thought for Americans, Kerouac occasionally built a straw man out of the Austrian doctor and psychoanalysis; the straw man justified inasmuch as it embodied and served to wage a war against the oppressive form of the dominating model of American psychoanalysis as well as against elitism. Although never heard of by Kerouac, Jacques Lacan enters the stage as the point of reference and the writer's silent partner in the criticism aimed at the institutional forms of American psychoanalysis, which often greatly diverged from what the clinic was meant to be for Freud.

If not fully compatible, the fields of Lacanian psychoanalytic practice and the Beat Generation poetics offer a fairly common understanding of spontaneous text production and text processing, which is the focus of Chapter Five, "*The Beat Analyst?* Jack Kerouac, Beat Models of Writing, and Lacanian Psychoanalysis: Textual Strategies and Comparative Perspectives." By highlighting some aspects of psychoanalytic free-association, the author hopes to demonstrate their affinity with particular textual strategies employed by Kerouac. The correspondence between Kerouac's poetics of spontaneity and Lacanian free-association is all the more meaningful when additionally referenced with Allen Ginsberg's and William S. Burroughs's literary tactics. What is more, in view of modern psychoanalytic criticism and its calls for substituting the all-too-predictive application of psychoanalysis to literature for applying literature to psychoanalysis, the author expects these fields to be offering spaces of mutual enrichment. Finally, as the book hopes to prove, both Beat models of writing and Lacanian psychoanalysis address issues relating to the philosophical and aesthetic assumptions of Surrealism.

The closing parts of the book aim at a close Lacanian reading of selected novels by Jack Kerouac. Much as the analysis of the chosen installments of the Duluoz legend shall offer a comprehensive Lacanian insight into its tissue, its primary focus will always revolve, just like Kerouac's prose, around the insufficiency of the paternal function. Often remarked upon by Kerouac scholars, the question of the absent father figure in the American writer's works has not yet, I believe, been given a proper, rigorous attention. The final part of my work falls into three chapters (Chapter Six to Chapter Eight) presenting to the reader different stages of tackling the (lack of) father figure, which correspond to particular works of Kerouac. Given the writer's strong dislike for psychoanalytic analyses of literary works, the offered reading perhaps ushers in a counternarrative to how Kerouac imagined his own works should be perceived. As such, it has the ambition of expanding Kerouac studies by reading Kerouac against Kerouac.

The primary sources given scrutiny in the present work encompass an extensive selection of both Kerouac's and Lacan's output. With regard to the American writer, the considered works include the non-fiction writings (letters, journals, magazine columns, theoretical essays) as well as the artistic body of work – the prose texts comprising Kerouac's Duluoz legend and, to a lesser extent, poetry.[4] While Kerouac's literary output is of paramount importance to the entirety of the following study, the non-fiction works bear special significance to the studies of Kerouac's personal attitudes towards psychoanalysis (Chapter Four) and the writer's poetics of spontaneity (Chapter Five). As regards Lacan, my work makes essential use of the complete edition of *Écrits* as well as a number of seminars available in English. Of not least importance is the number of scholars and secondary sources that proved illuminating in tackling the obscure and arcane thought of Jacques Lacan.

---

4 The question of which works actually make up the Duluoz legend, one vast book imagined by Kerouac to be comprising his entire oeuvre, has been raised by Kerouac scholars. The most common selection includes 13 novels and novellas (the years of composition are given in parentheses): *The Town and the City* (1946–1949), *On the Road* (1948–1956), *Visions of Cody* (1951–1952), *Dr. Sax* (1952), *Maggie Cassidy* (1953), *The Subterraneans* (1953), *Tristessa* (1955–1956), *Visions of Gerard* (1956), *The Dharma Bums* (1957), *Desolation Angels* (1956–1957), *Big Sur* (1961), *Satori in Paris* (1965), *Vanity of Duluoz* (1968), and such a choice is assumed by this study. Still, as aptly suggested by Michael Hrebeniak, rather than perceive it as a closed, unified body, "[i]t is … more appropriate to view the Legend as deliberately paratactic, a rejection of final form and homogenized schedule" (Hrebeniak 91).

1 The Development of Psychoanalysis in the United States

1.1 The Pre-war Period

It is now a common belief that psychoanalysis was brought to the United States by Freud himself. During his visit in 1909 the Austrian psychoanalyst gave a series of lectures at Clark's University in Worchester which rendered a vivid interest over his theories, allowed to establish some psychoanalytic associations in the following years, and were the first sign of highly successful adaptation of his work that was to come. However, the status of Freud's three-week conference visit to the Clark University in 1909 as the cornerstone of American psychoanalysis is nothing short of being mythical. As argued by Richard Skues, the event celebrating the twentieth anniversary of the university might have been something of a subject of a retroactive "act of displacement" when it comes to its significance for anchoring psychoanalysis in America (77). Prior to Freud's visit to the States, different forms of psychotherapy had already been present there and psychoanalytic theory was no exception; it "was only one of the competing techniques and did not stand out from the others" (Burnham, "Introduction" 14). Besides, it also "formed no coherent body of thought" (Skues 53).[5] Much as Freud was a name in the United States (albeit merely for a small group of professionals), psychoanalysis was mainly recognized in terms of being mistaken with other trends in the field of psychotherapy, which paradoxically might have helped it to gain some ground (Shamdasini 44). What is more, it would not be a far-fetched statement to call Jung the godfather of American psychoanalytical movement. The first English-translated psychoanalytic book was his *The Psychology of Dementia Praecox* (1909); what is more, by the time of its release Jung had published three articles in English and had been an authority among American psychotherapists with his new theories on dynamic psychiatry and word association (Shamdasini 46). One may therefore wonder why Jung's invitation to Clark University was not as great a matter of importance as Freud's since it was Jung who was generally more admired among American scholars of the psychotherapeutic field.

5 Shamdasini notices that some American theoreticians of psychotherapy called for unifying the field (38) and such could not have remained without importance for implanting psychoanalysis on the American soil.

As pointed by Richard Skues, Freud's visit was made possible thanks to a small and prominent group of experts acquainted with new European psychotherapeutic trends, who esteemed Freud's position on the scene. Thus, psychoanalysis would not probably have gained much support in the first two decades of twentieth-century American but for people like G. Stanley Hall, whose prominence and efforts allowed him to extend an invitation for Freud and confer on him an honorary degree (Skues 50). The first president of the Clark University and a scholar fluent in German, Hall was seriously interested in Freud's findings in the fields of child development and sexuality. His regard for the father of psychoanalysis went so high that, apart from awarding Freud, he made him his personal houseguest (together with Jung) and the primary speaker at the conference (Skues 54). What is more, he went as far as "to engineer favorable press coverage for Freud" (Skues 55). From this perspective, inviting Jung was also mainly confined to confirming the importance of psychoanalysis and its father; Jung was to act as Freud's "principal lieutenant" (Skues 72). Yet, as it has been said, Hall's enthusiasm was not shared by many at that time; Skues claims that it is highly probable that the majority of guests came to the Clark conference without the exact purpose of hearing Freud's lectures (64).

Demythologizing the event further, both Freud's interest in his visit and his own further contribution to the development of psychoanalysis in the States appear to be limited. For Freud, the gradual rise of anticipation of the trip and moderate satisfaction with its outcome, as proven by his correspondence with his daughter Mathilde and Jung, seemed to revolve merely around the pleasure that it was to bring (Skues 56–57). Skues argues that the Viennese psychoanalyst looked forward to the visit insofar as it was likely to bring little work and much enjoyment (57) and he was mainly preoccupied with being awarded the degree (78). Here, what might be worth mentioning is Freud's now-legendary despise for whatever America was ever to stand for. The Viennese psychoanalyst saw many a vice in the general image of the States, such as "the greed for money and the respect of public opinion" (Freud quoted by Falzeder, 91). The critique did not exclude the ways Freud presented his concepts: "no matter what subject Freud discussed – dreams, clinical theory, psychoanalytic treatment, history, or social issues – America emerged as an immediate association of what was bad" (Mahony, quoted by Falzeder, 90). In Falzeder's interesting record of the grudge Freud held against America and the Americans throughout years, the country he visited in 1909 emerges as a land mindlessly indulged with materialism ("Dollaria", as Freud called it in 1930 despite simultaneously counting on Americans' money), uncritical pragmatism, and a tendency to homogenize its society (91–94). As regards psychoanalysis, Freud complained about "unsatisfactory standard of psychoanalytic training" (Falzeder 104), disregard for an original text when offered 'source-books' (92), or making a "hotch-potch out of psychoanalysis and other elements" (Freud, quoted by Falzeder, 92) often in view of giving in to "dollar compulsion" (Freud, quoted by Falzeder, 104).

Not long after the Clark conference America witnessed a burgeoning interest in psychoanalysis. According to Skues, while Freud's visit to the States contributed only little to the growing popularity of the psychoanalytic field, there were a few other factors that turned out to be crucial. Most significantly, Freud's texts appeared in English at the end of September in 1909 (*Selected Papers on Hysteria and Other Psychoneuroses)* and in 1910 (*Three Essays on the Theory of Sexuality* and five Clark lectures) (Skues 75). The latter publication, in the overall history of the psychoanalytic field, "was the point at which psychoanalysis began to become not merely a method, but also a body of thought" (Skues 76), as it provided a comprehensive insight into Freud's work. The second reason for a successful implementation of psychoanalysis in America was the collective effort of other scholars, like Ernest Jones and Abraham Brill, to popularize Freud's thought. Among many actions taken, the former contributed to the field by lobbying for the psychoanalytic thought, organizing meetings and discussions, and by prolific publishing on the topic, while the latter focused largely on translating Freud and Jung (Skues 77). Skues also notes that the proliferation of psychoanalysis, both in America and elsewhere, could not have happened were it not for the lack of what could be labeled as "orthodox" psychoanalytic thought – there was no "notion of doctrinal purity or test of degree of commitment [that] was a prerequisite for membership of the early psychoanalytic associations founded from 1911 onwards" (81). Not least formative for welcoming psychoanalysis and establishing the psychoanalytic tradition in the United States was simply, as pointed by Kernberg, the "innate American optimism: the possibility to change people, the determinacy of the environment" ("Psychoanalysis in America").

Fundamental for the development of the European psychoanalysis and the unification of the Freudian field, the formation of International Psychoanalytical Association (IPA) in 1910 did not bring much but contempt and ignorance for the American clinical field (Makari 112). The first American psychoanalytic institution – the American Psychoanalytic Association (APA) – unifying smaller psychoanalytical societies (New York, Boston, Washington-Baltimore, and Chicago) was founded as early as in 1911; however, the leaders of the IPA shared all of Freud's feelings towards the American psychoanalysts. The latter were frequently as self-critical as to admit their own lack of originality and creativity in the field in the first two decades of the twentieth century, proving an absolute dependency on the European models of analysis (Makari 112).

The 1930s was the time of bitter clashes between American and European scholars in the field, with the peak of these clashes in 1938 when some American analysts decided to break from the IPA (and, accordingly, the APA as a subordinate and European-oriented body), training issues being the bone of contention (Makari 114). Under the 1938 agreement, the IPA granted the APA the exclusive right to train analysts and an exclusive recognition as an American partner. Importantly, only physicians could become trainees; the APA was thus extremely medically-oriented. The same year witnessed calling for the multidisciplinarity as a way for strictly American psychoanalysis, which would merge medicine and social sciences and do away with "obscure theoretical superstructures" (Makari 113). Much as the destination of American psychoanalysis might have been disrespected by its European proponents, ironically enough, history turned Americans into the saviors of psychoanalysis. Due to the rise of the Nazis in the 1930s, America witnessed a flow of refugees from Berlin. Many of them, like Franz Alexander, Sandor Rado, Karen Horney and Hanns Sachs, were among the most distinguished scholars in the field of psychoanalysis (Makari 113). Two months after the split of the IPA and the APA Austrian analysts faced the annexation of their country. Forced to exile and supported by the Emergency Committee on Relief and Immigration, they found home in America. Makari writes:

> In the decade leading up to 1938, a total of some 1,400 German, Austrian, and Italian doctors had immigrated to the United States, but after the annexation of Austria, the number of refugees ... surged to over 1,400 alone. (114)

As the refugee psychoanalysts moved mainly to New York, which was the central place for American psychoanalysis, Lawrence Kubie, the president of the New York Psychoanalytic Society, advised relocating them throughout the whole country to prevent an economic disaster; as a result, "[b]y 1943, 149 exiled psychoanalysts and psychiatrists had been relocated somewhere in the United States" (Makari 115). Consequently, American psychoanalysis gained new and influential centers all across the States. Soon, as expected, conflicts emerged within the APA, especially in the New York Psychoanalytic Society. The orthodox Freudians, such as Viennese Paul Federn, clashed with those, like Sandor Rado, who dared to revise Freud's body of thought. Burnham significantly observes that

> [m]any or most Americans were careless of theoretical and technical details. And they were notoriously given to eclectism, pragmatically taking only parts of psychoanalysis, not the whole, carefully considered edifice. (Burnham, "Introduction" 29)

Diverging from Freud might have reached its zenith with Karen Horney's *New Ways in Psychoanalysis* (1939), which, as noted by Makari, was "a book-length critique of psychoanalytic fundamentals" (130), such crucial ones as libido theory, the Oedipal complex, or Freud's second topography. Further schisms were unavoidable; breaking up from the APA resulted in the emergence of new institutes, such as the Association for the Advancement of Psychoanalysis, the American Institute for Psychoanalysis, or William Alanson White Institute.

At the same time, links between psychoanalysis and medical studies were getting tighter and tighter. Taking a wider look at the pre-war decades, one may notice that the main channels of popularizing psychoanalysis in the States were the fields of medicine and the intellectual and cultural avant-garde (Burnham, "Introduction" 3). Beginning with the 1930s, psychoanalysis started to gain impetus by encroaching into various fields. Most importantly, it was the top structures of psychiatric institutions which were basically taken over. All the major psychiatric departments (Harvard, Yale, UCLA, John Hopkins) and a large number of smaller ones were governed by either "psychoanalysts, or psychiatrists very favorable to psychoanalysis" (Kernberg, "Psychoanalysis in America"). Suffice it to say, The American Psychoanalytic Association and the American Psychiatric Association shared the same time and place of meetings from 1925 until 1974 (Barton 111). Prior to the 1920s, psychology, medicine, anthropology, arts and literature had started to incorporate psychoanalytical lexicon (Burnham, "Introduction" 4–5, 11). Many institutions and scientific trends which appeared at that time were heavily influenced by psychoanalysis; these included the Yale Institute of Human Relations, the child guidance movement, and culture and personality studies (Burnham, "Introduction" 26).

A separate phenomenon was the rising importance of Wilhelm Reich, one of Freud's best students. He first pursued his career and gained some recognition as a psychoanalyst and psychiatrist while belonging to the Freudian circle in Vienna of the 1920s. Reich focused on researching neuroses perceived as a disturbance caused by the conflict between sexual instincts and frustrating social repressions. In a transcendentalist manner, he believed in the inherent decency of human beings and any hindrance caused by society was perceived by him as a factor which stood in the way to people's health and happiness. Social repression was seen by him as a tool of power aiding in supervising people and exacting their obedience. Gaining renown, Reich soon proclaimed sexual energy to be the main aim of his research and created some clinics oriented towards proper understanding of sexuality and bringing down the socially imposed constraints. The peak of this stage of Reich's career was his most famous book, *The Function of the Orgasm* (1927), in which he elevated the orgasmic moment to the rank of a miraculous solution that alleviated troublesome tensions, rectified the balance, and was a prerequisite for proper functioning. Interestingly, being a Marxist, Reich joined political theories with psychoanalysis. Spending libidinal energies without any limit was necessary as

> 'compulsive [i.e. compulsory] sexual morality' compromised the natural human 'right' to orgastic potency, ... and went hand in hand with patriarchal power structures, reserving a monopoly on free sexual spending for the head of the bourgeois 'patriarchal-authoritarian family,' which in turn was the nucleus of the fascist state. ... Only the unreserved spending by all, which keeps libido in continual recirculation of exchange, could guarantee socio-economic health, obviating the depressions or recessions that result from the unequal distribution and hoarding of libido in capitalist society. (Bennett 44)

Reich's postulates led to a split between him and his master. Freud became very dubious about both Reich's fascination with solely sexual themes and his political activism; he was accused by Freud of being a "bolshevist" attacker, although the father of psychoanalysis later claimed that the conflict remained solely on scientific grounds. (Nitzschke, "Psychoanalysis and National Socialism"). Freud's craving for psychoanalysis to be a pure science inevitably clashed with Reichian ambition of joining psychoanalysis and sociology. Freud also saw to Reich's expulsion from the IPA and the DPG (German Psychoanalytic Society). As a result, one of the master's most favorite students continued his work in Norway, where he developed the idea of orgone energy – a bioenergetic version of libido similar to aether which was to be found in the atmosphere and gathered through specially constructed collectors. The fame of the so-called orgone accumulators was to flourish in the America of the 1940s when Reich began his experiments with a cure for cancer. The ban on his books, the removal of orgone accumulators, and the 1954 injunction filed against him shattered Reich's career and contributed to his early death.

1.2 The Post-war Period and Ego-psychology

Apart from the conflicts between orthodox Freudians (of Austrian origin), who often tended to be more fervent Freudians than Freud himself, and the so-called neo-Freudians (Berliners and Americans), the post-war period was marked by the rise and glory of Heinz Hartmann, the new president of the New York Society, and soon the president of the IPA (Makari 122). Together with Ernst Kris and Rudolph Lowenstein, "Hartmann set the theoretical agenda for American ego psychology for the following three decades" (Makari 122–123).

Much inspired by Freud's thoughts over the ego in *Inhibitions, Symptoms, and Anxiety*, ego-psychology could spread its wings in America because of a considerable number of respected European ego-psychologists who left war-torn Europe. C. Edward Robins claims that it was Adolph Meyer, an American psychiatrist and the president of APA in 1927–1928, whose philosophy of "occupational adaptation" (being simply "conformism" for Robins) fit ego-psychologists' goals (68). Scholars such as Hartmann, Rapaport, Kris, and Loewenstein, first and foremost, underscored the apparent autonomy and mediacy of the ego formation, which further allowed to claim its capability of setting defensive impulses against the id, and thus, integrating the subject's life. Ego-psychology seemed to be destined to perfectly succeed on the American soil as it took into account the American national character. Makari claims that Hartmann's

> emphasis on adaptation cohered nicely with American values of self-reliance, and his hope to link psychoanalysis to academic psychology would be taken up by allies, such as David Rapaport. (123)

Many opponents did not agree with tenets of ego-psychology, pointing to their incompatibility with Freud's teachings.[6] As a result, what faced a fierce critique was the apparent conformist approach aiming at making a subject as adjustable as possible. Asked about the common European perspective of blaming American psychoanalysis for its concern with apparent political conservatism, conformism, and its primary aim of adapting the patients to their social environment, Kernberg responds:

> It is partially justified: the early generation of Ego psychologists of this country (in particular Hartmann) insisted, theoretically and technically, on adaptation and on the environment, on psychoanalysis becoming a general psychology, on the adaptive functions of the psychic apparatus for the individual, and on the adaptive functions of defensive operations. Psychoanalysis became very fashionable in the US, sweeping through the universities and the departments of psychiatry in the 1950s and the 1960s; this produced a conservative atmosphere within psychoanalytic institutes, and a tendency to adjust to the cultural norms of society.
>
> But the accusation is only partially true. Some American psychoanalysts strongly criticized this tendency, and were concerned with the revolutionary nature of the knowledge of the unconscious. Even within psychoanalytic theory and technical approaches, there were counter-currents: Margaret Mahler, Edith Jacobson, Arthur Fennikel, and Hans Loewald from a different existential viewpoint, all criticized this adaptive quality of American psychoanalysis. ("Psychoanalysis in America")

---

6 Naturally, that was also the position of Lacan, who regarded the ego as nothing more than a set of unconscious identifications.

Also, side by side with the dominance of ego-psychology came the centralization of the APA, which turned "from a loosely knit federation into a central power that policed standards on teaching and training and no longer yielded authority on these matters to local societies" (Makari 123).

In addition to its adaptive and normative character, ego-psychology has been criticized for such issues as its take on the analyst's abstinence and the analysand's resistance during the treatment. Abstinence has been always one of central tenets of orthodox psychoanalytic method. Freud himself spoke of psychoanalysis as of a treatment that "must be carried out in abstinence," which is "a fundamental principle" (Freud, quoted by Lunbeck, 226). As it is pointed by Lunbeck, while never being taken rigidly by Freud himself, abstinence gained a crucial status with the dominance of ego-psychology in the middle of the twentieth century, when it was offered a special term, "rule of abstinence" (227). According to many of its proponents, a cool and unresponsive approach of the analyst was to furnish an emotionally neutral ground or ignite the analysand's frustration, both of which were favorable conditions for the patient's making some personal sense of the treatment. Much as abstinence has always been in the scope of theoretical interest of all analytical fractions, orthodox analysts, especially ego-psychologists, were criticized for employing it in an inflexible and excessively adamant way. Lunbeck glosses over the matter:

> Dissidents pointed to the "superfluous deprivations" exacted by "overzealous and indiscriminate" adherence to the rule of abstinence and chastised their colleagues for the austerity, aloofness, and authoritarianism that characterized their interactions with patients. The literature is peppered with accounts of analysts so under the sway of orthodoxy they cannot express any compassion over the fate of a patient's seriously ill infant or, conversely, congratulate a patient for a major achievement for fear that in doing so they might harm the patient. (228)

Orthodox to the limits, ego-psychologists, Lunbeck observes, did not notice the grotesque character of their actions. The place of resistance was treated in a similar fashion. According to Patricia Gherovici, resistances keep psychoanalysis alive and prove its effectiveness as an explanatory tool. They may be understood twofold, as "the analysand's resistance during the cure," which is a sign and clue to the analyst as where to proceed further, and as hostilities towards psychoanalysis in general (96). As for the place of resistance in ego-psychology, Gherovici notes that

> [b]y focusing on the dissolution of resistances, American psychoanalysis created an optimistic, adaptive technique, ego psychology (note that the word *psychoanalysis* has already disappeared). Its reading of Freud's second topic produced a misleading

> interpretation that stressed defenses and transformed psychoanalysis into an analysis of resistances. (97)

As Burnham observes, "the ego psychologists came slowly to an end ... because of attacks on the rigidity of their technical standards but also because of problems with theory" and those who spearheaded the critique were psychoanalytic theorists themselves ("Conclusion" 250).

Also, the lines between psychiatry, pharmacology and psychoanalysis were getting blurred further. As Louis Menand notes,

> between 1948 and 1976 the number of psychiatrists in the United States increased from forty-seven hundred to twenty-seven thousand. Between 1946 and 1956, the number of psychiatric residency programs doubled. . . . Most American psychiatrists employed Freudian assumptions (196)

The treatment of war-traumatized soldiers bore witness to the extent of medical and psychiatric reliance on psychoanalysis. Menand observes how many veterans were subject to a psychiatric treatment in the heyday of psychoanalysis:

> One million soldiers suffered neuropsychiatric breakdowns; ... for psychiatric conditions were two hundred per one thousand soldiers. (196)

What is more, pharmacology in the post-war period was no exception to the pervasive influence of psychoanalytic thought. "The advertisements for tranquilizers regularly used the language of psychoanalysis," Menand notes (202).

What mostly fostered the popularization of the psychoanalytic thought in the post-war America was its cultural impact, the label of "a new theory of human nature", which was first examined in and restricted to doctoral dissertations to reach its full impact with a great rise in post-secondary education in the post-World War II era (Burnham, "Introduction" 11–12). Between the 1940s-1960s, Burnham continues, "it was difficult to separate the core psychoanalytic movement from the pervasive cultural impact" ("Introduction" 4). For better or worse to psychoanalysis, Freudian nomenclature started to be (mis)used to gloss on new ongoing social and cultural processes (Burnham, "Introduction" 12). It was the time when people were advised to "learn about their hidden selves, whether formed from complexes and drives or grandular imbalances or childhood conditioning." ("Introduction" 26). As a result, a palimpsest of (mis)uses started to blur Freud's original thought; Americans finally had their own Freud(s). In the post-war years American psychoanalysis kept successfully venturing into such fields as sociology and popular culture. Burnham points out that the 1950s witnessed scholars' attempts to pick and choose those features of Freudian thought which could harmoniously fit with American pragmatism and serve society. For instance, "naturalism and biologism" of psychoanalysis was concurrent with American attitude, yet "irrationalism, dualism, and pessimism [was found to be] . . . incompatible with the American optimistic belief in the rational, progressive perfectibility of man and society" (Weisskopf, quoted by Burnham, "Introduction" 13).

The decline of psychoanalysis in America came with the 60s' social, cultural and political unrest concomitant with "the simultaneous resurgence of material, non-psychological ideas and new psychopharmaceutical resources for mental illnesses" (Burnham, "Introduction" 6). As Burnham continues,

> [i]n the years 1965 to 1975, as psychoactive drugs became well established in psychiatry proper, the new somaticism, along with waves of new psychotherapies, began to marginalize psychoanalytic practitioners in both medicine and society. ("Introduction" 6)

Menand corroborates the image:

> With the publication of Joseph Schildkraut's amine theory of depression in 1965, Freudianism began its professional death march. With the publication of *DSM-III*, in 1980, it met that death. (Menand 206)

Despite the general decline of psychoanalysis in the 60s and 70s, the person to leave a remarkable stamp in the field was Heinz Kohut, an Austrian psychoanalyst who worked in Chicago. In his attempt to domesticate psychoanalysis, Kohut

> challenged the primacy Freud had assigned to the drives ..., brought provision and gratification back to the discussions of analytic technique, and outlined a normal narcissism that was the wellspring of human ambition and creativity, values and ideals, empathy and fellow feeling. (Lunbeck 211)

Kohut's version of Freudianism was then perhaps the most optimistic one to have ever appeared; "self-psychology," as it was labeled, put emphasis on the themes of "growth and possibility that fueled the earlier stabs at analytic revisionism" (Lunbeck 213). This, however, was to be achieved at the expense of the liberatory potential of Freud. Kohut underscored the significance of social symbiosis (in the guise of morality) and strongly questioned the idea of an independent self (Lunbeck 214). For Lunbeck, Kohut is

> a pivotal or hinge figure between the bleak, drive-based theories of Freudian orthodoxy and the more generous, more hybrid, more plentitude-based therapies on offer today. (Agnew 234–235)

The late twentieth-century American mental healing, according to Burnham, is the victory of cognitive psychology, the substitution of methodical mental treatment with modern medications, and lack of financial support for psychoanalytic therapy ("Introduction" 7). Otto Kernberg observes that the last four decades of the twentieth century witnessed various "alternative theories to be studied and tolerated in the United States" owing to Heinz Kohut, whose career epitomized an individual approach towards psychoanalysis (Kernberg, quoted by Burnham, "Introduction to Part II" 161). Surprisingly, as noted by Burnham, the twenty-first-century psychotherapy has witnessed some vivid interest in psychoanalytic thought, despite having been largely ostracized ("Introduction to Part II" 162). Some, like Richard Rorty, held: "the revolution announced by Freud, rather than coming to its alleged end, has not yet taken place" (Gherovici 96).

1.3 American Psychoanalysis and Modernism

It is impossible to overlook the stamp that psychoanalysis left on the development of modernist thinking in the States. Kerouac, as well as other Beats who were students at Columbia, must have felt it too since

> [m]odernism was itself the coin, the currency – what we would now call the cultural capital – in which a New York intellectual could gain access to the university chairs and highbrow press ... . New York *was*, in the 1950s, a cultural capital; an international capital of modern art, cultural criticism, and, of course, psychoanalysis. (Agnew 242)

As it is aptly suggested by Dorothy Ross, "[t]he humanistic intellectuals who brought Freud to prominence during the 1940s and 1950s were advocates of modernism" and the peak of academic esteem for Freud came along with their dominance (2012, 163). With its focus on inwardness and various phenomena of consciousness, psychoanalysis won over modern literature and entered the center of modernist interests. Otto Kernberg corroborates the importance of links between modernism and psychoanalytic thought. As he claims, what helped psychoanalysis pave its way at that time was

> its emphasis on subjectivity, on the existential approach to psychological illness, and on its cultural relation to surrealist and anti-objectivist currents dominating both European and American culture at the end of World War II. ("Psychoanalysis in America")

Some modernist critics, like *Partisan Review* editor, William Barrett, were as daring and zealous as to confer messianism on the father of psychoanalysis and claim that Freud is the one who knows "how we are to live truthfully" and "how authenticity is to be achieved either in art or life" (Barrett, quoted by Ross, 168). Significantly, the Freudian thought was not a homogeneous notion in the academia. As further pointed by Ross, there existed the domesticated Freud of Erik Erikson and the Dionysian Freud of Herbert Marcuse and Norman O. Brown;

yet, the greatest prominence fell to its Apollonian mode (167).[7] Apart from Philip Rieff, its most notable advocate was no one else but Lionel Trilling, a professor of English at Columbia university, whose students included Jack Kerouac and Allen Ginsberg in the 1940s. Employing psychoanalysis in the 1940s, Trilling, on the one hand, wished to revise American political left, and on the other hand, advocated for making the best use of Freud's discoveries. He was the proponent of the Apollonian Freud, "the guardian of civilization . . . [which] worked to bring the irrational under control of the rational" (Ross 168). Jean-Christophe Agnew enumerates some other features of the Apollonian/Freudian character – "austere, abstinent, stoic, aloof, . . . a figure of discipline, a figure *for* a discipline" (241). A modernist artist (just as the subject of psychoanalysis) was someone that was to make their own sense in the world of chaos and discontent, Ross adds (169).

Notwithstanding Trilling's hopes, the implications of his essays were nothing but conservative, as some scholars claim (Ross 169). As for literary and academic discourse, Trilling perceived the Freudian subject in strictly modernist terms and, largely thanks to him, identifying Freud as a modernist thinker was a prevailing stance in the American academia of the 1950s. The decade also marked Trilling's move toward the liberating potential of Freud, which entailed that the tragic and dark residue of human nature might be seen as a force opposing the all-encompassing and homogenizing culture of the post-war America (Ross 171). In this sense, under the veneer of modernism, one might argue, there came a counterforce to a self-complacent, self-assertive version of ego-psychoanalysis. In the following decades modernism started to lose its dominance and so did Freud. Dorothy Ross observes that

> when many of his [Freud's] advocates blamed modernism for student radicalism and countercultural excess, his intellectual authority began to decline. The rise of feminism and postmodernism during the 1970s accelerated the decline, as Freud was linked by some to modernist/postmodernist vices and found by others to be lacking in the modernist virtues of a liberalizing culture. (188)

1.4 The Lacanian Clinic in the United States: A Brief Overview

The history of psychoanalytic movement in America bears witness to the fact that Jacques Lacan's presence in the American clinic has always been something of a nuisance. While it was more than welcomed in the American academia, the Lacanian thought in the clinical framework has been oscillating

7 For a more detailed study of modes of the modernist Freud in the mid-twentieth-century America, see Dorothy Ross (2012).

somewhere between a peculiarity and the object of ignorance. Taking a general look at the body of seminal works which handle the psychoanalytic heritage of the American soil, one seeking Lacan's contribution may feel somewhat confused. The first study in the field, C. P. Oberndorf's *A History of Psychoanalysis in America*[8] (1953), appeared four years after the first English translation of Lacan and did not allot any space to the French psychoanalyst. In the index of a monumental, two-volume and over a thousand-page history of psychoanalysis by Nathan G. Hale Lacan is mentioned once, in the context of a debate over analytical findings pertaining to women.[9] Not a reference more is featured by an illuminating collection of essays and the most up-to-date study of the history of American psychoanalysis, where Lacan appears alongside Derrida, Habermas, Ricoeur and the late Barthes as a representative of continental postmodernism.[10] The French analyst is either not mentioned at all in works relating to the history of mental treatment in America,[11] or again is referenced merely as a stamp of cultural influence.[12] Thus, as regards clinical practice, Lacanian psychoanalysis seems to be placed at the margins of the discourse and the history of American psychoanalysis. As is observed by Burnham, the shape of the latter has proved to be enough of a problematic, historiographical issue itself ("Introduction" 2–8). As observed by Judith Feher Gurewich at the break of the centuries,

> Lacan's contribution has been derailed from its original trajectory. No longer perceived as a theory meant to enlighten the practice of psychoanalysis, ... criticized so as to conform to the needs ... far removed from clinical reality. (xi)

The reasons for Lacan's conspicuous absence in American clinic are various. Firstly, the fact that "Freud and Lacan are read not as much by psychoanalysts as by humanists" (Gurewich xi), up to a point, is a result of a problematic status of the Viennese psychoanalyst in relation to the American psychoanalytic

---

8 See C. P. Oberndorf, *A History of Psychoanalysis in America*. New York: Harper and Row, 1953.

9 See Nathan G Hale, Jr. *The Rise and Crisis of Psychoanalysis in the United States: Freud and the Americans, 1917–1985*. New York: Oxford University Press, 1995; Nathan G. Hale, Jr. *Freud and the Americans: The Beginnings of Psychoanalysis in the United States, 1876–1917*. New York: Oxford University Press, 1971.

10 See John Burnham, ed. *After Freud Left: A Century of Psychoanalysis in America*. Chicago: The University of Chicago Press, 2012, 184.

11 See Donna R. Kemp, *Mental Health in America: A Reference Handbook*. Santa Barbara: ABC-CLIO, 2007.

12 See Michael Shally-Jensen, ed. *Mental Health Care Issues in America: An Encyclopedia*. Santa Barbara: ABC-CLIO, 2013.

discourse. As has been discussed before, in the United States Freud has always stood for something different for various scholars and analysts, which meant reshaping his body of thought for particular needs. The consequence of this was that "Americanizing" Freud made it difficult for Americans to access Lacan, whose body of work operated on what might be called "the European Freud" (Gurewich xiv). In other words, as claimed by various scholars, there exists a different Freud for European and for American psychoanalysts, which calls for a close and a separate scrutiny (Malone 7). Apart from now-legendary notoriety of Lacan's style, Gurewich also mentions the fact that whereas the American psychoanalysis has always been more of a reaction to Freud, Lacanian psychoanalysis has meant to rehabilitate the Viennese psychoanalyst in some way (xiv). Kareen Ror Malone adds that "there is little place for Lacanian psychoanalysis in North-American psychology" (3) since Lacan became some sort of a straw man; consequently,

> [i]t sometimes sounds as if American psychoanalysts, psychiatrists, and psychologists have to be protected against this phallocentric structuralist with his hordes of South American and Parisian analysts who, with the help of influential literary critics, eagerly await an impending colonization of the American clinical scene. (4)

Additionally, Malone continues, American psychologists and psychoanalysts have tended to leave Lacan behind the margin due to a few misconceptions. These either imply that because of its use of linguistics, Lacanian theory is too elitist to be practical, or reduce Lacan to "the most deterministic structuralism" (6). Finally, much as American psychology and psychoanalysis have remained open to reformulations and novelties, "the most vocal advocates for alternative psychological paradigms in North America are grounded in humanistic or hermeneutic perspectives" (Malone 12), according to which there seems to be an inerasable sign of equality between consciousness and subjectivity. By no means can this be Lacan's stance.

A perfect epitome for Lacan's mismatch with America may be the following anecdote relating to his 1975 visit to the States:

> Convinced that he was world famous, he wanted to be allowed to make a private visit to the Metropolitan Opera House: "Tell them I'm Lacan", he bade his three bemused companions. Pamela Tytell solved the problem with very "Lacanian" humour: she phoned the director of the Metropolitan and told him Jean-Paul Sartre wanted to visit incognito. The director was flattered and delighted to have such an eminent visitor and agreed at once. As if warning him about one of the great man's eccentricities, Pamela advised him not to address the philosopher by name. Despite her efforts, someone did ask after Simone de Beauvoir, but deception wasn't discovered: Lacan's English wasn't good enough to keep up the pretense. (Roudinesco, quoted by McQuillan, 216)

If one dared to treat the misnomer with psychoanalytic terms, the root of America's disparity with the Lacanian clinic is perfectly displaced and condensed in the above story: the expectations of both parties were of an imaginary and phantasmatic nature.

Although Malone does not hesitate to inform readers that Lacanian studies and the American clinic have not been on the same page (calling the relation between them a "premature" one) (5), there have been attempts to establish ground between the American psychoanalysis and Lacan. Some of the examples include the Lacanian Clinical Field publication series. Beside popularizing Lacan, its main aims have been, on the one hand, to provide the American clinic and academia with works already acclaimed in other countries, and on the other hand, to solidify the psychoanalytical community by encouraging encounters between various schools of analysis and demystifying prejudices against Lacan. Additionally, Lacanian heritage has been the focus of a few clinically-oriented works and collections of essays in which American psychoanalysts adapt it for their work with analysands.[13] Basically speaking, Lacanian psychoanalysis has been practiced in the States owing to a number of active analysts. Small as it is, the field of the Lacanian clinic is also relatively fresh; as noted by Martin McQuillan, in the mid-1970s Stuart Schneiderman was the only practicing Lacanian psychoanalyst in the United States (215).

1.5 Lacan and the Critique of Ego-psychology

Lacan's further links with American clinic may be extended in terms of his personal opinion on American psychoanalysts as well as his despise for the already-discussed ego-psychology. Although the French analysts referred to a handful of American theoreticians, or those residing in America, and their approaches (let the example be "Seminar I" with his either favorable or derogatory comments on Otto Fenichel, Hanns Sachs, Sandor Rado, Franz Alexander, Sandor Ferenczi, Herman Nunberg and Rudolph Loewenstein) (Roazen 51–54), the spearhead of his critique was the middle-of-the-century body of the psychoanalytic thought advocated by Heinz Hartmann.

Ego-psychology is subjected to Lacan's criticism on a number of major issues. Firstly, what matters in the context Lacan's experience with the American

13 See Raul Moncayo, *The Emptiness of Oedipus: Identification and Non-identification in Lacanian Psychoanalysis*, New York: Routledge, 2012; Judith Feher Gurewich, and Michel Tort, eds. *The Subject and the Self: Lacan and American Psychoanalysis*, Northvale: Jason Aronson, 1996.

psychoanalysis is the case of the analyst's abstinence in the analytical treatment. Being an important tenet of the treatment and a reaction to primary transference, abstinence was meant by Freud to frustrate the patient with one's reticence so that the symptoms would first reveal themselves, some suffering be maintained and finally a positive will for making changes be instigated. Yet, this tenet was never sharply delineated by the Austrian analyst. Confronting Freud with his orthodox American successors, yet again it is clear that rigidity and bureaucracy of the latter won over the common sense of the former. Liu claims that the post-Freudians'

> protocol for analysts to behave in a blank screen-like manner during all interactions with analysands is a practice that crystallized without Freud's personal endorsement, and only after his death. Freud's own couch-side manner, by many accounts, was any but orthodox, if it is to be judged by his successors' measure. ("Lacanian Reception" 116)

In Richard Sterba's view, being true and orthodox meant to encourage sterility, impersonality and strictness of the analyst (Sterba, quoted by Liu, "Lacanian Reception" 117). The opinion that the American post-Freudians were more orthodox than Freud himself is thus corroborated once again. Lacan noticed this well enough. For him, as earlier for Freud, abstinence was not the goal itself. Lacan understood that the analysand's perception of the analyst as the subject-supposed-to-know and a subsequent frustration that came with a lack of response for his demands opened the field of the analysand's unconscious desire. As he states,

> the analyst is he who sustains demand, not, as people say, to frustrate the subject, but in order to allow the signifiers with which the latter's frustration is bound up to reappear. (Écrits 516)

What is more, he highlights the value of listening as "simply the condition of speech" done by the analysand (Écrits 516).

Secondly, taking a more general perspective, Lacan believed that an inherent flaw in the dominating analytical discourse was the process of making the analyst itself. The "pass," a term he coined so as to describe a self-authorized and conscious moment of readiness for being an analyst, was, on the one hand, his response to the schematic character of training analysts, and on the other, a perfect epitome for what he thought practicing psychoanalysis was all about. For him, orthodox bureaucrats who were mindlessly initiated through a schematic authorization of some kind "compensate[d] for [their robotic approach] with the formalities of rank, an elegant way for them to establish themselves" and were eventually more interested "in their institutional relations than in their analytic practices" (Lacan, quoted by Liu, 119). As it is pointedly remarked by Liu, such "analysts have become bureaucrats and are no longer even capable of analysis" ("Lacanian Reception" 119), which marks a disaster for Lacan: "Freudianism has been institutionalized" ("Lacanian Reception" 119). What ego-psychology also implied, and what the French analyst could never accept, was the superior position and exemplary nature of the analyst. In such vein, psychoanalysis was otherwise represented as "the cure to be wrought by identification with the analyst" (Smith 35). Lacan never ceased to believe that "adaptation, in the pejorative sense of adjustment, is the proper goal of analysis propounded by Hartmann ... accepted by American analysts" (Smith 35). This adaptation, as put forward by Hartmann, necessitated reformulating Freudian ego as a behavioral formation to be shaped by the analyst and subjected to adaptive instructions. As the effect of a successful analysis, the ego as an entity would function "harmoniously in learning to adapt itself to external reality through the exercise of intelligence, through learning and through deferral" (Liu, "Lacanian Reception" 129). The ego then, as continued by Liu,

> becomes the hero of the day, regulating conflicts, engineering cease-fires between external conditions and instinctual drives in order to guarantee peaceful "internal development." ("Lacanian Reception" 129–130)

Liu makes an important point and reminds us that the adaptive strategies favored by ego-psychology stemmed from the needs of the European psychoanalytic Diaspora to adapt to new conditions on a new continent ("Lacanian Reception" 128). Naturally, reducing psychoanalysis to a form of adaptive strategy for immigrants cannot have deflected Lacan's severe criticism:

> The autonomous ego, the conflict-free sphere proposed as a new Gospel by Mr. Heinz Hartmann to the New York circle is no more than an ideology of a class of immigrants preoccupied with the prestigious values prevailing in central European society when with the diaspora of the war they had to settle in a society in which values sediment according to a scale of *income* tax. (Lacan, quoted by Liu, "Lacanian Reception" 128–129)

Liu makes a plea for the origin of ego-psychology as she observes that its roots are to be found in continental psychoanalysis, as early as in 1937 ("Lacanian Reception" 129), and that "Hartmann's work in Vienna was already based on poor readings of Freud" ("Lacanian Reception" 131). Yet, it cannot be denied that it was not until fleeing to America that Hartmann's idea of psychoanalysis came fully into force and being. In addition, similarly to Freud, Lacan emphasizes the commodified character of the dominant model of American psychoanalysis describing the setting of American psychoanalytic scene. It is thus again business married to psychoanalysis that comes to light as well. Naturally, by no means was Lacan a philanthropist, who offered his treatment for free, yet money seemed to have their special role in the treatment. Speaking over the matter of transference, Lacan states:

> [I]f love is giving what you don't have, it is certainly true that the subject can wait to be given it, since the psychoanalyst has nothing else to give him. But he does not even give him this nothing, and it is better that way—which is why he is paid for this nothing, preferably well paid, in order to show that otherwise it would not be worth much. (Écrits 516)

What we might make out of this statement is that money is then to make the analysand aware that love and, more generally, transference are imaginary identifications which are without any significant value and anchorage. In other words, money helps to contour nothingness and emptiness of an imaginary construction into a positive value to make it visible for the analysand.

Ego-psychology did much more to flatten the image of Freud let the best summary be Patricia Gherovici's opinion that ego-psychology is

> where the subject is divided between ego and unconscious, where the drive becomes instinct, sexuality becomes genitality, the phallus a penis, desire simple adaptation, the ego a biological construct, the analyst an ideal, repetition and resistance become defenses, and psychoanalysis consequently becomes a technique of suggestion. The attempt at dissolving resistances also dissolves psychoanalysis. (97)

Ego-psychology could not have bloomed had it not been bound by strict, overarching and comprehensive framework of institution. The 1963–64 period brought Lacan's conflict with the IPA, which resulted in his expulsion from the latter. At that time the IPA was presided over by Heinz Hartmann. The crux of the matter was Lacan's idea of a variable-length session as well as his ongoing criticism towards the orthodoxy of the IPA. The Société Française de Psychanalyse (SFP), a cooperator of the IPA and a body Lacan was a member of, faced an ultimatum by the IPA urging to expel Lacan under the pain of losing the opportunity to affiliate with the main body. Lacan's refusal to leave resulted in organizational splits. As observed by Catherine Liu,

> [t]he IPA's exclusion of Lacan appears as a defensive, bureaucratic move, designed to preserve a homogeneity in its ranks, and what could be called a reign of mediocrity in its operations; it proves itself unable to tolerate innovation on the level of either theory or technique. ("Lacanian Reception" 114–115)

The IPA "never analyzed its own status as an institution, the nature of its own decisions as such" (Liu "Lacanian Reception" 121). Lacan understood and bore disregard for bureaucratization, which in his eyes was an American phenomenon (Liu "Lacanian Reception" 122) and which cannot have left psychoanalysis alone. All in all, Hartmann's wish for an institutionalized psychoanalysis seems to have been a gargantuan need aimed at dominating the social, cultural and medical paradigm. Liu argues that

> Hartmann was ready to cooperate with sociology and psychology to establish the normative categories that would govern the administration of both mental health and education ("Lacanian Reception" 130)

With his "less technical and pragmatic understanding of authority" (Liu "Lacanian Reception" 123), Lacan found himself confronted with a highly hierarchical, authoritarian, and rigidly disciplined IPA. Liu finally adds that

> [t]his refusal of assimilation or adaptation to what was perceived as a largely American form of institutionalization allowed him to be viciously critical of post-war Freudians. ("Lacanian Reception" 123)

2 Fundamental Lacanian Concepts

2.1 Subjectivity

What is perhaps Lacan's most significant contribution not only to the field of psychoanalysis but also to literary/cultural criticism and philosophy is his exceptional conception of the subject. Although the term was picked by Lacan for various purposes over the years, its prime meaning was, in simple words, that of a person entwined in the symbolic register (language, law and order) and subjected to the unconscious. In his famous statement from "The Instance of the Letter in the Unconscious, or Reason Since Freud" (1957), the French psychoanalyst traverses Descartes' words: "I think, therefore I am" into "I am thinking where I am not, therefore I am where I am not thinking" (Écrits, 430). Being reformulated further, as we shall see, the statement is for Lacan nothing less than the indication that the actual subjectivity resides in the unconscious ("I am where I am not thinking" as opposed to the false subjectivity in "I am thinking where I am not") and is always at the mercy of the unconscious and the desire, which are elaborated in the further overview of the symbolic. The subjectivity emerges as such as the effect of the symbolic castration – Lacan bars the subject (thereby represented by the symbol of $\$$ in his formulas) to indicate its loss of pre-symbolic *jouissance* (explained further on the occasion of describing symbolic castration) due to the paternal prohibition and for the sake of entering into the realm of the language (the symbolic order). Apart from being the effect of castration, the barred, split subject, represented by "the slanted bar of noble bastardy" which is attached to "the S of the subject in order to indicate that it is this specific subject: $\$$ " (Écrits 530), takes a set of dialectical relations. On the one hand, it embodies the ego, that is, all of our imaginary, fantasized identifications with ourselves and other beings which further lead us to the false sense of our totality and of our self and ultimately equip us with the false impression of our agency. On the other hand, what is on the other side of the bar is the unconscious potential of language which is the true agent of our actions, and practically constitutes us as subjects. This is then its factual modus operandi which allows Lacan to famously claim that "the unconscious ... is structured like a language" (Écrits 737). The French psychoanalyst underscores the aforementioned illusions of the ego and the fact that being a subject entails (as much as it precedes[14]) being *subjected to* the power of the signifier, as he declares: "Such is the signifier's answer, beyond all significations: "You believe you are taking action when I am the one making you stir at the bidding of the bonds with which I weave your desires ..." (Écrits 29). The subject thus cannot constitute itself by any means; it is *barred* from doing so. In *The Lacanian Subject*, Bruce Fink elaborates on such a position and offers an interesting take on the Lacanian split when he maintains that the two sides of the bar are "I am not thinking" (upper, the ego part) and "I am not" (lower, the part of the unconscious). The postulate is based on Lacan's ideas in Seminar XV. What follows such a stance is denying the ego and the consciousness the primacy and authenticity of thinking processes insofar as they come as an offshoot; they are but secondary to the prior constitution of the subject. In other words, the ego and conscious thinking are not the cause but the effect of the appearance of the subject. Paradoxical as it may seem to be, there is *thinking*, Fink argues after Lacan, in the unconscious posited on the other side of the bar, and this is the "automatic functioning of language" (*The Lacanian Subject* 45) which is not preoccupied with establishing any kind of total self whatsoever (therefore, "I am not"). Slavoj Žižek's reading of the Lacanian subject corroborates with Fink's when he reminds us that in his seminar on *Logic of Fantasy* (Seminar XIV 1966–7) Lacan revised his own reading of *cogito* into "*I (*the subject*) am in so far as it (Es,* the Unconscious*) thinks*" (*For They Know Not* 147). Fink concludes that the Lacanian subject is the split itself and may exist only as something subjected to language. It is double barred – as a split "between two forms of otherness—the ego as other and the unconscious as the Other's discourse" (*The Lacanian Subject* 46) and as something which is denied making itself. In fact, it lacks itself, and as Fink argues,

> the subject fails to come forth as a someone, as a particular being; in the most radical sense, he or she is not, he or she has no being. The subject exists, insofar as the word has wrought him or her from nothingness, and he or she can be spoken of, talked about, and discoursed upon—yet remains beingless. (*The Lacanian Subject* 52).

Such is also Žižek's stance when he adds:

> The Unconscious is literally the "thing which thinks" and as such inaccessible to the subject: in so far as I am, I am never where "it thinks." In other words, I am only as in so far as something is left unthought: as soon as I encroach too deeply into this domain of the forbidden/ impossible thought, my very being disintegrates. (*For They Know Not* 147)

---

14 Here, I am referring to the Lacanian idea that, as subjects, we are born into the symbolic order to be further interpellated and summoned by it, which shall be explained in the analysis of the symbolic.

For the scholar, the true residence of the subject is in the very act of the Cartesian negation and thereby the loss of the world; as Tony Myers suggests: "this empty point of negativity is not 'nothing' but the opposite of everything, or the negation of all determinacy … . The subject is, in other words, a void" (Myers 37). We can therefore see that various scholars' approaches to the Lacanian subject do not essentially diverge: Žižek's point of negativity overlaps with Fink's bar. Looking at all the reformulations of Descartes' *cogito*, it is clearly seen that Lacan's initial formula from 1957 *had already included* their follow-ups. "I am thinking where I am not" indicates thinking "work" of the unconscious at the emptiness of the subject, and "… therefore I am where I am not thinking" indicates that I exist (of emptiness) insofar as I do not intrude into the unconscious with my thoughts.

2.2 Lacan's "Three Registers of Human Reality"

2.2.1 The Imaginary and the Mirror Stage

Before barring the subject, which equals the act of symbolic castration and entering into the realm of language, one faces the formative time of the illusory image of self and the other (the other, written small case, epitomizes for Lacan the image of another person): the aforementioned ego. This is the domain of what Lacan calls the imaginary order. Considering his topography of realms which govern the subject's life, there is a temptation to claim that the symbolic order is preceded by the imaginary one, yet this is merely an illusion.

It is in his early essay "The Mirror Stage as Formative of the *I* Function as Revealed in Psychoanalytic Experience" (1949) that Lacan develops his ideas pertaining to the formation of the imaginary order and speaks of the role of the eponymous mirror stage that holds a crucial part in it.[15] Although the concept lost its second-to-none importance in Lacan's later work, which witnessed a shift in focus from the order of the imaginary through the symbolic to the real, "it continued to provide a reference point to his thinking concerning the organization

---

15 Over the years Lacan reformulated his ideas on "mirror stage" several times. Also, the development of the concept is indebted to many scholars. One of them was Roger Caillois, a French thinker whose ideas and observations on the mimicry in the animal kingdom Lacan extrapolated to man. What is more, the idea of human prematurity was taken from Louis Bolk, the Dutch embryologist. Also, it was from Henri Wallon's 1931 article that Lacan borrowed the very term, changing *épreuve du miroir* (mirror test) into *stade du miroir* (mirror stage) and thereby eliminating "Wallon's reference to natural dialectic" (Roudinesco 29). For an extensive historical overview of the term see Elisabeth Roudinesco, "The Mirror Stage: An Obliterated Archive."

of the register of 'the imaginary'" (King 114). The starting point is Lacan's conclusion that human beings are always born prematurely as there are "(t)he objective notions of the anatomical incompleteness ... and of certain humoral residues of the maternal organism in the newborn" (Écrits 78). Faced with their helplessness regarding a major lack of communicative and motor functions resulting in their impression of a "fragmented body" (Écrits 78), infants cannot master the agency over their own bodies. The remedy for a newborn, argues Lacan, comes with the mimicry of the image of another child or a mirror image of oneself, which for him is the act in which in

> a series of gestures ... he [infant] playfully experiences the relationship between the movements made in the image and the reflected environment, and between this virtual complex and the reality it duplicates – namely, the child's own body, and the persons and even things around him. (Écrits 93)

Such a fresh perception for the infant is followed by the act of "*identification*, ... the transformation that takes place in the subject when he assumes an image, ... "imago"" (Écrits 76). Assuming the oneness of an image as one's own completeness equals what Lacan calls "ideal-I" (Écrits 76) (a counterpart of Freud's *Ideal ich*, which will be later on termed by Lacan as "the ideal-ego") which "situates the agency known as the ego, prior to its social determination"[16] and which will always be "the rootstock of secondary identifications" (Écrits 76) for the subject. Otherwise said, the coherence of the specular image, the ideal-ego, will serve for the subject as a paragon of excellence throughout the whole life and the subject will aim at becoming identical with it. Crucially, the perception of one's separateness and completeness is but a mirage as "the total form of his [infant's] body ... is given to him only as a gestalt" (Écrits 76) or, in other words, ""an orthopedic" form of ... totality" (Écrits 78). Also, it is underscored by Lacan that the before-mentioned identification is a form of being captured by the image. Its consequences are twofold as, on the one hand, on seeing such a unified image an infant gains motor coordination; yet, on the other hand, being trapped in the image of the other results in what Lacan refers to as alienation – "gestalt ... symbolizes one's mental permanence, at the same time as it prefigures its alienating destination" (Écrits, 76) where there will be "an inexhaustible squaring of the ego's audits" (Écrits 78). The ego, our projection of subjectivity through identifications, entails being lost in the other. The infancy, for instance, witnesses the phenomenon of transitivism – "the confusion of ego and other which is

---

16 It is again worth emphasizing that what we understand as the ego is *the effect* of such an operation.

inherent in imaginary identification" (Evans 216). As it is described by Evans, "a child can hit another child of the same age on the left side of his face, and then touch the right side of his own face and cry in imagined pain" (216). Alienation is also evident in the fact that "it remains a permanent possibility of adult human experience for us to speak and think of ourselves in the second or third person" (Sharpe). Alienation may thus typify a peculiar predicament of the subject when one's feeling of fragmentation is threatened by the totality of one's specular image, which may "give rise to an aggressive tension between the subject and the image" (Evans 118). Such a conflict may also bring the subject closer to the symbolic order. Namely, as Lacan's concept of identifying, or simply *falling in love*, with one's *imago* stems from Freudian ideas on narcissism, the subject in the mirror stage may either establish a relation with "the other in the form of a conflictual link" and this is where one "arrives at socialization" (and begins to be entwined in the symbolic), or turning back to primary narcissism, one "is lost in a maternal and deathly imago" (Roudinesco 30). It would be also useful to mention a Lacanian distinction between the ideal ego (Freudian *Ideal-ich)* and the ego ideal (Freudian *Ich-Ideal*). Differently than the first term, which has already been presented as the image one craves to be like and one craves to be seen as by others, the latter appears in the symbolic order, that is "the reign of the signifier" (Lacan, quoted by Glowinski, 84) and, as the ideal of the ego, pertains to the Other whom one tries to impress and who demands perfection. Hence, the primary narcissism in the imagined order is reinforced in the symbolic realm and there is no way to fully evade it. In Lacan's overall reckoning, the "spatial capture" taking place in the mirror stage gives evidence that there is nothing natural and inborn in the development of an infant; there is, conversely, "an organic inadequacy of his natural reality" (Écrits 77).

Importantly, apart from being an act which is said to happen at a certain period of development ("from the age of six months on ... up to the age of eighteen months") (Écrits 94–95), the phenomenon of the mirror stage is for Lacan an inherent hallmark of human subjectivity which will continue to define its imaginary identifications thereafter. Combining Kleinian "position" and Freudian "phase," Lacan reaches the "mirror stage" which "no longer has anything to do with a real stage or phase in the Freudian sense, or with a real mirror" (Roudinesco 29), and is "not a "stage" in the evolutionary sense" (Roudinesco 30) nor is it a single act. Fundamentally, the state of permanent restructuring of one's psyche throughout the whole life entails further repetitions of the mirror stage and the latter can be perceived as "a metaphor for the vision of harmony of a subject essentially in discord" (Ragland-Sullivan, quoted by Cruz, 105). This harmony, however, is never attained, and the mirror stage will "disrupt the seeming autonomy and control of the speaking subject later in life" (105). In other words, Ragland-Sullivan points to the fact that "the imagistic and fantasmatic subject of identifications continues ... to coexist ... with the subject of language and cultural codes throughout life" (Ragland-Sullivan, quoted by Cruz, 105). Therefore, the comforting image of the subject's "ideal unity" (S II 166) keeps blurring all the time, or as Lacan puts it in Seminar II, it "escapes him at every moment" (S II 166) when one is attempting to search for it in every object he perceives, for "all the objects of his world are always structured around the wandering shadow of his own ego" (S II 166).

Crucially, the mirror stage reveals that "an ontological structure of the human world" corresponds to what Lacan calls "paranoiac knowledge" (Écrits 76). The latter is the knowledge of imaginary objects among which the ego, "an imaginary production, a crystallization or sedimentation of images of an individual's own body or self-images reflected back to him or her by others" (Fink, *The Lacanian Subject* 84), takes the prime position (as an object). Knowledge is dubbed paranoiac as it works according to what Lacan calls "*the function of misrecognition*" of the ego (Écrits 80). Misrecognition creates a hiatus between the subject's ego and the other since the image the subject identifies with is in reality never as one imagines it to be. Fundamentally narcissistic and susceptible to objectifying self and others, the ego cannot reach any objective knowledge and its coordinates will always remain paranoiac, making one feel that everything is potentially possible.

Lacanian subjectivity, then, emerges in the middle of the complex interplay of images, which significantly are "not reflections of transcendental idea(l)s, but [are] strictly worldly and intersubjective" (Berressem 15). The subject emerges insofar as he or she is *seen* by others. Significantly, this pertains as much to the register of the imaginary as to the state where the language enters the subject's life. In relation to the said language, whose appearance is inevitable in the subject's life, such a formative act has to be understood as being summoned by signifiers and what Lacan calls the symbolic.

2.2.2 The Symbolic, the Signifier/Signified, the Other

Drawing clear inspirations from Claude Levi-Strauss's structural anthropology and its premise that social relations are governed by laws, pacts, kinships, and the exchange of gifts, the French psychoanalyst perceives the symbolic as the domain of language, which he regards as the founding ground for all of the above-mentioned. Since the language encompasses all three Lacanian orders (including the imaginary and the real), there is a need of greater precision; from its linguistic perspective, the symbolic dimension is constructed of signifiers in the Saussurean sense of a closed network of binary oppositions where there is not a single element with a positive meaning.

Although Lacan retains Saussure's distinction between the signifier and the signified (thus, between the phonological image and the alleged content of the sign, which together form a sign and constitute the most basic unit of the language according to Saussure), he partially questions the Swiss linguist's ideas by advancing a theory that it is only signifiers that compose the language (and not signs as it is suggested by Saussure). What is understood here and what adds another twist to Saussurean structural linguistics is a claim that it is the signifier that holds the primacy over the signified; moreover, the latter is not a given but merely a product of the former in the work of the chain of signifiers. What does Lacan mean by all this?

One may start with Lacan's substitution of Saussurean algorithm of the sign. The replacement, which "characterizes the modern stage of linguistics" (Écrits 415), is represented by an algorithm he offers in "The Instance of the Letter in the Unconscious:"

$$\frac{S}{s}$$

(Écrits 414)

Lacan modifies the Saussurean model not only by positioning the signifier (upper-case S) over the signified (italicized *s*) but also by disposing of arrows which originally meant to display relations between the elements in the Saussurean algorithm. What is put to the foreground, instead, is the bar which separates the signifier and the signified – a sign of a gap emphasizing highly arbitrary relation between a concept and its material realization, "a barrier resisting signification" (Écrits 415). Therefore, there is never a permanent bond unifying two elements, which is again signalized by the bar, as the meaning always depends on the position of the signifier in the symbolic; the meaning *slides* under the bar. It is ultimately the position that matters as the signifier is empty as such – it does not have any fixed referent whatsoever and consequently can be attached to any object; it "is a sign that doesn't refer to any object ... It, too, is a sign of absence" (S III 167). Referents of a given signifier are thus fully transposable and exchangeable. This may be visualized, for instance, by a closed system of military hierarchy in which various people may occupy the functions of lieutenant, captain or general yet the ranks and their position in the system always remain the same. Another exemplary system is that of a card game in which the function of a King or an Ace could be potentially represented by any other card depending on players' will. What is again maintained is the position, and this is Lacan's idea of the signifier.

For Lacan, there is no essential and fixed meaning manifesting itself by means of signifiers but a signifying chain (that is, a chain of signifiers) which establishes something of a constantly-fluid meaning, the signified. The latter may be labeled as a momentary feeling of comprehension and the effect of what in Lacanian nomenclature takes the name of a "quilting point." What is crucial, such a moment of possessing meaning is always directly linked to its prospective anticipation and a retroactive creation (Grigg 187). Unlike the Saussurean meaning always keeping pace with the signifier, the Lacanian sense is perennially delayed. Coming after a set of signifiers, none of which has an individual power of calling meaning into being (there need to be at least two of them to do so), a quilting point may shed a new light on the semantic understanding of a given situation, or even vary the subject's position in the symbolic (which is discussed in Seminar III). However, the meaning in its entirety cannot be closed by any means as the signifier leaves the possibilities of it open: "[y]ou can never say that this is what is being designated, for even were you to succeed you would never know what I am designating in this table – for example, the colour, the thickness, the table as object, or whatever else it might be" (S III 32). In other words, if "[t]he system of language ... never results in an index finger directly indicating a point of reality," then "a meaning always refers to another meaning, ... the meaning of ... words can't be exhausted by reference to another meaning" (S III 32–33). This is how the signifying chain works in moving from one element to another making the process of signification potentially endless; the signified created in the process of signification refers again to some signifier(s) which in turn refer further to some signifieds. As observed by Lacan, "[t]he sense ... always refers to something that is out ahead or that turns back upon itself, ... there is a direction" (S III 137). Importantly, being a "passage" from one signifier to another (S V, 23.4.58, 8), the signifying chain stems from and bears witness to insufficiency of any signifier and their fleetness; there is always "something which is beyond each one of the elements which are articulated, and which are of their nature fleeing, vanishing" (S V, 23.4.58, 8). The passage is insatiable; there is always yet another point of reference.

Besides drawing upon Levi-Strauss and Saussure, Lacan also makes use of structural linguistics of Roman Jakobson, especially when describing the passage of signifiers in the signifying chain. Namely, the French psychoanalyst employs Jakobson's distinction made in his seminal essay "Two Aspects of Language and Two Types of Aphasic Disturbances" (1956) between metonymy and metaphor as the two governing tropes in the construction of a message. For Lacan, the former figure represents the way signifiers are linked one to another owing to their contiguity and forming a horizontal chain of related elements as, for instance, when he writes of "thirty sails" understood as "thirty ships" in "The Instance of the Letter in the Unconscious" (Écrits 421). As he points, "the connection between ship and sail is nowhere other than in the signifier, and ... metonymy is based on the *word-to-word* nature of this connection" (Écrits 421). What is crucial, none of signification takes place therein as the metonymical movement takes place on the upper side of "signifier/signified" algorithm with the bar separating signifiers from any signified. Conversely, as "*one word for another*" (Écrits 422), the metaphor is capable of overcoming the bar and making signification possible. Unlike metonymy, it is a vertical movement in which one of the signifiers in one signifying chain "has replaced the other by taking the other's place" in another signifying chain (Écrits 422) and thereby constructed meaning – the signified. Both metonymy and metaphor (which are based on Freudian concepts of displacement and condensation) will be put into practice by Lacan in many of his concepts.

A natural consequence of the structural character of the symbolic universe is the symbolic perception of subjectivity. If any element in the symbolic order may be reduced to the work of signifiers, such is the destiny of the subject, which is for Lacan reduced to one of signifiers and as such is represented for the rest of them. The subject simply becomes *the effect of language* and

> [t]he effect of language is to introduce the cause into the subject. Through this effect, he is not the cause of himself; he bears within himself the worm of the cause that splits him. For his cause is the signifier ... [T]his signifier is what the signifier represents, and the latter cannot represent anything except to another signifier: to which the subject who listens is thus reduced. (Écrits, 708)

Hence, as the symbolic supplement to the imaginary, the subject emerges insofar as he or she is *signified* and only after such an operation on him or her can one operate on the outer reality. What is also underscored in the previous passage is the inert and passive status of the subjectivity; the subject emerges only insofar as "[t]he symbolic provides a form into which the subject is inserted at the level of his being" and "[i]t is on the basis of the signifier that the subject recognizes himself as being this or that" (S III 179). Interestingly, introducing the subject into the system, the signifier, as perceived by Lacan, is incapable of elucidating human procreation and "the subject's singular existence" (S III 179). Lacan enumerates the questions of ontological, epistemological, and teleological nature, which are left with no answer from the signifier:

> Why is he [the subject] here? Where has he come from? What is he doing here? Why is he going to disappear? The signifier is incapable of providing him with the answer, for the good reason that it places him beyond death. The signifier already considers him dead, by nature it immortalizes him. (S III 179–180)

If the symbolic "insists beyond the limit of life and death, as a logic that is by definition immortal," such questions that trouble the subject seem to "sit at an awkward angle to the movements of the signifier" (Eyers 113). Such a discord comes with one's awareness of the deficiency of the signifier as a provider of a stable identity in the face of the subject's "Real existence" (Eyers 112), another of Lacan's orders, which is unsymbolizable.

Importantly, even though the imaginary order is treated as a pre-linguistic state of nature and the symbolic register epitomizes the state of culture, by no means is there a gradual evolution from the former to the latter. If "[t]he human order is characterized by the fact that the symbolic function intervenes at every moment and every stage of its existence" (S II 29), then one is always already entangled in the symbolic register. It is only in a retroactive manner that the subject becomes aware that the symbolic *has already been there* and it *has always been there*. What is more, as it "isn't constituted bit by bit," the symbolic encapsulates the subject in a total manner – it is always "a universe of symbols" (S II 29) we find ourselves in and we cannot think outside of, as "[e]verything which is human has to be ordained" (S II 29) by the symbolic function. Hence, this positions also the imaginary order at the mercy of the symbolic; all the visual manifestations and identifications are structured by the domain of the signifier and the imaginary is already inscribed in the domain of the symbolic. Thus, the responsibility of the analyst is to avoid preoccupation with the imaginary realm of the analysand although the former "prefers to fall back on his ego" (Écrits 494). Instead, the only possible choice for a Lacanian practitioner is to deal with the symbolic register, where images may be converted to words.

Such for Lacan is the nature of language, which underpins as well as remains in inerasable affinity with the aforementioned social structures of the symbolic: laws, pacts, kinships, and the exchange of gifts. As he argues in Seminar III, "[t]he notion of structure is by itself ... a manifestation of the signifier" (S III 183). The most basic nature of any social structure is that of an exchange and, moving further, the most primal exchange comes for Lacan with communication. Namely, in his Seminar IV (1956–57), *The Object Relation*, he speaks of the exchange of words as of "the gift of speech" which is a prerequisite for entering and establishing social relations (Moore 48). What is further anchored in speech are rules, pacts, kinships and laws, which naturally work according to the language since the

> law ... reveals itself clearly enough as identical to a language order. For without names for kinship relations, no power can institute the order of preferences and taboos that knot and braid the thread of lineage through the generations. (Écrits 229–230)

Therefore, as it is argued by Lacan, "there is no society that does not include positive law, whether traditional or written, common law or civil law" (Écrits 103) which can always be traced back to the foundation of language.

The totality of symbolic structures and laws is perceived and termed by Lacan as the Other (the so-called "big" other as opposed to the "small-case other" discussed on the occasion of the imaginary order). If the other is understood as a reflective and specular counterpart of the ego working with it in a dual relation, then the Other works in a triadic structure with speaking subjects as an overall alterity (understood as otherness opposed to subjectivity) of the symbolic order. It is then, on the one hand, a kind of an individual subject-witness to other subjects' speech ("there is always an Other beyond all concrete dialogue, all interpsychological play" (S III 273)) and, on the other hand, the symbolic in its entire nature of law, language and order. The latter sense of the concept emphasizes its combinatorial and encompassing character that makes it "the overarching "objective spirit" of trans-individual socio-linguistic structures configuring the fields of inter-subjective interactions" (Sharpe). It may be also equalized with Wittgensteinian term of "objective certainty" understood as "the field of a symbolic pact which is "always-already" here, which we ""always-already" accept and recognize" (Žižek, *For They Know Not* 151). Such a perspective corroborates with Wittgenstein's comments on "objective certainty" as a feeling when " 'I have compelling grounds for my certitude.' These grounds make the certitude objective. What is telling ground for something is not anything *I* decide" (Wittgenstein, quoted by Vintiadis, 145). The Other is then an anchor the subject believes to be a residue of intersubjective rules, which one has no other way than to accept and obey. What is more, its system has to be believed by the subjects as a complete and the only one for "the one who does *not* recognize it, the one whose attitude is that of *disbelief* in the big Other, has a precise name in psychoanalysis: a *psychotic*" (Žižek, *For They Know Not* 151). A psychotic is the one who does not recognize the symbolic structure; he/she "is "mad" precisely in so far as [he/she] holds to attitudes and beliefs excluded by the existing "life-form [Wittgensteinian *Lebensform*]" (Žižek, *For They Know Not* 151). Understood as a code or mode of socio-linguistic/cultural existence, the Other may be also associated with or referred to as a narrative or system of beliefs, like God, Ideology, Science, Nature.

As the terms of language and speech often intersperse when the symbolic is scrutinized, it would be vital at this point to underscore the important distinction Lacan draws between the two. His prime focus on the concepts, as on the symbolic, falls on the 1950s, the time of his manifesto "The Function and Field of Speech and Language in Psychoanalysis," often referred to as "Rome discourse." Lacan's distinguishing into language and speech is first and foremost anchored in the opposition between what is respectively dubbed *langage* and *parole*. While the former "refers to the system of language in general, abstracting from all particular languages" (Evans 99), the latter is understood as any practical realization of this system by the subject.[17] What is more, it holds a prime importance in psychoanalysis as "psychoanalysis has but one medium: the patient's speech" (Écrits 206), which hints at the operations of the unconscious. Lacan importantly adds that "all speech calls for a response ... even if speech meets only with silence" (Écrits 206).

There is, however, an obstacle for the analyst as he or she has to separate what Lacan calls "empty speech" from the "full speech." Respectively, it should not be the ego which speaks, but the subject. If all the imaginary identifications and expectations of the ego are dismantled, the subject recognizes his/her true position in the symbolic order. This puts an end to the analytical treatment:

> One trains analysts so that there are subjects in whom the ego is absent. That is the ideal of analysis, which, of course, remains virtual. There is never a subject without an ego ... but that ... is what one must aim to obtain from the subject in analysis.
> The analysis must aim at the passage of true speech, joining the subject to another subject .... That is the final relation of the subject to a genuine Other, to the Other who gives the answer one doesn't expect" (S II 246).

It is often emphasized by Lacan that the Other is a locus; the locus "in which is constituted the I who speaks along with he who hears, what is said by the one being already a reply" (Écrits 358). The Other is thus a residue of speech for any subject taken, a sort of umbilical cord with the system of language when the psychoanalyst argues that it "extends as far into the subject as the laws of speech

---

17 What is significant, Lacan diverges from Saussure in putting aside *langue* referring to a particular language.

reign there, … [it] is well beyond the discourse that takes its watchwords from the ego, since Freud discovered its unconscious field and the laws that structure it" (Écrits 358). It is significant that the Other as a locus is prime to aforementioned Other as a subject. As it is put by Lacan, "[p]ersons ... must come from somewhere" and "[t]hey come first in a signifying" (S III 274) after which they may personify the Other for another subject. It could be claimed that by hypostatizing this *somewhere* as a locus Lacan already underscores the witnessing nature of the Other.

It is thus in the speech that we are left with the traces of the unconscious, which is primarily "structured like a language" (Écrits 737), as famously claimed by Lacan. In our linguistic experience language always already contains us, crucially, with all the ambiguity that comes with our speech, and it is in this ambiguity that a psychoanalyst tracks down the unconscious at work. What is more, pointing to the fact that "the unconscious is the Other's discourse" (Écrits 316), Lacan yet again underscores the passivity and incapacitation of the subject, who is only at the mercy of the Other (and the unconscious) as a dispenser of speech; the subject as if exists outside itself as it is merely owned by the Other in linguistic and symbolic sense and may emerge only as such. Perhaps the most radical sense of such a moment of emergence comes with what Lacan calls founding speech, which "envelops the subject, is everything that has constituted him, his parents, his neighbours, the whole structure of his community, and not only constituted him as a symbol, but constituted him in his being" (S II 20).

All the aforementioned ideas may be complemented with another of Lacan's observations which posits that "language is as much there to found us in the Other as to drastically prevent us from understanding him" (S II 244). What may be inferred thereof: "[w]hen we use language [thus, speak], our relation with the other always plays on ... ambiguity" (S II 244). The Other, in Lacanian understanding, is to serve as a point of reference *par excellence* in the symbolic, yet it is simultaneously unfathomable, with the ambiguous speech of other subjects as the best exemplification. As it is famously claimed by Lacan, the Other "does not exist" (Écrits 700) before the subject in a single given form or totality and as such is ungraspable. In other words, the ambiguity and mystery that comes with the other using language is ultimately the ambiguity and mystery of the symbolic and the Other. Here lies the task of the analyst: to take the position of the Other and make the analysand aware of the unconscious (and desire, as we shall see) by pinpointing to ambiguities of his or her speech. This, hence, is the meaning of Lacan's confusing words that *what is said* is *already a reply* – speech already includes answers for any questions it may pose. The Other anchored in speech knows the subject's desire.

We may see that the idea of the Other is for Lacan a fluid concept carrying various connotations on a given occasion. As Grigg observes, Lacan describes the Other

> variously as the discourse of the unconscious; as ... the guarantor of the truth; and as the treasure of signifiers upon all speech acts must draw. The common element in all these formulations of Lacan's is that the Other is the third place in discourse, radically external to both speaker and listener. (Grigg 190)

2.2.3 The Real

Like many other Lacanian concepts, the real entered Lacan's theoretical apparatus to be further reformulated and take the prime focus of Lacan's interests in the final stage of his life and work. The term first appears as early as in a 1936 paper, as is noted by Evans, in the spirit of early twentieth-century philosophy and its representative, Emile Meyerson, who defined the real as "an ontological absolute, a true being in itself" (Meyerson, quoted by Evans, 162). However, it is many years later, in 1953, that the real obtains its status as one of three orders governing subject's life and becomes a well-covered and commented concept ever since, perhaps acquiring most attention in Lacan's seminal seminar discussing *The Ethics of Psychoanalysis* (1959–60).

Regardless of the shifts it has undergone throughout years, the crucial aspect of the real has always been its unsymbolized and unsymbolizable nature. Lacan claims that the real "is what resists symbolisation absolutely" (S I 66), and therefore, it evades both the imaginary and symbolic order.[18] However that does not exclude a degree of interrelation between the three realms. Through the resistance of the real emerges the fundamental difference the psychoanalyst makes between "reality" and "the real." Namely, in Lacan's own words, "reality, the whole of human reality, is nothing other than a *montage* of the symbolic and the imaginary" and "the desire, at the centre of this apparatus, of this frame, that we call reality, is ... what covers ... what must be distinguished from human reality, and which is properly speaking the *real*, which is never more than glimpsed" (S XIV 7). Hence, in a general overview, the reality is to be perceived as a network of symbolic and imaginary identifications as opposed to the real being a matter that eludes such operations. The desire, a concept which shall be elaborated later on, is for Lacan an inherent element of the symbolic which merely hints at and

18 This, in the early 50s, allows Lacan to claim that the real is not within the scope of psychoanalytical interest as the foundation of a treatment relies on language and speech, which are excluded from the real.

reminds one of the insufficiency of the reality as a symbolic and imaginary construct as confronted with the self-sufficiency of the real. If the symbolic order is built upon a chain of signifiers whose deficiencies render a sense of lack and instability, the real is characterized as something "absolutely without fissure" (S II 97) and complete. Moreover, both imaginary identifications of the ego, which aim at an accordant unity with an image, and the never-ending presence/absence dialectics characteristic of the symbolic (one element is to fill the absence of another, yet it only starts to mark the absence) cease to matter in the real as "[t]here is no absence in the real" (S II 313). In other words,

> [i]f the imaginary is a question of sameness, and the symbolic one of difference, this unrepresentable vanishing point of humanity, to which Lacan gives the name of the Real, is a matter of both sameness and strangeness, allowing us to find ourselves mirrored in the very alienness, unrelatedness or deathly singularity of the other. (Eagleton, *Trouble with Strangers* 272)

What then also emerges from the Lacanian perspective on the real is its congruence with the concept of the other. Namely, the other is real in so far as it cannot be discerned beyond its symbolic and imaginary identifications; it is always an alien neighbor whose desire remains enigmatic to a subject. This has been the reading taken by many scholars, Žižek and Eagleton among others,[19] who, after Lacan, employ Freudian *das Ding* as the unfathomable element in the other.

Das Ding – "the Thing" – is something belonging to the realm of the real and as such remains unscrutinizable and unassimilable for the symbolic or imaginary register of the subject since the real is "that which resists symbolization absolutely" (S I 66). Since Lacan perceives it as "the-beyond-of-the-signified" (S VII 55), the Thing remains outside the system of language, and consequently, outside the unconscious. As it is elucidated by Evans, *das Ding* may be only *represented* in the symbolic (the language and the unconscious) as *die Sache* (another German word for "thing") in *Sachvorstellungen* ("thing-presentations) (207) while in its nature it is an incomprehensible and inconceivable "dumb reality" (S VII 55).

What is perhaps of second-to-none importance when considering Lacanian understanding of the Thing is that it is the founding for the symbolic, all signification, and a sense of loss experienced by the subject. Relying on Heidegger's thoughts on the emptiness of a vase as its founding factor in "Das Ding," Lacan postulates similar ideas pertaining to signifiers in "On Creation *ex nihilo*" in

---

19 See Eagleton, *Trouble with Strangers* and Slavoj Žižek, *How to Read Lacan*. New York: W.W. Norton & Co, 2007. Print.

Seminar VII. Just as the emptiness of a vase is precisely what makes it an object (also, a signifier) to be used, "the emptiness at the center of the Real that is called the Thing, this emptiness as represented in the representation presents itself as a *nihil*, as nothing" (S VII 121). This is the condition for the beginning of signification as the Thing becomes a signifier of signifying; like a vase it is "a hole with something around it" (S VII 121) – a void in the center of the real which begins to be visible as some signifiers start to revolve around it. Lacan even advances a metaphor of himself as "the potter" who "creates the vase ... around ... emptiness" (S VII 121) by speaking to the audience. Significantly, signifiers only prove that there is a void never to be filled, which renders a sense of irrevocable loss in the subject, never to be recuperated. Emphasizing once again the founding character which engenders a never-to-be-filled nature of *das Ding*, Lacan points out that "the fashioning of the signifier and the introduction of a gap or a hole in the real is identical" (S VII 121). From there on, the subject's progress "will be oriented around the *Ding* as *Fremde*, strange and even hostile on occasion" (S VII 52) and will be a "progress that seeks points of reference ... with the world of desires" (S VII 52) that cannot be satiated. As a regulator, the pleasure principle makes sure that the subject faces "an optimum tension" to establish a constant "state of wishing for it [the lost object] and waiting for it" (S VII 52). Ultimately for Lacan the lost object stands for the forbidden, incestuous relation with the mother who "occupies the place of ... *das Ding*" (S VII 67), and "the law of prohibition of incest" is what was believed by Freud to be "the law of which all other cultural developments are no more than consequences and ramifications" (S VII 67). The mother is thus elevated to the status of the Real Other, commented on by Johnston:

> In the beginning of the psychical-libidinal subject's ontogenetic life history, the maternal caretaker is, at one and the same time, both overwhelmingly, stiflingly present or near and, in her strange, impenetrable alterity, also frustratingly, uncontrollably absent or inaccessible; there is either too much or too little of her, never the right balanced amount. With the passage of time and the temporal transformations of the libidinal economy, the mother, as this archaic Real Other, becomes the forever unattainable "Sovereign Good," the fixed vanishing point, of all desiring. (Johnston)

This double nature of something simultaneously missing from the subject's life and displaying a perplexing and overwhelming presence lies at the nature of *das Ding* and anything that attempts to represent it.

The French psychoanalyst also claims that "the Thing only presents itself to the extent that it becomes word" (S VII 55), *le mot* which hints at something which "remains silent; ... in response to which no word is spoken" (S VII 55). Metaphorizing it further as Harpo Marx's smile which is "absorbing, ...

disruptive, ... nauseating, ... [and] sufficient to sustain the atmosphere of doubt and of radical annihilation" (S VII 55), Lacan hints at the Thing as inextricably linked with the sublime, or more precisely, sublimation in his nomenclature.[20] The operation of metaphorizing is not without importance as in sublimation, according to Lacan, an object (in any sense of the word) is raised "to the dignity of the Thing" (S VII 112); thus, the subject may imagine and elevate a given signifier as a representation of *das Ding*. The object of sublimation imbues one with terror as, by means of sublimation (for instance, in a poetic act), we find ourselves "positing an object I can only describe as terrifying, an inhumane partner" (S VII 150). On the other hand, such an object is perceived as the one capable of satisfactorily filling the sense of loss accordant with the void of the Thing. Yet, it is always inaccessible, "in its nature ... the object as such is lost" (S VII 52). Lacan exemplifies sublimation with the troubadours practicing an impossible courtly love to the Lady. As he argues, "courtly love was ... a poetic exercise, a way of playing with a number of ... idealizing themes, which couldn't have any real concrete equivalent" (S VII 148); a prime ideal was precisely that of an ethereal Lady. Significantly, the love-object of sublimation is for Lacan of feminine nature – it is a vaginal object whose emptiness is turned into a presence and ultimately "courtly love [is] the elevation of the woman into the place where her absence or inaccessibility stands in for male lack" (Rose, quoted by Breitenberg, 180). Finally, as an act of ascribing imaginary features to *das Ding*, sublimation is "fundamentally narcissistic in character" (S VII 151). Lacan perceives it as an anamorphous act and a mirror in which one may see their ideal yet may not cross its surface of separation to reach the desired object. Summing up, as it is put by Ronen,

> Sublimation is located between the narcissistic object and the Thing. At its foundations, sublimation retains the primary loss, the culturally imposed loss of an object, which is why in sublimation one cannot distinguish the Thing from its social-cultural imaginary adaptation. The imaginary object in sublimation – whether in the form of the ideal ego, in the image if the lady of the knights in medieval culture, or in a formless sublime object of nature – constitutes a place of a momentary repose in the company of *das Ding*, a moment in which the subject attains the domain of instinctual satisfaction by means of imaginary schemes.

---

20 For a detailed discussion over the distinction between the sublime and sublimation, often perplexing in Lacanian criticism, see Catherine Belsey, *Culture and the Real: Theorizing Cultural Criticism*. London: Routledge, 2005.

So for Lacan ... *das Ding* can be recruited to locate the object of sublimation, to show that sublimation is not without an object, and yet its object cannot be identified with the imaginary presentation. (Ronen 129)

With such modus operandi, the sublimation is located "beyond the pleasure principle, where anxiety in front of the Thing is imbued with satisfaction" (Ronen 129).

Returning to "the other," we may now see that it intersects both the imaginary and the real order. Performing its functions in the former domain, it is an idealistic and narcissistic projection of one's neighbor aimed to be dominated by the subject's ego. Of such a tenet of the other Lacan speaks: "What I want ... is the good of others provided that it remains in the image of my own" (Lacan, quoted by Eagleton, *Trouble with Strangers* 159–160). As an unfathomable neighbor located in the realm of the real, the other petrifies the subject with the question of its desire and mysterious enjoyment that we will later call *jouissance*, and as such is "a traumatic alterity" (Reinhard 99). According to Lacan, the Freudian *Nebenmench*, neighbor, "expresses powerfully the idea of beside yet alike, separation and identity" (S VII 51). It may be treated as one's very first contact with the real when Lacan speaks of "original division of the experience of reality" (S VII 52) after approaching the real in the other. This sense of strangeness/alikeness shapes the subject's further progress. What Lacan means is that such confrontation engenders first imaginary identifications as well as leaves a leftover, a sense of something forever unfathomable – *das Ding*, which will always be at the center of the subject's interest. Finally, the other as *das Ding* allows Lacan to demand the existence of "the prehistoric Other that ... is impossible to forget – the Other whose primacy of position Freud affirms in the sense of something *entfremdet*, something strange to me, although it is at the heart of me" (S VII 71). What makes a way to bridge this gap of a traumatic alterity is love in Lacanian sense:

> "to love our neighbor as our self" is to encounter what is most singularly strange and disturbing in the other person, what is most rageful, perverse, or disgusting, and unknowable, ... – yet to acknowledge that dark abyss as the figure of our own unconscious desire. (Reinhard 99)

For Lacan, it is not loving "in spite of," but precisely "for" the sheer horror of alterity that comes with the other (Reinhard 100). Ultimately, it is not the artificiality of the symbolic, but this traumatic alterity that constitutes both the subject and the other; the search for *das Ding* is the search for a true common ground.

It is thus no surprise that it is the realm of the real that Lacan points at when commenting on Freud's notion of "truth" which "cannot be approached in terms of true and false representations or in terms of symbolic order and reality, for truth is linked to the real, and not to reality" (Shepherdson 32). Interestingly, as Shepherdson notes, the psychoanalyst coined the word *le vréel* to emphasize such a bond between the truth and the real (32).

For Lacan, such a status of something strange and outer at the heart of the subject, the phenomenon of simultaneous insideness /outsideness, is ascribed to the real as a kind of "intimate alterity" relying on an exclusion (Shepherdson 2). Namely, Lacan speaks of "the centre only in the sense that it is excluded" and, in a reciprocal way, of something which is "excluded in the interior" (Lacan, quoted by Shepherdson, 2). According to Shepherdson this obscurity points to something which is not outside of, but "missing *from* the structure" (2). Here again we turn back to a lost object, the Thing, missing from the reality of the symbolic, but nonetheless exhibiting its *representations* in the aforementioned realm. As an intimate alterity it "is an element that appears without appearing, emerging "inside" of the structure without belonging to the structure" and it "persists in "presenting itself"" (45) and this is the answer to the curious paradox.[21]

What is perhaps symptomatic of the gnomic nature of the Lacanian real, Lacanian studies approach the concept of the real in a heterogeneous manner. In a predominant way, it "remains an inaccessible, prediscursive reality, while reality is understood as a symbolic or imaginary construction" (Shepherdson 32). Yet, Charles Shepherdson gives evidence that the perception of the real as "an external domain that *precedes* representation and remains unknown" (34) or something "abolished as soon as it is spoken" (Kojève, quoted by Shepherdson, 33) is but one tendency (albeit a prevailing one in Lacanian-oriented criticism) to juxtapose it with "reality." As we are reminded by the scholar, a no less significant aspect of the real is its nature of a "lack, ... a *postsymbolic* phenomenon, a void that arises *through* the symbolic order, as an effect of the symbolic order which is nevertheless irreducible to the imaginary or symbolic" (34). As it is added by Žižek in the same spirit, the real emerges with the thinning of the symbolic; it

> is ... not an inaccessible kernel hidden beneath layers of symbolization, it is *on the surface* – ... a kind of excessive disfiguration of reality, like the fixed grimace of a smile on Joker's face in *Batman*. (Žižek *Looking Awry*, 172n2).

---

21 Interestingly, Shepherdson also reads the "intimate alterity" of the real as a post-structuralistic maneuver of Lacan's in the fashion of Derridean "the law of the law" – the real is the failure of the symbolic (and of structuralism in a way) which nevertheless (as a gap, a failure) may serve for theoretical ponderings (9).

According to the scholar, this pertains to what is referred to by Lacan as the "grimace of the real" (Lacan, quoted by Žižek, *Looking Awry* 172n2). The real is then a sort of gap in the symbolic. In consequence of its disturbing nature and lurking out of the symbolic, it is perceived as the source of trauma in the subject's life and the cause of psychopathological phenomena.

It is since 1964 and his seminar on *The Four Fundamental Concepts of Psychoanalysis* that Lacan begins to approach the realm of the real with yet another set of metaphors, which eventually make the traumatic nature of the real more evident. In the said seminar the psychoanalyst ponders upon the real as "an essential encounter – an appointment to which we are always called with the real that eludes us" (S XI 53). Lacan makes it clear that the character of this encounter is traumatic when he indicates that "[t]he function of ... the real as encounter – the encounter in so far as it can be missed, in so far as it is essentially the missed encounter – first presented itself in the history of psychoanalysis in a form ... of the trauma" (S XI 55). This encounter with the real, Aristotelian *tuché*, which is borrowed by the psychoanalyst, is situated in the opposition to *automaton* understood as the network of signifiers, or more precisely, "the return, the coming-back, the insistence of the signs, by which we see ourselves governed by the pleasure principle" (S XI 53–54). By saying that the real eludes us and arguing that the subject's encounter with the real is always missed, Lacan insists that the presence of the real can never be felt but in its belated, contingent effects. These are merely what Freud calls *Vorstellungrepresantanz*, and Lacan translates as "that which takes place of [real] representation [*Vorstellung*]"[22] (S XI 60), that is, signifiers. In his seminar Lacan expatiates on a case described by Freud in *The Interpretation of Dreams* portraying the father who, resting in a room next to the one with the corpse of his dead son, is awakened in his dream by the dead son asking: "Father, can't you see that I'm burning?" (S XI 58). As further explained by Lacan, the son's words pertain to the actual reality of the bed that caught fire, yet also to the actual cause of the child's death, the fever. Lacan claims that the message contains the (real) reality which is missed in a double sense – it is what is lacked by the symbolic reality and what comes too late to change anything. For Lacan such an awakening is synonymous with "the waking state of

22 Translating Freudian *Vorstellung* into English, as well as interpreting it from the Lacanian perspective, has been a problematic matter. Bruce Fink keeps interpreting it as "representation" and underscoring its real nature as something [real] which is represented by signifiers, yet is by no means a signifier itself as opposed to *Vorstellungrepresantanz*, which is a signifier. This analysis follows Fink's stance. See Bruce Fink, "The Real Cause of Repetition"

subject's consciousness in the representation of what has happened" (S XI 59), which again pertains to the fact that consciousness is something separated from and denied a direct access to the reality of the real. *Tuché*, therefore, epitomizes the inaccessibility of the void of the real, a fundamental lack in the symbolic, which misses the real and fails to find signifiers that could fill it. What we get in a discussed dream is merely "an act of homage to the missed reality – the reality that can no longer produce itself except by repeating itself endlessly, in some never attained awakening" (S XI 58). Fink indicates that "the real's representation [*Vorstellung*] is lacking and what we find in the dream is its place-holder, its stand-in"; the former is merely "represented but never presented" (Fink, "The Real Cause of Repetition" 227). This representation is ultimately the symbolic revolving around the lack of presence of the real. Thus, the traumatic reality can only be hinted at and repeat itself in the function of *automaton* – the reality of signifiers, of the symbolic, and of the unconscious – in a distorted and always belated manner. As Fink observes, "it is the missing *Vorstellung* (missing in the symbolic, in the representational space of the dream, not something missing in the real) that leads to repetition" ("The Real Cause of Repetition" 227) as a search for something lost. The scholar continues:

> It is the non-representational nature of the real that brings on repetition, requiring the subject to return to that place of the lost object, the lost satisfaction. Every other satisfaction pales in comparison with the one that was lost, and the subject repetitively returns to the site of that absence in the hope of obtaining the *real Thing*, and yet forever missing it. (228)

Here we notice that the traumatic character of the real must eventually intersect with the lost satisfaction and the lost sense of completeness which need to be compensated for; thus, the traumatic real enters a dialectical relation with the search for retaining the object which guaranteed totality and which the subject allegedly lost.

What is more, Lacan argues that repetition is fostered by the deficiency and inability of signifiers to hold once and for all to what is signified; therefore, the aim of significance has a tendency to be forgotten. Any traumatic content, thus, in a way reappears, as the symbolic constantly proves to be incapable of inscribing it in itself once and for all. The reason, Shepherdson believes, is that "there has been no sufficient symbolic or imaginary network in place for representing it" (34). As is observed by Verhaeghe, any subsequent attempt to lock the real in a system of signifiers ends up with a greater number of signifiers and moving further away from the real; thus Lacan speaks of the real as of "what does not stop not writing itself" (Lacan, quoted by Verhaeghe, 8). It is also significant that, in the spirit of the belatedness of and the missed encounter with the real, a given event is traumatized only in a retroactive manner to indicate that something cannot be grasped with the symbolic up to a present moment. Commenting on Freud's case of the Wolf Man, Lacan observes that the subject may even become fixated on the question of the origin of the trauma, the "anguish [of his] question – what is the first encounter, the real, that lies behind the phantasy?" (S XI 54). Accordingly, the lost object, the sense of perfect completeness, in fact, has never existed, but "is retroactively constituted as having had to have been lost" (Fink, "The Real Cause of Repetition" 228), which makes repetition, as well as the realm of symbolic possible at all.

Hence, the post-symbolic nature of Lacanian real is evident; the real "is traumatic, not in itself, but only in relation to the established order of representation" (Shepherdson 34). It is not

> the immediate contact with an external reality [of the unknown], ... but a new signification that has retroactive effects on the past, [the result of] a shift in the symbolic" [due to which] "the past suddenly appear[s] as traumatic, as false and slanted and full of holes. (Shepherdson 36)

For Freud and Lacan alike, these limits of (traumatic) memory are related to the real and they foster repetition:

> Let us take a look, then, at how Wiederholen (repeating) is introduced. Wiederholen is related to Erinnerung (remembering). "The subject in himself, the recalling of his biography, all this goes only to a certain limit which is known as the real." (Lacan, quoted by Fink, "The Real Cause of Repetition" 224)

Fink points out that the real is "impossible to say" and "impossible to think" ("The Real Cause of Repetition" 225) as it cannot be consciously encountered; it "comes back to the place at which the subject ... does not come across it" (225). This is then the meaning of Lacanian real as "that which always returns to the same place" (S XI 49) when the subject, in the manner of repetition, attempts to give it a symbolic presence.

Finally, repetition at the level of *automaton*, according to Lacan, is not a "return of need" (a biological necessity) but something that "demands the new" (S XI 61) and "occurs ... *as if by chance*" (S XI 54). Elucidating Lacan's words, Fink indicates that Lacan's idea of repetition differs from what we used to take it commonsensically for; namely, it is not a return (of the same), but a "return with a difference" ("The Real Cause of Repetition" 224). In the course of the search for the lost object, the said difference may be called a repetitive failure of the symbolic to reach this object; it is the difference of heterogeneous things or events which attempt to cover the loss and which nevertheless "may be equated because one signifier covers all of them" (Fink, "The Real Cause of Repetition" 224). Fink gives the example of blue eyes of one's mother as an object of fascination:

> while no two sets of eyes are ever absolutely identical, and no two shades of blue either, ... the word "blue" allows [one] to equate his mother's blue eyes with a partner's blue eyes and thus to transfer his fascination with the former to the latter. Language allows for such equations, ... (*The Lacanian Subject* 26)

Repetition is thus the reappearance of diverse elements under one signifier; it is "a misnomer, consisting in the return, not of the same, but of the different" (Fink, "The Real Cause of Repetition" 223). Fundamentally, as Fink observes, it is "the return of that which remains self-identical, and that can only be object *a*" (224).

2.3 Object a

As it is pointed by Shepherdson, the emergence of the real leaves us with a feeling that, on the one hand, there is a void or lack in the symbolic, and on the other hand, that the symbolic experiences some kind of surplus, "a certain excess it cannot adequately contain". The real is then something "simultaneously too little and too much" (Shepherdson 38) and here appears the role of object a (also known as "object petit a"). Having been introduced by Lacan in the 50s, *l'objet petit a* (alike many other terms) was to undergo some elaboration throughout years and become one of the key concepts of Lacanian theoretical apparatus.[23]

Importantly, object a may be characterized by its strong bond with the subject's fantasy as can be observed with Lacanian matheme referring to the latter. Namely, the Lacanian algorithm for fantasy ($ ◊ *a*) teaches one that it emerges as soon as the subject ($) is barred by the signifier (thus becoming a desiring subject) and subsequently launches attempts to make up for some undefined, alleged loss. The symbol "*a*," which is established in a mutual rapport (◊) with the subject, is *objet petit a*, the object-cause of the desire to fill the lack which has been caused by barring the subject. Crucially, what must be underscored is that object a is by no means something attainable, but something causative for the search of a factor that would redeem the loss which is experienced. The appearance of such a construct as a potential solution consequently results in a number of real-life objects entering the libidinal dynamics of the subject and being desired by him or her. These objects, however, always prove to be merely an ersatz of something

23 Bruce Fink indicates that the invention finds its roots in Freudian idea of "lost objects" yet, as he adds, these were never said to be always inexorably lost (*The Lacanian Subject* 93).

yet more fulfilling and all-encompassing which was allegedly lost. This proves the phantasmatic nature of object a, which in Lacan's own words is "the presence of a hollow, a void, which can be occupied" (S XI 180) and which is surrounded by drives revolving around it (S XI 243). Also, its position at the intersection of unsymbolizable real and phantasmatical imaginary is reflected in what Fink calls its "unspecularizable" nature (Fink, *The Lacanian Subject* 92), which practically means that

> you cannot see them [the manifestations of object a] per se, they have no mirror images and they are extremely difficult to symbolize or formalize. ... They are nevertheless closely related to the subject's most crucial experiences of pleasure and pain, excitement and disappointment, thrill and horror. They ... are related to jouissance that defines the subject's very being. (92)

As with the real, we may speak of object a as of both contributing to the lack in the realm of the symbolic and as being the result of the deficiency of the symbolic to symbolize everything. This deficiency may be exemplified by experiencing emotions which are impossible to be put into words. From such a perspective, *l'objet petit a* is what remains and reminds the subject of the insufficiency of the signifier. Being not "a past that has been lost, but something that presents itself in the present" (Shepherdson 45), it nevertheless leaves the subject with phantasmatic feelings that it is something coming from the past and that there once was a time when there were no such discrepancies. Shepherdson insightfully remarks that object a

> is not a leftover that remains from the past, or the "return" of an original state, but the temporal paradox in which we find the return of something that did not originally exist, but only emerged "after the fact" ... as an *effect* of symbolization. Its apparently "original" status is thus strictly mythical. (47)

Object a is thus the embodiment (despite not having a body of its own) of the surplus-effect of the real, the part of reality which defies symbolization. From such a stance it is known by the name of the surplus-of-enjoyment (*plus-de-jouir*), a surplus which the process of symbolization cannot deal with because it "is what resists this assimilation to the function of the signifier" (S X, 13.03.1963, 5). In other words, *plus-de-jouir* may be treated as the function of object a, that is as an excess, or excessive enjoyment, which is produced by the subject's repetitive and endless revolving around the lost object.

Freud argues that "[t]he finding of an object is in fact a refinding of it" (Freud, quoted by Fink, *The Lacanian Subject* 222) which is to mean that "an initially encountered object is found anew at some later point in time" (*The Lacanian Subject* 94) and that the subject will make every effort to re-find the exact satisfaction. Lacan's novelty is the claim that the subject pursues a pure phantasm as object a is merely a leftover of the process of distinguishing between a subject and an object. Fink claims that repetitions of this behavioral pattern arise due to the loss of "hypothetical mother-child unity", of which object a is a reminder (*The Lacanian Subject* 97). As such, the latter engenders cathexing subsequent objects of desire, all reminding the subject of the loss of mother's breast (primal cathexed object), Fink adds.

2.4 The Oedipus Complex, the Phallus, Castration

Another approach to the logic of the symbolic leads through Lacan's ideas on the Oedipus complex and what is known as the symbolic castration. To begin with, Lacan retains the Freudian sense of centrality of the Oedipus complex in psychoanalytic theory. His understanding of it, however, takes its own way. First, while for Freud the child is attracted to the parent of the opposite sex, Lacan argues that it is always the mother that the subject in the parental triangle leans towards while the father functions as a blockage. This Oedipal triad commences to work as a prime structure of the symbolic since the passage from the dual relation with the mother to a feeling of a third presence is the very epitome of switching from the imaginary realm to the symbolic one. The third presence is what Lacan calls the phallus, the imaginary and symbolic functions of the biological organ, rather than the organ itself. The idea of the phallus emerges, again crucially for Lacanian theory, with the subject's feeling of a lack in the mother as well as in himself or herself. To be precise, on entering the so-called pre-oedipal stage, the child begins to sense that its presence does not suffice to satiate the mother's desire (the subject lacks something), which is imagined to be directed elsewhere (the mother lacks something). The alleged object desired by the mother is the (imaginary) phallus, which the child attempts to learn of and stand for. Lacan indicates that such endeavors make the child "never really there at the place where he is, and ... never completely absent from the place where he is not" (Lacan, quoted by Evans, 152). As it is further pointed by Evans, there is a point where attempts take on anxiety, and it is the biological emergence of the child's sexual drives, the emergence of the real, which makes it clear for the child that the imaginary phallus is insufficient in the face of necessity of the real phallus (131). What should ultimately happen is the intervention of the paternal figure as the representative of the symbolic with its law, order and language. Whether real or purely symbolic in his function, the father as the possessor of the phallus *castrates* the child of its futile effort to be the phallus for the mother. All the imaginary exchanges "established around the imaginary lack of the phallus" (S

III 319) cease to take place as there is a father, who "has its own and ... he neither exchanges it nor gives it" (S III 319). Such a break of the deadlock of the Oedipal complex is beneficial for the development of the subject as the acceptance of father's power takes off the burden of an impossible task. The phallus, as that which would allegedly allow to reach the forbidden *jouissance*, occupies a crucial position in a father-mother-child triangle to the extent that Lacan speaks of a "(father)-phallus-mother-child" relationship (S III 319).

In the course of Lacan's development of the concept of castration, the phallus becomes more and more the epitome of the very effect of language on the subject's life. What then eventually takes place in the act of castration is identification with both the symbolic order and the father as an superegoic figure administering the law. Castration in due course manifests itself as the *symbolic* castration; the act of sacrifice related to "the human being having to use the signifier in speech which can never match the thing exactly, thus necessitating a loss of the complete *jouissance* of the Other" (Levy-Stokes, "Castration" 47). The signifier which emerges with primacy is the phallus itself, the signifier of castration. Since it introduces the realm of signifiers, for Lacan it is synonymous with the bar of signification (Écrits 581), which makes it impossible to reach the signified, the sense of exactness. Significantly, the phallus "can play its role only when veiled ... once it is raised ... to the function of the signifier" (Écrits 581), which results in the sense of lack experienced by the subject and engenders desire. The phallus, then, is also the signifier of lack and desire, which in an inseparable manner are being perennially displaced within the symbolic and the unconscious of the language. As such a signifier, a veiled hint that there is a sense of fulfillment one step further, it is always already lost so that it may operate. In this sense, for Lacan there is in fact no one who owes the phallus "for both man and woman always receive it from another, another who can bestow it only because he or she has as the signifier of his or her desire" (Borch-Jacobsen 214). The unconscious may actually come into existence owing to the operation of the phallus, when Lacan indicates that the subject "designates his being only by barring everything it signifies" and the primarily repressed part of his being "finds its signifier by receiving the mark of the phallus's *Verdrangung* [repression] (owing to which the unconscious is language)" (Écrits 581). Being both the repressing and the repressed, the phallus stimulates the subject's making up for the sense of fracture and loss in the symbolic.

The language, order and law, which bar the subject from the sense of potential yet forbidden satisfaction, are disposed by the paternal figure. The "no" of the father, *non du père*, is for Lacan both homophonous and synonymous with the "name" of the father, *nom du père*, and therefore Lacan does not simply speak of the father, but of the Name-of-the-Father. Not to be taken as a real father or an imaginary one, the Name-of-the-Father is the symbolic realm of the paternal figure; importantly, rather than a fixed occupier, it is a position in the symbolic that a subject might take and exercise. It is, in other words, a signifier which exchanges the possibility of incestuous relation with the Mother with the safety valve of signifiers and the law of prohibition which is to establish a "symbolic distance" (Lacan, quoted by Evans, 62) between the mother and the child. The inspirational character of Freudian mythical father in *Totem and Taboo* is clear – killing the person of the primordial father does not stop his function; conversely, the prohibition of women is felt more acutely. Lacan underscores the unique status of the symbolic father, as compared with other concepts of the father, when he argues that

> it is in the *name of the father* that we must recognize the basis of the symbolic function which ... has identified this person with the figure of the law. This conception allows us to clearly distinguish ... the unconscious effects of this function from the narcissistic relations, or even real relations, that the subject has with the image and actions of the person who embodies this function (Écrits 230)

What is more, the instance of the Name-of-the-Father, also referred to as "paternal function" (Écrits 230), is a prerequisite for the subject's unhindered progress and successfully entering the culture; it is to position him properly within the realm of the symbolic.

In contrast with the Name-of-the-Father and its functions in the triad, the imaginary and the real father derail the subject's sense of belonging to the symbolic. The former is merely a phantasm built up of the subject's imaginary expectations and reflections and, as such, it has a dual relationship with the subject. As Lacan points, the subject assumes an imaginary father when it is impossible to fulfil "the realization of the signifier *father* at the symbolic level" (S III, 204). As a consequence, the subject may have to identify throughout life with what he or she *imagines* to be the representative of the law and

> will have to bear the weight of ... dispossession of the signifier and adopt compensation for it, ... over the course of his life, through a series of purely conformist identifications with the characters who will give him the feeling for what one has to do to be a man. (S III 205)

As Evans comments, being phantasmatic, the imaginary father may take the guise of either an ideal father, who is believed to be a kind, God-like protector, or a cruel figure, who forces the incest taboo and who performs the so-called privation (in short, depriving a woman of the symbolic phallus) (63). Finally, the real father might be simply treated as the biological father and as such the holder of the real phallus and the one who castrates the child ending the Oedipal stage; Lacan goes as far as to call him the "Great Fucker" (S VII 307), which indicates the material status of the figure. Summing up and taking all the subdivisions of the father into consideration, it is the Name-of-the-Father whose importance is crucial in the development of the subject. Any failure of installing the paternal function in the subject results in psychopathological phenomena.

As we have seen, for Lacan the symbolic castration is inherently connected with and revolves around the terms of *jouissance* and desire, which occupy central positions in his version of psychoanalytic theory. As he indicates, "[c]astration means that *jouissance* must be refused, so that it can be reached on the inverted ladder of the Law of desire" (Lacan, quoted by Berressem, 24). Castration also "creates the lack on the basis of which desire is instituted [and] [d]esire is desire for desire, the Other's desire, ..., in other words, subjected to the Law" (Écrits,723). How should these arcane comments be understood?

2.5 Jouissance

Often incorrectly mistaken for simple "enjoyment" or "pleasure," *jouissance* is the special type of fulfillment which, especially since the 1960s, epitomizes for Lacan satisfaction spiked with pain. It is, in other words, a transgression of the "pleasure principle" and as such an excess of enjoying, more than one is allowed to, which ultimately brings the subject to pain. It may be even treated as a transgression relating to the limits of subjectivity as indicated by Lacan:

> If the living being is at all something thinkable, it will be above all the subject of the *jouissance*; but ... the pleasure principle is very soon to create a barrier to all *jouissance*. If I am enjoying myself a little too much, I begin to feel pain and I moderate my pleasures. The organism seems made to avoid too much *jouissance*. (Lacan, "Of Structure")

Thus, it is the function of the pleasure principle and pleasure to "[set] limits to *jouissance*" as it "binds incoherent life together" (Écrits 696).

Again, typically for many of Lacanian terms, *jouissance* operates in various realms. For instance, on the level of the imaginary it is the object of the subject's nostalgia, which longs for the phantasmatic, prediscursive mother-child oneness and satisfaction that must have been lost due to having entered into the symbolic and having accepted the paternal metaphor. As one finds oneself always-already in the symbolic, such status of *jouissance* is unverifiable and therefore is merely a sort of myth and illusion. In this sense, the act of paternal prohibition is responsible for and truly engenders longings for what was allegedly lost (Evans 94). Regaining satisfaction proves to be, in turn, as illusory as its loss. Such longings are for Lacan nothing other than desire, an incessant attempt to transgress the chains of the symbolic and reach what has been prohibited *on the side of the Law*. It is thanks to desire that any subject may "approach, . . . test, this sort of forbidden *jouissance* which is the only valuable meaning that is offered to our life" (Lacan 2014).

What is more, Lacan makes it clear that "jouissance is prohibited to whoever speaks" (Écrits 696); therefore, it may not be approached in signifiers that constitute the speaking subject. As a further consequence of operating only with signifiers, the subject may never know the Thing, which resides at the core of each subject and which has been previously discussed. *Das Ding* is in such sense another term for *jouissance* of other subjects, or of the Other, that cannot be scrutinized. The subject may experience merely the *jouissance* of the real organ in a sexual act, which comes down to an experience of narcissistic and masturbatory nature without any link to the *jouissance* of the body of the Other. This is why Lacan famously claims that "there is no sexual relation" (S XVII 116), which, as elucidated by Serge André, means that

> [t]he sexual act of coitus takes on ... the figure of an eternal missed act where repeatedly the absence of the sexual relation, the failure to reunite the subject with the Other to form one body, is verified. The resulting satisfaction can only be defined as the failure of the *jouissance* of the body and the return to the *jouissance* of the organ. (98)

Imagining and craving unity with the Other, which is related to accessing what Lacan calls signifier "One" and which tempts one with the possibility of one's unity with what is beyond the language and signifiers (André 96), the subject always finds him- or herself separated from what is the unnamable *(jouissance)* in the Other. The only *jouissance* to be experienced by a symbolically castrated being is what Lacan calls symbolic or phallic *jouissance*, the one which is the consequence of language. Given the banned body (that is, *jouissance*) of the Other, what remains to describe one's sexuality and make up for the loss are words. In this sense phallic *jouissance* is something which cannot reach the *jouissance* of the Other: "[j]ouissance, qua sexual, is phallic – in other words, it is not related to [it does not reach] the Other as such" (S XX, 9). It is, in fact, "the obstacle owing to which man does not come *(n'arrive pas)*, ... to enjoy woman's body, precisely because what he enjoys is the jouissance of the organ" (S XX 7).

> With the symbolic castration as its source, the *jouissance* in the symbolic is I-centered and masturbatory by nature; as it is argued by Levi R. Bryant, it "strives to avoid any detour through the Other for *jouissance*" and "can be detected in all those social and signifying formations that strive for completeness, totality, and a theory of everything" (Bryant), which is to cover up the lacking character and the incoherence of the symbolic

> order. For Lacan this incoherence, Levy-Stokes adds, is "both the cause of *jouissance* and what creates a limit to it" ("*Jouissance*" 101). As she further points out, the fundamental lack in language is the impossibility of a fit between the sexes, of a fit between the drive and the object ..., of a fit between what is said and the fit itself. This impossibility creates a push to repeat, a repetition which is founded on a return of *jouissance* and which always produces a failure, a loss. ("*Jouissance*" 101)

The subject entwined in the symbolic order and, consequently, in the phallic *jouissance* as the only *jouissance* to be experienced is left with a feeling that something has been lost, yet it remains unnamable. This is what is known by the term of surplus-*jouissance*, which

> is a loss that takes place as a result of language but that cannot be detected within language. As a result, the subject perpetually pursues this lost *jouissance through* language, only to find the loss further exacerbated and thereby finding himself increasingly alienated within language. (Bryant)

Since the 70s, his seminar *Encore*, and the introduction of the graph of sexuation, Lacan begins to draw attention to another side of *jouissance*, which he calls feminine *jouissance*. The novelty value is introduced by a claim that not all *jouissance* must run under the power of the phallus and signifiers as there is a feminine side to it which is not subject to the phallus. Whilst all men are subject to the signifier and strive after an object as the lost object, some part of the feminine is able to circumvent the phallus and experience a non-phallic *jouissance* (without the loss of experience of the phallic *jouissance*). This allows the analyst to theorize woman as ""not whole" with respect to phallic jouissance" (S XX 7). Also coming under the term of the Other *jouissance*, the feminine *jouissance* is a proof for Lacan that

> there is something essential about language that renders impossible putting the essence of femininity into words. Someone with a feminine structure, according to Lacan, is defined by the presence of real order Other jouissance in addition to symbolic order phallic jouissance. (Swales 58)

A woman is thus capable of breaking the deadlock of pursuing the object and may have access to the Other's *jouissance*, which does not know such a pursuit. In this sense for Lacan "*woman* does not exist" (S XX 7) as a symbolic construct, as some essence of fixed features of womanhood, which is why in Lacan's crosses out the definite article *la* in *la femme*.[24] Bryant elucidates more on the topic:

---

24 The English counterpart of the term is often rendered as the barred Woman, or "t/he Woman"

> Insofar as not-all of those speaking-beings are subject to the phallic function, there is always something resistant to naming among those subjects that fall on the feminine side of the graph of sexuation. It is this that will lead Lacan to argue that "La femme n'existe pas" or that "The Woman does not exist." By this Lacan does not mean that *women* do not exist, but rather that there is no generalizable category or signifier within the symbolic order capable of defining or naming woman. Each subject sexuated according to the feminine side of the graph is absolutely singular. As such, feminine identity is experienced as a non-identity or a state in which identity is perpetually precarious. (2014)

The barred Woman may be unaware of the feminine *jouissance*, "a jouissance that is hers about which she herself perhaps knows nothing if not that she experiences it" (S XX 74). What may also be inferred from Bryant's words is that the French analyst does not set fixed rules of sexuation with regard to biological sex; both males and females alike may be structured in accordance with the feminine model. In any case, as the one given access to the Other *jouissance*, the woman in Lacanian system achieves crucial functions. She may obtain the status of the phallus, "the signifier of the Other's desire" (Écrits 583), provided that she "rejects an essential part of femininity" and pretends to be what she is not "to be desired as well as loved" (Écrits 583). As a consequence of such a masquerade, as put by Lacan, woman is a symptom of a man (S XXII 28) insofar as she remains the object of his fantasy. As such, she is the phantasmatic *objet a*, the cause of one's desire which, as argued by Lacan, is "[a] manifest example of the hole, of what is only supported by the object *a* – but always by a misdeal, by a confusion" (S XXII 29). Lacan exemplifies his thesis with the case of James Joyce and his beloved wife, Nora Barnacle, who always epitomized the ideal object of fantasy. The analyst points out that "[t]here is only one woman for Joyce, she is always the same model" (Lacan, quoted by Kaltenbeck, 118). Elaborating on Lacan's idea of woman-as-a-symptom and a symptom as a means of consolidating subjectivity, Žižek goes as far as to claim that the very ontological status of man depends entirely on his relation to woman/ the symptom. When

> the symptom is dissolved, the subject itself disintegrates … . [Man's] very ontological consistency depends on, is "externalized" in, his symptom. In other words, man literary *ex-sists*: his entire being lies "out there," in woman. (Žižek, "Rosselini" 21)

Lacan also points to the fact that there is specific enjoyment stemming from the language and meaning and he coins the neologism of *jouis-sens* to describe this phenomenon. Being located at the intersection of the imaginary and the symbolic, *jouis-sens* is the way the subject enjoys his/her unconscious, that is, all the free-associating and substituting processes that take place within the system of signifiers. The driving force behind such enjoyment is what Lacan calls *lalangue*, another neologism reminding one of a child's babble ("lallation"), referring to a play on words, and incorporating all the inconsistencies and imperfections of the spoken language. These may include parapraxes, unwanted sounds, mumbling and stuttering, all revealing the subject's desire. Consequently, each *lalangue* is an idiosyncratic experience and as such is unique. Lacan also indicates that *lalangue* is a means to approach *jouissance* and give it a literal form in the course of analysis by free-associating. This, as he believes (drawing on a Joycean phrase), is an endeavor to turn litter into a letter.[25] What is more, being the motor of *jouis-sens*, *lalangue* is more concerned with pure "satisfaction derived from engaging in verbalization, the urge to say something for the sake of saying than for a communication of a message (Nobus and Queen, 77). Taking a different angle, the message which does get communicated through "lallation" is the one of the unconscious and, therefore, of one's desire. In this way, *lalangue* may be called "a crowd of swarming ramifications to which the subject attaches its desire" (Milner, quoted by Nobus and Queen, 77).

2.6 Desire and the Death Drive

As it has been mentioned, the symbolic castration, the acceptance of the Name-of-the-Father, and the consequent renouncement of *jouissance* bring about a subversive element, which feeds itself on symbolic prohibition. This phenomenon and one of the central concepts in the Lacanian theoretical apparatus is the subject's desire. Being dubbed by Lacan as "the essence of man" (S XI 275) and operating under the symbolic Law, it emerges as the possibility of transgressing this Law and approaching the always-already forbidden *jouissance*. This then is the essence of the aforedescribed "inverted ladder of the Law of desire" (Lacan, quoted by Berressem, 24); symbolic castration becomes "a condition for satisfaction" (Levy-Stokes, "Castration" 42).

Stemming from the lack in the symbolic, desire may be envisioned as the subject's unconscious way along the chain of signifiers that expects (hopelessly) to regain what was allegedly lost and is the result of the emergence of the aforedescribed object a, the cause of desire. As a formation which flows through the signifying chain, desire operates in the symbolic and makes the subject occupy certain positions in this realm, which indicates that it is not of a biological character. On the contrary, it resides purely in the unconscious and remembering

25 See Jacques Lacan, "Lituraterre"

that the latter "is structured like a language" (Écrits 737), desire may be partially traced in the practical realization of language, that is speech. According to Lacan, being the motor behind human activity, desire is also the core of psychoanalysis, which is all about the articulation and learning of one's desire by means of free-associating (as observed in the case of the aforementioned *lalangue*) and "talking cure." The aim of the analysis is then based on "getting an analysand to dream, daydream, and talk, however incoherently, about a traumatic "event," we make him or her connect it up with words, bring it into relation with ... signifiers" (Fink, *The Lacanian Subject*). The echoes of desire are found in parapraxes, puns, jokes and dreams. It is, however, as observed by Evans, impossible to articulate the whole of desire just as speech and the unconscious are not entirely compatible. The latter "*cannot be known*" (37) by definition and it always characterized by "a leftover, a surplus, which exceeds speech" (37).

Desire itself may also be defined as a leftover of its own sort when juxtaposed with the concepts of need and demand. Lacan's distinction among these was one of his great contributions to psychoanalytic theory. Being born with needs, purely biological requirements which call for fulfillment so that a person can survive, human beings strive to satisfy them; yet they may only rely on others to do so as they find themselves in the state of infantine hopelessness and incapacity. This necessitates articulating the needs to O/others and although the infant uses only inarticulate and primitive means, like screams or gestures, such behavior is already a sign of being at the mercy of language and the O/others who have to interpret the signals. Soon, needs cease to be simply needs and on establishing a certain rapport with O/others, each need takes on an additional value of demand, which is that of love required by the subject. The emergence of demand is in fact the entrance into the field of the Other and the state of culture, as when Lacan argues that "[d]emand already constitutes the Other as already possessing the "privilege" of satisfying needs" (Écrits 580). All the satisfied needs of the subject lose their atavistic character and become proofs of the Other's unconditional love:

> Parents of children are all too familiar with seemingly endless series of demands from the little ones ("I want a sandwich," "OK, here's a sandwich"... "I want a lollipop," "OK, here's a lollipop"... "I want a new toy," "OK, here's a new toy"... and on and on until an exhausted parental "No" is pronounced and wearily defended against vigorous protests). Adults, whether parents or not, also are aware of a similar desiring restlessness in themselves, an inability to acquire an object or attain a success that would be "IT" (with-a-capital-I-and-T), the final be-all-and-end-all *telos* of wanting and wishing satisfying them for good forever after. Similarly, an adult in a romantic relationship is never content with being told that he/she is loved by the beloved only once; he/she insists upon

> repetitions *ad infinitum* of the affirmation by the significant other that, "I love you" (as if no affirmation is ever quite enough). (Johnston)

What is demanded as love is the impossible-to-be-reached real core of the Otherness, which cannot be objectified as a single object but which nonetheless becomes one through the fantasy of achieving it at some point, as further pointed by Johnston. In Lacan's own words, demand entails "the radical form of the gift of what the Other does not have – namely, what is known as its love" (Écrits 580) As love may not be fully satisfied, desire emerges; it is

> neither the appetite for satisfaction nor the demand for love, but the difference that results from the subtractions of the first from the second, the very phenomenon of their splitting (Écrits 580).

The place of the splitting becomes the space of fantasizing; it is the aforementioned real "void, which can be occupied" by the subject's ideas on what the lost object a may be like (S XI 180). The real and imaginary nature of object a must be compensated by the symbolic order; desire exists only as a self-reproductive and futile attempt to find a match for the lost object a. Its reproduction, as a symbolic structure, is metonymical as it is an unquenchable longing for consecutive objects in a signifying chain.

Perhaps the most frequently discussed phrase of Lacan's is the one relating to human desire and stating that "[m]an's desire is the desire of the Other" (S XI 235). The ambiguity of the formula calls for various readings. First of all, man's desire is the desire for being recognized by the Other and becoming the object of the Other's desire. Put another way, "[d]esire is desire for desire" (Ecrtis 723); it is the wish to be seen as one able to fill the lack in the Other. Dylan Evans indicates that the archetypical longing of this sort is the oedipal desire to stand for the phallus in a mother-child relationship (39), which corroborates with Lacan's own claims on the role of m(O)ther in the subject's desire:

> [T]he child, in his relation to the mother, a relation constituted in analysis not by his vital dependence on her, but by his dependence on her love, that is to say, by the desire for her desire, identifies himself with the imaginary object of this desire in so far as the mother herself symbolizes it in the phallus. (E: AS 155)

In later life, such a model is repeated as

> for each of the partners in the relationship, both the subject and the Other, it is not enough to be subjects of need or objects of love – they must hold the place of the cause of desire. (Écrits 580)

What is more, the formula indicates that the subject's desire is the one *belonging* to the Other; thus, there is no other way than to desire *through* the Other. The consequence is that the objects of desire are desired by the subject insofar as they have already been made desirable by somebody else. As it is argued by Evans, desire is not engendered by any "intrinsic quality" of the object, but "the fact that it is desired by another" (39), which makes it the effect of intersubjective dialectics, not of nature. As the dynamics of dialectics change, so does the desirability of objects; desire is thus metonymical for it is "what makes objects equivalent and exchangeable" (Evans 39).

A concept which is also to be located by Lacan in the symbolic and not among biological instincts, which was the case with Freud, is death drive. The French psychoanalyst deviates from Freudian *Todestrieb*, understood as a natural tendency of human beings to return to the primordial state of inanimateness, and argues that the death drive runs along the repetitions necessitated by the symbolic order to break the barrier of the pleasure principle and experience the utter state of *jouissance*, which for Lacan is nothing but death. What is more, the analyst claims that all drives are ultimately related to death drive (Écrits 719) as with a self-complementary manner, on one hand, death drive is the death of the thing (turning real into symbolic) and, on the other hand, the wish to turn the symbolic into the real. Taking a different perspective, Freudian division into the sexual drive and death drive ceases to make sense for Lacan as *jouissance* is what involves the two in its incomprehensible combination of pleasure and pain. Yet, the true nature and satisfaction of a drive comes with its failure to achieve the goal. Just as desire, drives are to be located in the symbolic realm as they do not relate to biological needs but are intertwined in a dialectic process with desire. It may be claimed that drives prey on and draw satisfaction from the failure of desire to get satiated; their true aim and enjoyment taken thereof is to circle repetitively around the consecutive objects. Considering this, Žižek poses an interesting question:

> Is not desire as such already a certain yielding, a kind of compromise formation, a metonymic displacement, retreat, a defence against intractable drive? 'To desire' means to give way on the drive — insofar as we follow Antigone and 'do not give way on our desire,' do we not precisely step out of the domain of desire, do we not shift from the modality of desire into the modality of pure drive? (*Looking Awry* 172)

3 Literary Studies and American Literature: Lacanian Perspectives

3.1 Literature with Lacan

The usefulness and validity of the psychoanalytic thought for the sake of literary analysis has been perhaps the most discussed and divisive issue in the history of literary theory. Nevertheless, it would not be an exaggeration to call psychoanalysis the most influential theoretical underpinning literary criticism has had up to the present day. Recent examples would include the 2014 *Cambridge Introduction to Literature and Psychoanalysis* and *A Concise Companion to Psychoanalysis, Literature, and Culture* published in the same year. Over a hundred years, if still perplexed over the matter of applicability of psychoanalytic theories to its field, literary criticism seems to have solved the problem at least partially. In the course of time, some ways of applying psychoanalysis to literary studies have been questioned, mainly due to their incompatibleness, implausibility and far-fetched conclusions drawn thereof. Such have been the cases of Marie Bonaparte and of Charles Mauron, whose model of psychobiography, that is psychoanalyzing the writer through his literary work, has been verified as simplistic and anachronistic. Having given up a questionable extrapolation of literary characters onto the person of the author, literary studies needed and welcomed language-oriented bodies of psychoanalytic thought, theories of Jacques Lacan being undoubtedly among the most seminal and influential ones. As observed by Elizabeth Wright,

> [w]hereas the deliverances of classical psychoanalysis were used towards providing interpretations of actual texts, the effect of Lacan's work has been to revitalize literary theory. With the help of such new theoretical understanding, approaches may indeed be made to actual texts, but it is as a result of the light they cast upon language and communication that they are most valuable. (111)

Lacan's famous likening the structure of the unconscious to language, which paved his way to literary studies, placed an equals sign between symptoms and signifiers, proving that the former appear either as a condensed metaphor or are displaced in a metonymical chain. By this token, one is able to perceive a symptom as a trope (Stoltzfus 7) and analyze the dynamics of the unconscious, desire and "narrative symptoms" of a given textual rhetoric. As further elucidated by Ben Stoltzfus,

> Lacan's analysis of narration begins with language and proceeds to rediscover the discourse of the Other that is embedded in speech and literature. The blockage of desire, along with its corollary, repression, produce a neurosis whose narrative symptoms are metaphorical. In the production of narrative, unconscious content is condensed as metaphor and displaced as metonymy. (2)

The role of the critic here would be to track down the logic and dynamics of the aforementioned discourse of the Other, some type of a repressed or muted voice/narrative, characteristic for symptomatic places, to use the label given by Terry Eagleton, in the text. These places might include

> evasions, ambivalences ... points of intensity in the narrative – words which do not get spoken, words which are spoken with unusual frequency, doublings and slidings of language ... [which] ..., like an unconscious wish, the work both conceals and reveals. (*Literary Theory* 158)

As posited by Rabaté, "Lacan always insisted that a psychoanalytic symptom could be treated by linguistic ambiguity" (*Jacques Lacan* 18). What, then, appears to be "absent, marginal or ambivalent about it may provide a central clue to meanings [of a given text]" (Eagleton, *Literary Theory* 155). Eagleton's understanding of psychoanalytic criticism seems to concur with Lacanian thought, which correspondingly underscores the problem of both surplus and lack. Such symptomatic spaces of text often hint at "the relationship between sexuality and social role" (Wright 4) and conflicts prompted thereof. It is the focus on the politics of (repressed) body which makes psychoanalysis a distinctive field among other theories. Finally, it is also the mode of production that might be addressed psychoanalytically since "what [a text] does not say, and *how* it does not say it, may be as important as what it articulates" (Eagleton, *Literary Theory* 195) and how it articulates it. Summing up, such spaces of ambiguity and repression seem to hint at text of the unconscious and, as posited by Derrida, "writing is unthinkable without repression" (Derrida, quoted by Wright, 120).

Taking a more general perspective on what makes tenets of Lacanian psychoanalysis practical for examining literature, on the most basic level, the French psychoanalyst asks questions which are fundamental in literary criticism and theory. As it is put by Rabaté,

> Lacan's lifelong confrontation with literature has always hinged on basic and almost naïve questions, such as why do we write? Why do we read? What touches us in this apparently simple process? ... When and how are our bodies touched by the 'letters' of literature? (*Jacques Lacan* 3)

It seems that offering an equally elementary answer is possible. Approaching life and its narratives (regardless of the taken stance, be it a deconstructivist or an essentialist one), one incessantly longs for understanding. Mellard observes that "as interpreters, we are always in search of master codes" that could govern our lives (xii). As it provides a comprehensive theory of what it means to be a human subject, Lacanian body of work is fully capable of presenting itself as such a master code. Lacanian concepts offer themselves as allegories and metaphors, helpful in encompassing human experience by liking its manifestations to certain psychoanalytical processes. However, what is important, Lacanian psychoanalysis does not forget that there is no understanding outside language and, therefore, it cannot overlook the textual character of its own interpretative matrix. Mellard aptly comments that

> all interpretation is essentially allegorical in the sense that interpretation "translates" one set of data into another set of terms. The structure of allegory or interpretation underlies all Lacanian thought. ... [A]ll interpretation is finally textual and is allied to what can only be called a textual unconscious. (xii)

Hence, given the textual character of any interpretation in light of the Lacanian thought, a claim that a symptom operates like a metaphor is ultimately a metaphor itself.

It may be surmised that the general allegory arising from Lacanian theory is that of language being a handicapped, imperfect, and limited, yet the only available means through which one experiences the world. What such imperfectability engenders is, on the one hand, some experience that fails to be expressed though language and, on the other hand, incessant attempts of the subject to overcome such limitations and predicaments. As it is put by Markowski on the occasion of describing the affinity of Gombrowicz's oeuvre and Lacanian psychoanalysis, "it lies in the nature of life that sooner or later it reveals something which craves to be symbolized, yet eludes the process and becomes unbearable" (55).[26] It is thus one of the main roles and endeavors of using language and creating literature, as well as of Lacanian psychoanalysis, to pursue the goal (however heroic it may be) of inscribing the unsymbolizable (what Lacan calls "the real") into our symbolic, that is linguistic, dimension (labelled by Lacan as "the symbolic"). As Markowski concludes, "the escape from the real and the trauma (regardless of what it is) is the main subject of Lacanian psychoanalysis" (55). Azari refers to Lacan's comment on writing as a "form, in which one can grasp the limits, impasses, and dead ends that show the real acceding to the symbolic" (Lacan, quoted by Azari, 63), and corroborates Markowski's understanding:

26 All translations here and henceforth of Markowski as well as of Jarniewicz are by the author.

> [t]he acceding of the real to the symbolic means that writing makes it possible to bring the real into the symbolic. The letter is one such real object in the symbolic. (63)

The unrepresentable, which one struggles to represent, lurks as much from within the language as from within the castrated (that is, reduced to the symbolic) body, which does not know how to conform to the unbearable excess. Therefore, as added by Wright, "[t]he psychoanalysis of Jacques Lacan ... could be said to found itself on the failure of language to match the body" (97). Taking a different angle, such a battle fought by the subject may be also metaphorized in terms of attempts at recovering some blissful state one has allegedly lost. The narrative, taken up as a weapon against the real, would then be

> a source of consolation: lost objects are a cause of anxiety to us, symbolizing certain deeper unconscious losses ..., and it is always pleasurable to find them put securely back to in place. (Eagleton, *Literary Theory* 161)

Hence, a loss or a lack of some sort appear to be prerequisites for any narrative to happen; as aptly observed by Eagleton, "[s]omething must be lost or absent in any narrative for it to unfold: if everything stayed in place there would be no story to tell" (*Literary Theory* 161). According to Eagleton's reading of Lacanian theory:

> it is an original lost object – the mother's body – which drives forward the narrative of our lives, impelling us to pursue substitutes for this lost paradise in the endless metonymic movement of desire. (Eagleton, *Literary Theory* 161)

Lacan's liking the unconscious to language might be now seen in a different light when one thinks about the importance of loss. Wright notes that

> the dictum 'the unconscious is structured like a language' is more than an analogy, for the unconscious is born to be no more than its linguistic birthmarks. The fact that every word indicates what it stands for intensifies the frustration of this child of language, since the absence of satisfaction has to be accepted. Language imposes a chain of words along which the ego must move while the unconscious remains in search of the object it has lost. (102–103)

Language thus functions paradoxically both as an intruder which takes the place of some original satisfaction which is felt to have been lost and as a sense of hope on entering the scene of writing that the loss is recuperated.

Concluding, we may easily see how the above-mentioned Lacanian concepts of the symbolic, of the real, or of loss of the original object, among many others, work metaphorically inviting comparisons between the functioning of literature and the psyche. Although, as believed by Rabaté, providing literary, cultural or film examples to illustrate psychoanalytic concepts partially engenders the problem of coming back to "applied psychoanalysis" (*Jacques Lacan* 9), Lacan's theories, as we have seen, appear to have never aimed at offering a totalizing metalanguage. Constantly re-worked and fully aware of the their textuality, they perform the instability of meaning and systems of meaning themselves (let the best indicator be the bulk of criticism making use of Lacan for contradictory purposes), or in Rabaté's words, are "not just ... an instrumental means of communication, but as an active medium" (*Jacques Lacan* 9). Thus, as one of many master codes that we pick from in our lives, the Lacanian thought is similar to other master codes; it offers interpretation and is simultaneously dissimilar since it does not aim at totalizing and cannot be totalized itself.

Another point of focus which might be offered by the Lacanian thought is that on the relation between the writer and the reader/critic/interpreter. Having accepted the premise that the unconscious is of textual nature and a text includes the unconscious, Mellard posits that

> [a] psychoanalytic theory of interpretation ... rests on a theory of a textual unconscious, an unconscious that is shared by both text and critic, ... one created between text and critic (as between analysand and analyst) in a process like the analytic transference. (5)

Mellard's commentary echoes Eagleton's claim that "[a]ll literary works contain one or more ... sub-texts, and there is a sense in which they may be spoken of as the 'unconscious' of the work itself" (Eagleton, *Literary Theory* 155). To be elucidated, the sub-texts, which are, basically speaking, potential meanings of a given text, require not only the literary work itself but also the addressee, who, in the act of transference, stimulates the potentiality of the text, for instance, by interpreting its indeterminate spaces. As explained by Stoltzfus,

> [t]he reader is invited to collaborate in the creation of a parallel text to the one the writer has scripted and in doing so the reader forms his or her own tropic network using the holes, traces, words, repetitions, sentences, structures, paragraphs, and figural motifs. Underlying all this is the voice of the Other caught in the folds of the text and which the reader unfolds ... .(8)

Given its textuality, the unconscious (the discourse of the unreachable Other as an ungraspable potential of language) is thus capable of becoming a common ground for the writer/the analysand and the reader/the analyst, a field in which the latter might see and understand something more in the text than the former being its originator. It is in "the dialogic struggle and collaboration of the two" (Brooks, quoted by Stoltzfus, 4) that the literary work gets concretized. In this respect, Lacanian literary criticism might well be understood as the epitome of literary criticism per se.

It is worth adding here that in light of the Lacanian thought the textuality (of the unconscious), where there exists the potential for the encounter between the writer and the reader, is often spoken of in terms of identity. Mellard posits that "one's identity is a text formed mainly by language" (xi); Stoltzfus observes that "the structure of the unconscious is the invisible text that determines our role(s)" (6). Lacan himself adds:

> certificate tells me that I was born. I repudiate this certificate: I am not a poet, but a poem. A poem that is being written, even if it looks like a subject (Lacan, quoted by Rabaté *Jacques Lacan*, 13).

Given the textual character of one's identity, Wright proposes to entirely erase the distinction between the writer and the reader claiming that

> the reader/writer distinction is no longer valid because making sense of the sign-system implicates both: each is caught in the net of signs, is up against language. Reading, writing and criticism are part of continuum whereby readers write in the act of reading and writers are shown to read in the act of writing. (112–113)

Yet another perspective that the Lacanian thought offers is a focus precisely on the reader/ the analyst who, being exposed to the text, is offered both a reflection of the self and a self-reflection. In Ellie Ragland-Sullivan's words,

> the literary work represents a reader's ego to itself through the language of the text – a text that exerts a "magnetic pull" on the reader "because it is an allegory of the psyche's fundamental structure." (Ragland-Sullivan, quoted by Stoltzfus, 1)

With the premise that a literary composition may function as a mirror in which the reader's images of oneself and the other get either solidified or misrecognized, the relation between the writer, the text and the reader invites a comparison with another element of the Lacanian triad, the imaginary, which, basically speaking, involves all the fantasies that the subject has of him- or herself and any identifications arising thereof. The constituents of imaginary are phantasms, which according to Rinon's definition, open

> a zone of reciprocity between the I and its surroundings. The problem is that this kind of relationship is possible only as a potential never realized, for the phantasm by nature is only potential. (139)

It is then possible that the writer's fantasizing on a given topic may seek a dialogue with the interpreter's phantasmata; in light of the Lacanian imaginary, literature would thus constitute a field inviting a confrontation of the two.

Concluding, Lacanian literary criticism proves its value as body of work capable of handling a literary text on various levels. The space which binds all the layers of analysis is language, "the one agency that 'contains' the author, reader, work, and world" (Mellard 36), which is yet, as believed by Lacan, highly deficient as a means of human experience. Regardless of it being more focused on the tissue of the text or more reader-response-oriented, the Lacanian thought offers itself as a study of how "visible language ... [exerts] invisible effect" (Ragland-Sullivan, quoted by Stoltzfus, 7). Furthermore, it might well be viewed as a commentary on what it means to be a literary critic; Lacan's lesson that a "man's desire is the Other's desire" (Écrits 525) is by all means pertinent to literary studies with its struggle for what a text, a fathomless reservoir of the Other's potential and mystery, could mean, want to do with us, or want from us.

3.2 Lacan with Literature

Although for Lacan, just as for Freud, psychoanalysis was meant to serve the domain of the clinic, their comments on art and literature have never ceased to inspire literary scholars and foster the mutual correspondence between psychoanalysis and literary works. Pondering over masterpieces of the Western literary canon, including the works of Joyce, Shakespeare, Sophocles and the surrealist poets,

> [n]ot only does he [Lacan] show how much Freud and other practitioners rely on literary effects in many case studies, with all the subsequent narratological problem they entail, but he also follows Freud in suggestion that there is not opposition but complementarity between the literary domain and 'the real cases.' (Rabaté, *Jacques Lacan* 2)

One of the most serious charges brought against psychoanalytic criticism has been the claim that its theoretical apparatus is authoritarian and unproductive in so far as psychoanalytic readings are always-already preconditioned, ready to merely impose an already-existing theoretical matrix onto a given text. Such were the worries of Jacques Derrida, who advised against the psychoanalytic thought which would await a literary work to prove its theoretical assumptions, and thus act in a predetermined way; such was the warning of Geoffrey Hartman, who stated that "theory must first conceive of itself as productive ... rather than as a metalanguage" (Hartman, quoted by Vice, 6). Faced with its sins, psychoanalytic criticism found itself in a deadlock of what Shoshana Felman describes as

> Hegel's master-slave relation of struggle between two entities for recognition where psychoanalysis has been the subject, literature the object: a 'unilateral monologue of psychoanalysis *about* literature.' (Felman, quoted by Vice, 7)

As discussed before, a number of critics find Lacanian theory to be far from a "totalizing system" (Rabaté 6). It is also worth calling upon the words of Lacan himself, who was fully aware that "there is no metalanguage" (Écrits 688). Given this textual awareness and blurring the distinction, or even deconstructing, the relation between the fields of literature and psychoanalysis, Lacanian criticism puts writing and literature in mutual partnership. Rabaté points that, bringing literary examples, Lacan

> refuses to psychoanalyse either the writer or the works [which has been the case of a classic Freudian literary criticism] … . What he does with texts … is similar to what he does with patients: he treats 'the symptom as a palimpsest' and tries to understand the 'hole' created by the signifier, into which significations pour and vanish. (Rabaté, *Jacques Lacan* 3–4)

It is easy to notice that Lacan does not avoid discussing the author of the text, yet it is by no means a priority in his critical work. As observed by Ehsan Azari,

> [i]t is … worthwhile to note that Lacan in his analysis doesn't deny altogether the consideration of the life and personality of the author. He himself refers to the lives of Gide and Joyce in his literary analysis … . He ventures from the textual networks of Gide and Joyce into their lives rather than other way round … . (60)

Lacan's ambition is therefore neither to master the author nor a literary text but to draw conclusions that could possibly offer insights into psychoanalytic approach. The latter are perhaps best noticed in Lacan's later teaching and his introduction of concepts such as *lituraterre, littoral*, and *sinthome.*

As posited by Sue Vice, "it is possible to offer a detailed reading of a text … as part of the same project as considering the wider implications of the psychoanalytic approach" (6). Elizabeth Wright adds that an exemplary psychoanalytic reading should focus on "pursuing the interrelationship of psyche and text, without either one mastering the other, as was the case with classical applies psychoanalysis" (119). Lacanian criticism seems to meet both of these expectations raised by modern psychoanalytic studies.

3.3 Lacan in the Anglophone Academe: An Overview

Lacan first appeared in English in 1949 with the publication of his "The Mirror Stage, Source of the I-Function, as shown by Psychoanalytic Experience" in *International Journal of Psychoanalysis.* 1953 came with the publication of his "Some Reflections on the Ego," originally, a speech given two years earlier, yet it failed to stir much interest in the Anglophone academia. It was not until 1966, as most critics posit, that the French psychoanalyst's theories found acclaim among the Anglophonic intellectual elites. The breakthrough year was the result of a few crucial events: the English translation of "The Insistence of the

Letter in the Unconscious" in *Yale French Studies* 36/37, Lacan's participation in the now-legendary Baltimore conference, "The Languages of Criticism and the Sciences of Man," (along with Jacques Derrida, Roland Barthes, and Lucien Goldmann), where he delivered a lecture entitled "Of Structure as an Inmixing of an Otherness Prerequisite to Any Subject Whatever," and finally, publication of his *Écrits*.[27] The English translation of the selection of the latter, as well as of "Seminar XI," came in 1977, and by that time Lacan had already been a name in the academic circles. The time between the 1970s and the early 1980s also proved to be the glory days of Lacanian thought as considered by Anglophonic literary critics; speaking about the period, Mellard claims that Lacanian psychoanalysis was "one of the most stimulating areas of development in European and Anglo-American literary studies" (1). When thinking about particular scholars whose merits helped the Lacanian thought to enter the Anglo-American literary criticism at its earliest, Mellard mentions four names. One of them is Anthony Wilden, a scholar who "invented Lacan for Americans" (ix) and whose

> *The Language of the Self* (1968) ... included a translation of Lacan's landmark "Function and Field of Speech and Language in Psychoanalysis," the report on his theory that Lacan delivered in Rome in 1953 [often referred to as "The Rome Discourse"] at the first Congress of the newly founded Société Française de Psychanalyse. Wilden's book also included what is perhaps the first substantial piece in English on Lacan, his long essay "Lacan and the Discourse of the Other," and it included as well roughly seventy pages of Wilden's notes to intricacies in Lacan's text and his thought in general, and, to top it off, a bibliography ... that much facilitated entry to those vexed areas of theory and practice. (2)

Anika Lemaire's *Jacques Lacan* (translated into English in 1977) "offered the first book-length explication, one that in the seventies became easily available to Anglo-American readers" (Mellard ix). Another significant scholar in the field is Stuart Schneiderman, who "published the important 'Afloat with Jacques Lacan' in *Diacritics* in 1971, ... and became the only American ever trained by Lacan" (Mellard 2). Finally, one should not overlook Eugen Bär, the author of a 1971 essay "The Language of the Unconscious According to Jacques Lacan" and an exhaustive 1974 article entitled "Understanding Lacan" (Mellard 2).

Considering other founding fathers of American Lacanian studies, Mellard mentions: Robert Con Davis, Shoshana Felman, Ellie Ragland-Sullivan, whose

---

27 Lacan visited the United States two more times. In the year of the Baltimore conference he had guest lectures at Columbia, MIT, Harvard, and Chicago. 1975 witnessed his talks at Yale, Columbia, and MIT (McQuillan 214).

book *Jacques Lacan and the Philosophy of Psychoanalysis* (1986) he calls "the most complete synoptic overview of Lacan in English" (ix), Bice Benvenuto and Roger Kennedy, Christine van Boheemen, Catherine Clement, Jerry Aline Flieger, Jane Gallop, Andre Green, Julia Kristeva, Annette Lavers, Juliet Flower MacCannell, David Macey, Jeffrey Mehlman, John Muller, William Richardson, Antoine Vergote (Mellard ix).

Another milestone in both adopting Lacan to American ground and applying his theories for the sake of literary studies was a 1972 volume of *Yale French Studies* (vol. 48), "French Freud: Structural Studies in Psychoanalysis". It proved to be crucial since, apart from psychoanalytic and deconstructivist contributions, it contained the English translation of Lacan's "Seminar on 'The Purloined Letter'," which "forced Americanists to consider Lacan and Derrida" (Mellard 3).

It is also with the 1970s that a controversial issue of whether one could speak about Lacanian literary criticism arose. Mellard enumerates seminal collections which, although offering no precise definition of Lacanian literary theory, prove that there has been much interest in applying Lacan's concepts to studying literature since mid-1970s. The first anthology of what could be labeled as Lacanian literary criticism was a 1977 double issue of *Yale French Studies* entitled *Literature and Psychoanalysis* and edited by Shoshana Felman. Apart from that publication, there have appeared *Psychoanalysis and the Question of the Text* (1978, edited by Geoffrey Hartman), a 1981 issue of the journal *Humanities and Society* focusing on psychoanalysis and interpretation, and a special 1984 issue of journals *Style* and *Poetics* on psychopoetics (edited by Mieke Bal) (Mellard 33).

Between the 1970s and the early 1980s Lacan proved to be as much stimulating for literary studies as for other fields of the humanities. Tom Eyers speaks of the return to psychoanalysis,

> initiated by feminist scholars and activists of the 1970s, keen to furnish feminism with a theoretically sophisticated account of the gendered subject. Lacan seemed to offer ... an account of the psyche that rejected any stable link with biology, and thus a vision of subjectivity and ideology that refused to naturalize sexual difference. (6)

Many theoretical formulations have proved to be exceptionally valuable for feminism. However, as Freud, Lacan did not avoid strong criticism from feminist thinkers. Deborah Luepnitz observes that many Anglophone female scholars and practitioners

> felt that Lacan's reliance on the concept of the phallus and the "paternal metaphor" returned them to all the wrong aspects of Freud ... . Lacan seemed to be carrying on the Freudian tradition of ignoring mothers and the pre-Oedipal. (222)

In her seminal work *Speculum of the Other Woman* (1974, translated into English in 1985) Luce Irigaray pointed to Lacan's phallocentrism that would entail a male fantasy over the feminine, a flawed version of the masculine. These, as well as many other bones of contention, have been dealt with by such critics as Luepnitz (in her exhaustive article quoted above), Tim Dean, Jane Gallop, Ellie Ragland-Sullivan, Elizabeth Grosz, Elizabeth Wright. Perhaps the greatest merits for bringing Lacan and (the American) feminism close to each other are to be awarded to Jacqueline Rose and Juliet Mitchell, whose *Feminine Sexuality: Jacques Lacan and the ecole freudienne* (1982) "marked a turning point in the encounter of English-speaking feminists with Lacan" (Luepnitz 222). As suggested by Rabaté,

> Jacqueline Rose asserts very cogently that only psychoanalysis allows women and men to question their political fate as gendered beings. Mitchell and Rose's careful edition of Lacan's essays on feminine sexuality has led to a more balanced account of Lacan's alleged 'phallocentrism' and of the rift with early American feminism. (*Jacques Lacan 26*)

Finally, it is also queer studies which are undoubtedly indebted to Lacanian theory since they have underscored the performative character of sexual identities, determined by the unconscious (Rabaté, *Jacques Lacan* 26).

The universality of Lacan's thought soon opened him the way to film and cultural studies, among others Laura Mulvey's canonical, yet questioned, discussion of Lacanian concept of "the gaze" in cinema and Colin MacCabe's blend of Marxist criticism and Lacan's ideas on signification (Eyers 6). According to Eyers, Lacan's "phenomenological concern for identity and the struggle for recognition" (Eyers 7) drew the attention of philosophers and scholars, most notably David Macey, Malcolm Bowie, and Peter Dews, attempting to inscribe it into a wider, post-Hegelian phenomenology (7). Finally, in the United States critics such as Charles Shepherdson and Joan Kopjec

> combined a critical theoretical reading of Lacan, mobilized as a thinker who could usefully complicate the historicism and culturalism that had grown up in the US 'Continental' thought .... (Eyers 9)

There has been hardly any field of the Anglophonic humanities which would be left untouched by Lacan's theories. As claimed by Mellard, by the 1990s Lacan was already significant in

> structuralist and post-structuralist, deconstructionist and post-deconstructionist, as well as Marxist, feminist, and postmodernist, critical theories of English and American ... academics. (3)

Azari adds that Lacan's strong presence helped psychoanalytic literary studies to fully belong to the humanities and achieve a much needed holistic shape:

> [a]fter Lacan, psychoanalysis is no more a foreign discipline to literary studies. Lacan's contribution to criticism and the literary use of his theories are important in the fact that he integrated psychoanalytic literary criticism in the overall project of poststructuralist literary and cultural studies. ... It is not accidental that in North America, Lacan was first discovered by professors of literature, not psychoanalysts. (74)

Perhaps the most obvious manifestation of such universality and, at the same time, the greatest contribution to popularizing Lacanian theory came with the 1990s and the scholars of the so-called Ljubljana School of Psychoanalysis, most notably Slavoj Žižek, Alenka Zupančič, and Mladen Dolar. As claimed by Eyers, "[a]rguably, prior to the publication in English of Žižek's *Of Sublime Object of Ideology* in 1989, Lacan's star had faded considerably in the Anglophone academe" (8). Onward from then, the Slovenian philosopher's work, focusing mainly on deconstructing ideology and discussing popular culture with a blend of Lacan, Marx, and Hegel, found many enthusiasts and much acclaim, gaining much ground for Lacan as well. As claimed by Rabaté,

> Žižek has been successful where more classical Lacanians have failed ... [f]or Žižek had the productive idea of beginning at the end with Lacan, that is, from the last seminars, taking his cue from a moment when the master was at his most gnomic, speaking enigmatically in mathemes and parables. Žižek managed to make sense of this mode of utterance, illuminating the 'gists' and riddles by examples taken from popular culture, to which they in turn provided a deeper meaning in a constant give or take. (*Jacques Lacan* 11)

In 1991 in the preface to his *Using Lacan, Reading Fiction* Mellard stated that

> [w]hile there are now many books on the psychoanalytic theories of the French-Freudian Jacques Lacan, most of those books focus on theories as theories. They are on Lacan, not on the ways in which Lacanian principles might be used in the reading of literary works. (ix)

A decade later, in his 2004 article, Santanu Biswas maintained Mellard's claims and partially repeated his postulates. The scholar argued that there had been still few full-length critical books concerned with Lacanian literary criticism. He also underscored that a considerable part of Lacan was still due to be published, which promised new critical perspectives, and petitioned for

> a close, sustained and systematic Lacanian reading of all those littérateurs who had been influenced by Freud and psychoanalysis, such as, W H. Auden, Thomas Mann, Eugene O'Neill, and the like. (2004)[28]

---

28 Alike many other scholars before him, Biswas has raised the question of what can actually be defined as the Lacanian literary criticism and he partly disapproves of any "literary readings of Lacanian theory."

Since that time various publications seem to have responded to Biswas's request and proven that the tenets of Lacanian psychoanalysis are indeed applicable to and useful with literary text analysis. Within the past decade there have appeared several books of literary criticism which deal strictly with Lacanian readings of literature (not to mention those works which do it partially).[29] Although often divergent in their perception of Lacanian theory, their authors share Lacan as a common denominator for their work. In conclusion, though still not unanimous about the shape of Lacanian literary criticism, literary critics and theorists appear to hold Lacan tight in the field of their interest. It may be observed that, like Lacan himself in the 1970s, Lacanian criticism has recently shifted its scope of interest from the symbolic to the real, bringing to the fore the mystery of the latter and its topological bonds with the rest of the triad, as well as the concepts of *jouissance* and *sinthome*.

3.4 American Literature with Lacan

Having entered American consciousness not as much through the clinic as through cultural and literary studies, Lacan has been extensively used in American literary criticism, notwithstanding the lack of a sharp definition of Lacanian literary criticism. Lacan's theories have been the theoretical basis for collections of essays as well as single articles dealing with the works of American literature. This subchapter first attends to these scholarly works which are now considered innovative and canonical in extensively exploring American literature with Lacan. It then follows with an overview of particular American writers whose works either have been given Lacanian readings and commentaries in single essays and dissertations or have been briefly referenced with Lacan's concepts in critical books.

A number of scholars have been credited with pioneering work in the field of discussing American literature with Lacan. Robert Con Davis edited and contributed to *The Fictional Father: Lacanian Readings of the Text* (1981) and *Lacan and Narration: The Psychoanalytic Difference in Narrative Theory*

29 Some important examples of the most recent publications are: *Lacan and the Destiny of Literature* (2011) by Ehsan Azari, which handles Shakespeare, Joyce, Donne and Ashbery, *The Orders of Gothic: Foucault, Lacan, and the Subject of Gothic Writing, 1764 – 1820* (2007) by Dale Towshend, which examines Gothic Fiction, or *The Literary Lacan: From Literature to 'lituraterre' and Beyond* (Ed. Santanu Biswas, 2013) looking at the relationships between Lacanian psychoanalysis and literature.

(1984), two seminal volumes of Lacanian literary criticism. The former, with the overall theme of fatherhood, comprises six essays on the Anglophone fiction, among which one may find Lacanian examinations of father figures in Melville, Faulkner and Barthelme. Discussing the first writer, Régis Durand scrutinizes the links between father figures and institutional authorities. Faulkner's works are the focus of André Bleikasten and John T. Irwin's essays, which put emphasis on the Lacanian symbolic father (Bleikasten) and the substitution of the symbolic father for the real one (Irwin). Finally, Davis devotes a text to Barthelme and the matters of literary paternity as confronted with the father figure of Barthelme's "The Dead Father." The other volume scrutinizes the implications of Lacanian notions related to language for the theory of the narrative, shaping the concept of a repressed scene of writing and discussing, among other writers, Edgar Allan Poe. Poe's "The Purloined Letter" was also discussed by Shoshana Felman in her *Jacques Lacan and the Adventure of Insight: Psychoanalysis in Contemporary Culture* (1987), which takes a more clinical angle. Felman was the editor of a number of volumes related to psychoanalytic criticism, *Literature and Psychoanalysis: The Question of Reading: Otherwise* (1982) remaining perhaps the most influential one. The volume contains her now-canonical, widely quoted and frequently reprinted "Turning the Screw of Interpretation" in which, discussing Henry James's *The Turn of the Screw*, Felman proves the deficiencies and the ultimate failure of any psychoanalytic criticism (such as represented by Edmund Wilson) that makes attempts at mastering the final meaning of a literary text. The structure of James's novella, as well as the relations between its characters, are for Felman the very epitome of the unconscious at (a literary) work, always evading being pinned down. A widely recognized essay from the same collection is Barbara Johnson's "The Frame of Reference: Poe, Lacan, Derrida," a closing of a debate between Lacan and Derrida over the status of signifier in Poe's story. Arguing that Derrida does exactly what he criticized Lacan for, which is totalizing the role and meaning of the signifier (even if Derrida's deconstructivist point is that a signifier cannot be totalized), Johnson offered

> a compelling account of how the process of critical disagreement illustrates the transferential process of reading: exposing what the other missed exposes you in turn, as you find yourself pulled into that position in the structure, repeating what you denounce. (Culler 74)

Other significant collections of essays dealing strictly with Lacanian readings of literary works and devoting much of their focus to American literature include James M. Mellard's *Using Lacan, Reading Fiction* (1991) and Ben Stoltzfus's *Lacan and Literature: Purloined Pretexts* (1996). Employing Lacan to read Hawthorne's *The Scarlett Letter* and Henry James's "The Beast in the Jungle," Mellard presents the four modes of Lacanian subjectivity based on four fictional characters in the former and studies the way in which the repetitions of Lacan's mirror stage shape the fictional subject in the latter. Stoltzfus's volume includes Lacanian examinations of Hemingway's *The Sun Also Rises*, *A Farewell to Arms*, and *The Garden of Eden*. In the scholar's view, Hemingway's first novel demonstrates the affinity of moving and writing which, in the light of Jake Barnes's impotence and the characters' peregrinations, bring one to the always-deferred, unfulfilled desire. *A Farewell to Arms* deals with the unstable and deferred (textual) identity of the narrator as well as his experience of loss and the retrieval of the lost object that is ultimately always, as Lacanian theory posits, the mother. Finally, Hemingway's posthumous novel and its eponymous garden symbolize, in Stoltzfus's eyes, the space of liberation from the chains of desire in a paradoxical affirmation of the effects it takes.

As regards particular American writers whose works have been offered a Lacanian approach in single essays and dissertations, possibly the most frequently commented authors have been Melville, Faulkner and Poe. In addition to the aforementioned Régis Durand's work, Melville has been given Lacanian readings by Dennis Williams[30] (an examination of Ahab's lack of essence and his interiorization of Moby Dick), Chris Wiesenthal[31] (Moby-Dick and the Lacanian concept of paranoiac knowledge), Harold Beaver[32] and Jennifer Mary Wing[33]. Moving further, Faulkner has been examined by Chad Eugene Lewis,[34] Doreen Fowler,[35] John T. Irwin,[36]James M.

---

30 See Dennis Williams. "Filling the Void: A Lacanian Angle of Vision on Moby-Dick." *Ungraspable Phantom: Essays on Moby Dick*. Ed. John Bryant, et al. Kent: Kent State University Press, 2006.

31 See Chris Wiesenthal. *Figuring Madness in Nineteenth-Century Fiction*. New York: St. Martin's Press, 1997.

32 See Harold Beaver. "Melville and Modernism." *Dutch Quarterly Review of Anglo-American Letters* 13.1 (1983).

33 See Jennifer Mary Wing. *Resisting the Vortex: Abjection in the Early Works of Herman Melville. Diss.* Georgia State University, 2008.

34 See Chad Eugene Lewis. *Faulkner's Construction of Quentin Compson's Identity: A Lacanian Reading. MA thesis.* North Carolina State University, 1995.

35 See Doreen Fowler. *Faulkner: The Return of the Repressed*. Charlottesville: University Press of Virginia, 1997.

36 See John T. Irwin. *Doubling and Incest/ Repetition and Revenge: A Speculative Reading of Faulkner*. Baltimore: John Hopkins University Press, 1975.

Mellard,[37] Linda Kauffman[38] and Ronald Schleifer.[39] Finally, one should also not forget about critics such as Dennis Pahl,[40] Gita Rajan,[41] Renata R. Mautner Wasserman[42].

Apart from Poe or Melville, other nineteenth-century American writers whose works have offered a fruitful ground for Lacanian criticism include: Charles Brockden Brown (Allan Gardner Lloyd-Smith's comments on *Wieland*), Nathaniel Hawthorne (discussed by James M. Mellard, John Dolis, Eric Mottram, Itala Vivan, Elizabeth Wright), Mark Twain (John Bird's discussion of the metaphor in Twain) and Stephen Crane (Sheldon George). It is also the pioneers of American poetry who were commented upon with Lacan. Walt Whitman's *Leaves of Grass* were looked upon from the point of view of Lacan's concept of desire and mirror stage by Michael Moon[43] and Emily Dickinson's oeuvre, evidenced a Lacanian potential as well, which was demonstrated by Mary Loeffelholz[44].

As regards the twentieth-century American literature, all of the seminal writers have been looked at from a Lacanian perspective just as it has been done with the American writers of the prior century. As well the before-mentioned and extensively commented Faulkner, Hemingway, and James, other major modernist writers have been in the focus of Lacanian examination. These involve Eliot (Harriet Davidson),[45] Pound (Robert

---

37 See James M. Mellard. "Lacan and Faulkner: a Post-Freudian Analysis of Humor in the Fiction." *Faulkner and Humor*. Eds. Doreen Fowler and Ann J. Abadie. Jackson: University Press of Mississippi, 1986; "Faulkner's Miss Emily and Blake's 'Sick Rose': 'Invisible Worm,' *Nachtraglichkeit*, and Retrospective Gothic." in: *The Faulkner Journal* 2.1 (1986).

38 See Linda Kauffman. "Devious Channels of Decorous Ordering: A Lover's Discourse in *Absalom, Absalom!*" *Modern Fiction Studies* 29 (1983).

39 See Ronald Schleifer. "Faulkner's Storied Novel: *Go Down, Moses* and the Translation of Time." *Modern Fiction Studies* 28 (1982).

40 See Dennis Pahl. "Recovering Byron: Poe's 'The Assignation'" *Criticism* 26.3 (1984).

41 See Gita Rajan. "A Feminist Rereading of Poe's 'The Tell-Tale Heart.'" *Papers on Language and Literature* 24 (1988).

42 See Renata R. Mautner Wasserman. "The Self, the Mirror, the Other: 'The Fall of the House of Usher.'" *Poe Studies* 10.2 (1977).

43 See Michael Moon. *Disseminating Whitman: Revision and Corporeality in Leaves of Grass*. Cambridge: Harvard University Press, 1991.

44 See Mary Loeffelholz. *Dickinson and the Boundaries of Feminist Theory*. Urbana: University of Illinois Press, 1991.

45 See Harriet Davidson. "The Logic of Desire: The Lacanian Subject of The Waste Land" *The Waste Land: Theory in Practice*. Eds. Tony Davies and Nigel Woods. Philadelphia: Open University Press, 1994.

Casillo),[46] Djuna Barnes (Christine E. Coffman),[47] H.D. (Elizabeth A. Hirsh),[48] Gertrude Stein (Cynthia Merrill),[49] Hart Crane (Veronica Morgan),[50] W.H. Auden (David Cowart),[51] and Wallace Stevens, who was the subject of a full-book Lacanian monograph[52]. Lacan's theory has also been applied to the Southern writers, mainly Kate Chopin (Patricia Yeager and her Lacanian reading of *The Awakening*)[53] and Flannery O'Connor (essays by James M. Mellard).[54] What is more, numerous critics found Lacanian psychoanalysis useful when dealing with ethnic literature. In Raphael Comprone's 2006 *Poetry, Desire, and Fantasy in Harlem Renaissance* Lacan is employed to elucidate the subjectivity in Langston Hughes and Zola Neale Hurston, among other writers. Hughes, as well as W.E.B Du Bois, Richard Wright, Nella Larsen, Emma Dunham Kelley, are examined by Claudia Tate in her 1998 *Psychoanalysis and Black Novels: Desire and the Protocols of Race*. Lacanian examinations are given to Toni Morrison's novels (Sheldon George, Evelyn Jaffe Schreiber)[55] and Alice Walker's works (Daniel W. Ross).[56] As regards Asian-American literature, an unprecedented work has been done by Fu jen-Chen and her Lacanian readings of Maxine Hong Kingston

---

46 See Robert Casillo. *The Genealogy of Demons: Anti-semitism, Fascism, and the Myths of Ezra Pound*. Evanston: Northwestern University Press, 1988.

47 See Christine E. Coffman, *Insane Passions: Lesbianism and Psychosis in Literature and Film*. Middletown: Wesleyan University Press, 2006.

48 See Elizabeth A. Hirsh. "'New Eyes': H.D., Modernism, and the Psychoanalysis of Seeing" *Literature and Psychology* 32 (1986).

49 See Cynthia Merrill. "Mirrored Image: Gertrude Stein and Autobiography" *Pacific Coast Philology* 20 (1985).

50 See Veronica Morgan. Reading Hart Crane by Metonymy. Diss. University of Michigan, 1986.

51 See David Cowart. *Literary Symbiosis: The Reconfigured Text in Twentieth-Century Writing*. Athens: University of Georgia Press, 1993.

52 See Chetan Deshmane. *Wallace Stevens: A Lacanian Reading*. Jefferson: McFarland & Co, 2012.

53 See Patricia Yeager. "'A Language Which Nobody Understood': Emancipatory Strategies in The Awakening." *Novel: A Forum On Fiction* 20.3 (1987).

54 See James M. Mellard. "Flannery O'Connor's Others: Freud, Lacan, and the Unconscious" *American Literature 61* (1989)

55 See Sheldon George. "Approaching the *Thing* of Slavery: a Lacanian Analysis of Toni Morrison's *Beloved*" *African American Review*. 45 (2012); Evelyn Jaffe Schreiber. "Reader, Text, and Subjectivity: Toni Morrison's *Beloved* as Lacan's Gaze qua Object" *Style 30* (1996).

56 See Daniel W. Ross. "Celie in the Looking Glass: The Desire for Selfhood in The Color Purple" *Modern Fiction Studies 34*.1 (1988).

(*Tripmaster Monkey: His Fake Book*), Joy Kogawa (*Obasan*), and John Okada (*No-No Boy*).[57] Native American literature has also been the subject of Lacanian criticism; Gretchen Ronnow examined Leslie Marmon Silko's *Ceremony* for the Lacanian concepts of desire and the death drive present therein.[58] Other post-war American prose-writers and poets whose works have been subjected to Lacanian interpretations include: J. D. Salinger, Bernard Malamud, Joseph Heller (James M. Mellard's essays on all of them),[59] Sylvia Plath (Paul Mitchell),[60] John Updike (Robert H. Detweiler),[61] John Ashbery (Eshan Azari's discussion of *jouissance* and *littoral* in his texts).[62] Among the postmodern fiction writers who have been given Lacanian scrutiny are (apart from the aforementioned Barthelme): Thomas Pynchon (Sanford S. Ames, Robert N. Watson)[63] and John Barth (Christopher D. Norris).[64]

---

57 See Fu-jen Chen. "Asian-American Literature and a Lacanian Reading of Maxine Hong Kingston's Tripmaster Monkey" *Comparative Literature and Culture* 6.2 (2004); "A Lacanian Reading of *No-No Boy* and *Obasan*: Traumatic Thing and Transformation into Subjects of Jouissance" *The Comparatist* 31 (2007).

58 See Gretchen Ronnow. "Tayo, Death, and Desire: A Lacanian Reading of *Ceremony*" *Narrative Chance: Postmodern Discourse on Native American Indian Literatures*. Ed. Gerald Vizenor. Albuquerque: University of New Mexico Press, 1989.

59 See James M. Mellard. "The Disappearing Subject: A Lacanian Reading of The Catcher in the Rye" *Essays on J. D. Salinger*. Ed. Joel Salzberg. Boston: G. K. Hall, 1989; "The 'Perverse Economy' of Malamud's Art: A Lacanian Reading of Dubin's Lives" *Critical Essays on Bernard Malamud*. Ed. Joel Salzberg. Boston: G. K. Hall, 1987; "*Something Happened*: The Imaginary, the Symbolic, and the Discourse of the Family" *Critical Essays on Joseph Heller*. Ed. James Nagel. Boston: G. K. Hall, 1984.

60 See Paul Mitchell. "Reading (And) The Late Poems Of Sylvia Plath" *Modern Language Review 100*.1 (2005).

61 See Robert Detweiler. "Updike's *A Month of Sundays* and the Language of the Unconscious" *Journal of the American Academy of Religion 4* (1979).

62 See Eshan Azari. *Lacan and the Destiny of Literature: Desire, Jouissance and the Sinthome in Shakespeare, Donne, Joyce and Ashbery*. London: Continuum, 2008.

63 See Sanford S. Ames. "Pynchon and Visible Language: *Ecriture*" *International Fiction Review 4* (1977); see Robert N. Watson. "Who Bids for Tristero: The Conversion of Pynchon's Oedipa Maas" *Southern Humanities Review* 17 (1983).

64 See Christopher D. Norris. "Barth and Lacan: The World of the Moebius Strip" *Critique: Studies in Modern Fiction 17* (1975).

3.5 Lacanian Criticism and Beat Studies

There has been a number of attempts to approach the literary output of the Beat Generation writers with a psychoanalytic frame of reference. Most of them, however, were strictly Freudian. The Beat writer who has been most extensively examined with the Lacanian theoretical matrix is William Burroughs. This should not come as a big surprise since the Burroughsian poetics of instability, fluidity and indeterminacy invite a post-structural reception. The studies which need to be mentioned in this respect are: Serge Grünberg's *A La Recherche D'un Corps": Langage Et Silence Dans L'oeuvre De William S. Burroughs* (1979), Oliver Harris's *William Burroughs and the Secret of Fascination* (2003), Michael Sean Bolton's *Mosaic of Juxtaposition: The Narrative Strategy of William S. Burroughs* (2014) and his essay "From Self-Alienation to Posthumanism. The Transmigration of the Burroughsian Subject" in *The Philosophy of the Beats* (2012). Being most likely the first application of Lacanian concepts to any of the Beat Generation writers, Grünberg's work examines closely the Burroughsian themes of language, power, and body. It ultimately acknowledges the body as the sphere of one's true expression as opposed to a textual discourse in which the subject always does not belong to itself. Not intending to deliver a strictly Lacanian reading of Burroughs, Oliver Harris's book seems to take a different angle and offer a look on the status of Burroughs and his oeuvre within the canon of American literature. While Lacan's ideas are used rather as a pretext, the question that dominates Harris's book is what makes the American writer so fascinating for critics and readers despite his work's gnomic, unapproachable language and form. By linking *Queer*, *Junkie*, *Yage Letters* and *Naked Lunch*, Harris examines the mythical status of the Burroughs himself as well as the readers' process of reading and understanding. The conclusion that arises is that of Burroughs being

> [t]he Lacanian Real of American literature and reflecting back the very fantasy identity projected in his work and image; as the irredeemably other, forever unassimilable and always out of place. (Harris 19)

Making use of the poststructuralist body of critical references (Lacan, Derrida, and Baudrillard), Michael Sean Bolton's recent publications examine the trajectories of Burroughs's fluid subjectivity and the narrative strategies employed in his novels. Lacanian concepts, mainly these of the gaze and desire, are used to offer an understanding of Burroughsian revolutionary approach to words and images. What is more, Bolton finds Lacan and Burroughs's concepts of subjectivity convergent since both underscore a self-alienating, fundamentally divided and estranged character of the subject. What engenders the estrangement, as observed by Bolton, is the Lacanian Other, the instance of the Symbolic, which finds its equivalent in the Burroughsian "Other Half".

Another Beat writer who received a comprehensive Lacanian reading is Gary Snyder, a poet who has often been associated with Buddhism and ecocriticism in the present day. Snyder is the focus of Tim Dean's *Gary Snyder and the American Unconscious: Inhabiting the Ground*, a 1991 rigorous reading of his poetic body of work in which Lacanian concepts serve to probe America's mythologies, including the myth of the "American consciousness," and locate the poet's agency therein. As observed by Daniel L. Buccino,

> Dean masterfully explores the early work of Jacques Lacan in order to engage the American cultural consciousness with the poetry of Gary Snyder to illuminate the repressed anti-mythologies in each. ... Dean is remarkably sophisticated not only in his use of Lacan as a means of reading Snyder and American culture, but most particularly in his reciprocal demonstrations of what Gary Snyder reveals for psychoanalysis. (1062)

As delineated in the Introduction, although not bereft of psychoanalytic critical perspectives, Kerouac studies have not yet come into contact with Lacanian theory, which calls for expanding both fields, the more so in light of the abovementioned criticism.

4 Kerouac and Psychoanalysis in America: Direct Encounters

4.1 1940–1945

Jack Kerouac came into fuller contact with psychoanalytic writings during his studies when reading and having intellectual disputes with his friends absorbed much of his time. The early 1940s also mark Kerouac's first real life experience with psychotherapy, yet a rather psychiatrically-oriented one. In 1942 after having enlisted to join the United States Navy, the writer as well as – ironically enough – his novel *The Sea Is My Brother* were examined by psychiatrists at a boot camp in Newport, Rhode Island. This was mainly the result of Kerouac's antics which were carefully crafted in order to get dismissed, since the writer became quickly disillusioned and appalled by what his responsibilities were to be after the training (Nicosia 104). Such behavior further took him to the naval hospital at Bethesda, Maryland, where his case was diagnosed as *dementia praecox*. Nicosia adds that the latter was finally changed to ""schizoid personality" with "angel tendencies" (an early epithet for unrealistic self-aggrandizement)" (106). Kerouac's image of himself was another matter. Anne Charters notes that at that time he perceived himself as being troubled with what he labeled himself as "complex condition" of his mind, which meant being torn apart by contradictory feelings and which hoped to find final welding in the act of writing (SL1 57–58). In a letter to his friend, George J. Apostolos (April, 1943), he states that what he considers "a good book on psychology" (SL1 59) is *Human Behavior and Human Mind* by H.G. Wells, Julian Huxley and G. P. Wells. Being a part of a bigger series entitled *The Science of Life* (1929–1930), which offered a comprehensive insight into the discoveries in the field of biology up to the first decades of the twentieth century, the work deems Freud's name

> as cardinal in the history of human thought as Charles Darwin's. Psychoanalysts, under his leadership, have created a new and dynamic psychology, one that thinks in terms of activities and strivings, of impulses and conflicts, in the place of a flat and lifeless picture of mental states. (Wells, Wells and Huxley, quoted by Zweig, 295)

Learning from the book that "all persons wear a mask" (SL1 59), Kerouac might have recognized the clash between one's need for a conforming social image and their inner, often-repressed impulses, which psychoanalysis taught about. In consequence, doing away with what was believed to be artifice and hypocrisy of social agreement and exploring the inner, hidden, and – according to Kerouac and his fellow writer – true self was to become one of the Beats' key agendas in the following years. The same hospital stay brings about an unsent letter to a friend, Cornelius Murphy, in which the writer is mocking at his psychiatrist and recognizes his condition as psychoneurosis, which can explain "idiosyncrasies" of his personality. He also admits having tried "a searing self-analysis," which leads to a series of aphorisms and a list of books (SL1 61–63).

What can be made of the above-mentioned records is Kerouac's distrust of psychiatrists as opposed to his liking for psychoanalysis, whose usefulness is being tentatively signaled in the letters. His medical report prepared by lt. cmdr. B. L. Allen bears no explicit signs of psychoanalytical language: *dementia praecox* is characteristic for psychiatry rather than for psychoanalysis, whose choice for the term would have rather been "paraphrenia" (Dalzell 119). The writer also makes fun of the doctor's attempts to fish out any non-normative behavior and perceives it as a chance for a pun or two. Conversely, his holding some esteem for the above-mentioned *Human Behavior and Human Mind* as well as aiming at self-analysis allows one to believe that the psychoanalytic thought, be it not precise enough, was of some importance to Kerouac. It is also the writer's choice of words that supports such a thesis – Kerouac judges his condition as "psychoneurosis," whose connotations are principally psychoanalytical if related to conflicts in one's psyche (Shorter 192).

Kerouac's esteem for psychoanalysis is sustained as long as up to 1945. In May, 1944 he was instructed in Freudian dream interpretation by his friend, Duncan Purcell, a student of psychology. As put by Nicosia, Kerouac was interested in dreams mainly "as a means of fortune telling and a source of ... mysteries" (126). In addition, he "acknowledged his oedipal complex," yet "never saw fit to worry about it" (Nicosia 126). In the same year he went to the public library in Grosse Pointe every day in order to expand his knowledge of literary criticism and masterpieces of literature (Nicosia 131). He also used to employ some of psychoanalytic nomenclature to describe his past experiences, e.g. claiming that he had had an "inferiority complex" at Horace Mann preparatory school (Nicosia 131). In New York at the end of 1944, along with Ginsberg, Kerouac paid numerous visits to Burroughs, who lectured them on such various fields as semantics, Mayan codices and Italian philosophy. It was also him who offered his younger friends a reading list, including among many others Goethe, Nietzsche, Koestler, Wells, and Freud (Nicosia 134), whom he studied diligently.

At the beginning of 1945 Burroughs, who himself was undergoing a depth analysis, employed some techniques to analyze Kerouac and Ginsberg, who "spent an hour every day on the living-room couch, free-associating in Burroughs' presence" (Nicosia 138). Done in an amateur and informal way, it mainly included speaking one's mind and acting out various characters (Nicosia 138). Burroughs's diagnosis was that Kerouac "resented a slap in the face [given by his brother, Gerard] and wished Gerard would die, and he died a few years later" (SL1 259). On the other day, Kerouac also heard that he was "tied to [his] mother's apron strings" and that it would get stronger and stronger, which left him shaken by its aptness and resulted in a desperate need to talk it thoroughly over with Ginsberg (Nicosia 139). Due to his maladjustment at Columbia, Ginsberg himself had already been recommended joining Karen Horney League by his friend, Bill Lancaster. Kerouac also believed many of the answers to the question of his troubling personality (e.g. homosexual drives) to be residing in his "subconscious."[65] Hidden homosexuality and childhood sexual experiences were the prime issues to be raised by group analysis administered by Kerouac and his friends at Columbia. Kerouac's "neurosis," as he called it himself, was to be dissolved either by transgressing the norms of behavior or finding an artistic method "capable of unleashing the inner life" and having "the ambiguities in his character ... resolved" (Nicosia 142). Art was thus to be a cure. According to Kerouac, unconsciousness was also a vital feature of the American land, as its life and culture brought together various paradoxes in one body, which Kerouac deemed as valuable and worth sustaining (Nicosia 155). In a letter to his sister, Caroline (March 1945) Kerouac expressed some trust he put in psychoanalysis. Troubled by the cycles of fleeing and returning to his relatives, he states:

> [a] psychoanalyst I recently met is much interested in all this and claims that what I need is ... a psychoanalytical operation on my will – before I can get out of this ever-revolving prison circle. He says I don't want to be successful, that something destructive in me, in my subconscious mind, works against all that, which explains why I never finish important projects or why I don't stick to jobs or anything for that matter. (SL1 87)

It is more than likely that the psychoanalyst was Burroughs himself, as there are no records whatsoever of Kerouac's reliance on a professional psychoanalytic therapy. The writer continues:

> [a]nd what is most fantastic, that the reason I have this subconscious will to failure, a sort of death-wish, stems from something I did before I was five years old and which stamped upon me a neurotic and horrible feeling of *guilt*. ... The psychoanalyst figured

---

65 As regards the terms "subconscious" and "unconscious," they were initially transposable for Freud. As pointed by Eagleton, "[i]n popular English speech, the word 'subconscious' rather than 'unconscious' is often used; but this is to underestimate the radical *otherness* of the unconscious, imagining it as a place just within reach below the surface." See Eagleton, *Literary Theory* 136.

> that I hated Gerard and he hated me – as little brothers are very likely to do, since children at that age are very primitive and aggressive – and that I wished he were dead, *and he died*. So I felt that I had killed him, and ever since, mortified beyond repair, warped in my personality and will, I have been subconsciously punishing myself and failing at everything. (SL1 87)
> psychoanalysis can make me remember the kind things Gerard did to me, and the kind feelings I had for him – which would thus balance against the terrible guilt complex and restore normalcy to my personality. Nothing else can make me remember the kindness I felt for Gerard … . Psychoanalysis is a sort of ingenious method which helps you to remember by piecing clues from dreams, by semi-hypnosis, and so forth. … [T]hroughout Freud, Adler, Karen Horney, and Krafft-Ebbing, and all the other psychologists, I can find more data. … The truth is I've studies these people long ago, but now for the first time, I find that their knowledge can help me. So they're not just books, but salvation. (SL1 87–88)

Kerouac's letters are a sign of their time as they appear to prove the already-discussed American dilution of Freud's thought: psychoanalysis is being used interchangeably with psychology and Freud appears side by side with Karen Horney, a complete rejectionist of Freud's basic psychoanalytic ideas.

4.2 The Break: 1945–1953

It seems that Kerouac's distrust of psychoanalysis begins after 1945. While there is no record of the writer's direct disappointment with it, his letters, journal entries, and prose bear evidence that a change in perceiving the psychoanalytic thought has taken place. Although varied in itself, Kerouac's distrust might be traced to one root, which is his links with Columbia University intellectuals and his New York friends, both of whom were a stronghold of psychoanalysis those days.

The most serious disillusionment Kerouac seems to have experienced at that time was insincerity and artificiality of the intellectual milieu he came into contact with. As a much endeared trend, psychoanalysis was, as we have already seen, an inherent part of the academic life at that time, and simply might have been swept into Kerouac's criticism. Despite dropping out from the university in 1941, the writer kept returning to its campus to join his friends (including Allen Ginsberg and Lucien Carr) until he was finally banned from it in 1945 under allegations of "unwholesome influence." Kerouac's turning away from psychoanalysis might have been caused indirectly by its affinity with high academic authorities, who on the one hand greatly promoted the Freudian thought, yet were also responsible for a police-state discipline in the American academy of the 1940s, which, for instance, included homophobic feelings among the academic staff. New York psychoanalytical circles appear to have been no different. In 1950 Allen Ginsberg, who was being institutionalized in Columbia Psychiatric Institute, would hear that in order to regain his mental health he had to become heterosexual (Nicosia 328).

As regards Columbia intellectuals, Kerouac's growing disregard for psychoanalysis might have been a sign of the writer's personal grudge against one of the most prominent professors, Lionel Trilling, who was an ardent advocate of Freud and a rather harsh critic of Kerouac at the same time. The writer's letter to Allen Ginsberg and his journal entry bring a conspicuous change in tone. Back in September 1945 Kerouac accords Trilling esteem by naming him "an entrenched man of letters" who "represents something I'd like to happen to me someday, namely, to be liked and admired by someone like him" (SL1 95). Yet, in December 1949, the writer remains nothing but critical towards the Columbia professor giving a record of a situation that took place a few years earlier:

> The only time I knew Trilling he pulled the most absurd irrational mask it has been my honor to observe: after Ginsberg was thrown out of college, and I had been mixed up in this downfall and barred from the Columbia campus, Trilling refused to recognize me on the street in the most farcical way, because so solemn, as if I'd suddenly acquired leprosy and it was his rational duty to himself a Liberal Enlightener of Intellectuals to repair at a safe distance from the area of my septic running sores … .
> This is what I saw him do. I can take no crap from such men about my own work, especially when I am no longer barred from that imaginary campus-club of theirs. (WW 253)

Kerouac's critique of Trilling appears to thrive on a blend of artistic, intellectual and personal charges. What brings about the writer's disheartened words is Trilling's rationalism and liberalism, which, at least according to Kerouac, lay their claims to be a truly enlightening way for an intellectual to take, yet at the same time, ostracize any undesirable viewpoints, behaviors, and, as we may see, people themselves. What is more, an advocate of rationalism, Trilling in Kerouac's eyes emerges as a hypocrite, who does not play by the rules he drew up. Whereas Trilling's *The Middle of the Journey* (1947), which receives some of Kerouac's criticism, advocates a liberal, emphatic attitude of tolerance, discussion and integrity, its author appears to be personally unsympathetic for and ignorant of the low-brow society that Kerouac stands by.

Kerouac's stance towards Trilling is alluded to in later journal entries. In February 1950 the writer returns to his critique of false liberalism and intellectualism of America, whose representatives "write about "criminals" but don't want the Neals [an allusion to Neal Cassady] in their houses" (WW 270). Shortly after dropping such a hint about Trilling, the writer condemns psychoanalysis as well. For Kerouac, liberalism of this sort is an indication of neither America's progress nor openness, but a sign of its disintegration. Also, the writer's aggravation towards psychoanalysis might have become stronger with Trilling's further turn to Freud and psychoanalysis as regards literary and cultural studies (*The Liberal Imagination* (1950), *Freud and the Crisis of Our Culture* (1955)).

Finally, what Kerouac also experienced was an artistic let-down, which might have had bearing on his attitude to Trilling and his perception of literature.

> Trilling's earlier critique of a 20-page typescript titled "God's Daughter" elicited a curt written response that Kerouac was "trying to blend realism with symbolism." (Maher and Amram 153)[66]

Again, this might have been the reason for Kerouac's disillusionment with what Trilling stood for at that time, including, on the one hand, Modernism, which the writer often considered to be pretentious and far removed from real life, and psychoanalysis as one of its favored bodies of thought, on the other.

The intelligentsia of New York, which brought Kerouac a great deal of disillusionment, also to some extent meant his bohemian friends. Occasionally, an irritating mode of intellectualism was apparently represented by Ginsberg, who would at times become a "self-aggrandizing weasel" (SL1 99) displaying his intellectual superiority, imbuing the writer with some sense of guilt and pushing him into psychoanalysis. Also, "Reichians" and "Orgonists" (WW 147–148), which might be an allusion to Burroughs, are for Kerouac just another fashion that tries to be against 'Bourgeois culture,' yet their progressiveness is merely superficial. His friends' zeal for the new craze is compared by Kerouac to that in France over "Existentialism and Dolourism and what-not" (WW 142). The writer apparently begins to voice his reservation about the superficiality of bohemian community he has been a part of and struggles to leave the vicious circle of progressing trends, which in his opinion takes one nowhere. In November, 1947 he states:

> Went out on dull carousals, forced into them, really. Missed the football game, and instead got involved in a silly argument with Burroughs and Ginsberg in the afternoon, about psychoanalysis and about "horror." They are still wrapped up in the same subjects as a year, two years, ago. (WW 30)

---

66 In the later years, according to Trilling's widow, Diana, "Trilling had hated himself for lacking the wildness he scorned in Kerouac, and he blamed his failure to write fiction successfully on the very qualities that he was esteemed for: his conscience, decency, quietness, moderation, and reasonableness." See Ellis Amburn, *Subterranean Kerouac: The Hidden Life of Jack Kerouac*.

Kerouac's discontent with psychoanalysis gets even greater as its apologists make efforts at fitting his psyche into a psychoanalytical frame. Around 1949, when charged with his religiousness as a manifestation of a death drive, Kerouac responded to his friends with an intriguing, meta-comment "that neurosis theory was itself a manifestation of anxiety" (Nicosia 263). Generally adverse to religion, psychoanalysis might have therefore strengthened his Christian stance, even if from spite. All things considered, Kerouac had his reasons for despising the novelty of psychoanalysis entering post-war American life. This is corroborated by Gerald Nicosia, who claims that in 1948, while going out with Bea Franco, the writer was simply "contemptuous of people who depended on psychoanalysis" (236) and used to quarrel with his girlfriend, who got psychoanalyzed at that time.

Kerouac's doubts about the psychoanalytic thought get reflected in his work created at that time. The first signs come with his first-published novel, *The Town and the City* (1950), whose writing process is dated back to the late 1945. Much in the vein of Thomas Wolfe's sentimental prose, the work sets out to depict the lives of the Martin family (heavily based on Kerouac's relatives) with two eponymous places as the setting for the story – Galloway, Massachusetts (representing Kerouac's hometown, Lowell) and New York City. The main protagonist, Peter Martin feels torn between the simple and modest life of the former and the irresistible charm of bohemian circles that the latter offers. It is also with the latter that Kerouac associates psychoanalysis. Considering the context of the whole novel, the New York intelligentsia and psychoanalysis as one of its new religions are put in a rather bad light. Not long after Peter joins the intellectual community, the bohemian and intellectual circles of New York begin to be epitomized with cynicism, nihilism, and depravity of the rich and wealthy. In addition, Leon Levinsky, a character based on Allen Ginsberg, urges Peter to become less sentimental and "smalltown" and "get psychoanalyzed" in order to do away with "his own ignorance and blindness to things" (TTATC 366). Kerouac equips Peter Martin with some stoicism and "smiling indulgence" that helps him to put up with Levinsky's agitation (TTATC 366).

It is also Francis Martin, Peter's brother who gets accepted into Harvard, who becomes allured by the new language of "contemporary thought" (consisting, among many, of Freud, Krafft-Ebing, and Jung) and those who use it (TTATC 116). The intellectual jargon unravels before him

> a whole new exotic world suddenly discovered in the vast midst of a drawing, stammering, brute-like America. He could hear the words, the terms – "frustration," "compulsive neurosis," "Oedipus complex," "anxiety," "economic exploitation," "progressive liberalism," … .(TTATC 116)

More and more remote from and disrespectful for his family and simple values they stand for, Francis appears to be contributing to the eventual downfall of the Martin family.

Interestingly enough, in Kerouac's literary account of the mental check up at the boot camp, found in *The Town and the City*, the words "psychiatrist" and "psychologist" are used interchangeably (TTATC 319), which might serve as yet another proof for the mishmash of various therapeutic trends and concepts in the 1940s. In addition, some of the doctors who examine Francis Martin reveal their "blank disinterestedness" and "Don Juan-ish[ness]," while others are competent and humble (TTATC 323).

Among other charges Kerouac matches psychoanalysis with the show-business of those days. Perhaps, yet again, this might be accounted for by Kerouac's perceiving psychoanalytic body of work as a passing trend offering no more than some cheap intellectual amusement. Around 1947–1948, in an undated entry of his journal, the writer likens the intellectuals of New York, who are "embarrassed by Freudian slips of speech" (WW 140), to a "'show-business' crowd ... embarrassed by Jimmy Durante malapropisms" (WW 140) and, importantly, claims that there is not a single difference more.

What is also comparable for Kerouac is their refinement and sterility; both focus on the low-brow only when it is to be criticized or taken advantage of. The writer's accusation is serious – "sophisticated, ... suave" TV shows and "suave Viennese psychoanalysis," which additionally aims at inflicting guilt upon one, contribute to "a disintegrating America" (WW 270). Psychoanalysis, therefore, is seen to be standing in the way of integration and true progress of the nation; it is "impractical and destructive" (WW 193), as the writer adds in May, 1949. The solution is to be sought not in Freud, or whatever he would stand for, but in "the true optimism of Twain and Whitman" (WW 270).

What is interesting, Kerouac's criticism appears to have another side. While there is a Kerouac who is quick-tempered and harsh in his skepticism, there is also one who demonstrates a deeper reflection, be it still a critical one, on the psychoanalytic thought and makes something out of it for himself. In addition, however despised for what form it took in America, psychoanalysis must have intrigued Kerouac insofar as in its core it was much aligned to his literary agenda of self-inquiry and spontaneity of (artistic) language.

In August, 1948 he is upset that he causes some misunderstandings and offence with his confessions while aiming at something he labels as the "palpitation of pride," which comes down to dismantling one's sense of self-importance (WW 127). On this occasion he observes that

> [o]ne of the interesting things about these disclosures of dark self is that all emerges without Freudian pornography, almost…it's terribly "clean" and human. (WW 127)

Although unalterably derogatory, the tone is less mockery. Also, Kerouac is critical in a reasonable way when he claims that psychological self-scrutiny and spontaneity of mind do not principally need to invoke sexual connotations. What finds reflection in Kerouac's words is the unfortunate tendency of American society to connote Freud with sexual symbols on every occasion.

Around the same time, psychoanalysis lends Kerouac a hand insofar as it helps him to shape his own life philosophy by providing some contrast to it. Pondering the value of psychoanalytic practice, the writer concludes:

> as far as psychology vs. morality is concerned, I take the position morally, that psychology is a hesitation-in-analysis and not an action-in-the-world. Knowledge has its place, but the work of *life* needs to get done. (WW 149)

Thus, for Kerouac, a true way of self-inquiry means an immediate act of participation in the world on as wide a scale as possible. The work of psychoanalytic (psychological?) talking cure is useful as long as it remains secondary to the work of life, which absorbs one in acting out one's desires. Having already thrown himself into cross-country journeys, Kerouac jots down the following words on his way from New York to Denver in 1949:

> The bus zoomed on along Kansas River to Manhattan. The prairie grew more desolated – it was dark out there. … I slept a little. That psychiatrist who had traveled to St. Louis – what in the hell for was he coming out here to psychoanalyze such wonderful people like that motorcycle kid? Which is best – wreck a motorcycle on a Saturday night, or stay home reading Freud? What is the earth for – what is the night for – what is food & strength for – what is man for? For joy, for joy. (WW 345)

Apart from being another proof of close links between psychiatry and psychoanalysis in the mid twentieth-century America, the image one gets is the primacy of pure force of life over the existing order of knowledge. For Kerouac, plunging into the former, which is nothing more than validating some pre-existing knowledge in practice, is a more accurate verifier of what is undisclosed in oneself. In the end, practice is put back into knowledge. If Kerouac's method of automatic writing aims at creating spontaneous prose, which is to be a record of achieving greater self-awareness, then it would not be an exaggeration at this point to claim that it was psychoanalysis which, at least partially, triggered the writer's need for confessional mode of (artistic) expression. In September, 1948, while conceptualizing *On the Road*, the writer discovers the value of the "subconscious mind" in the process of artistic creation:

> Fourteenth Day of lazy work on the last chapter. What a joke. The life of a mind? – not 'rational' thought, but the mere *process* which is undergone when the subconscious mind breaks through to the conscious mind. Hooray! Hooray for me! (WW 129)

Hence, at the break of the 1940s and 1950s, Kerouac's attitude to psychoanalysis becomes complex inasmuch as it begins to be driven by contradictory forces. On the one hand, psychoanalytic practice, its theories and institutional presence in the American life are perceived by him as an elitist hobby capable of disintegrating the country and, on the other hand, psychoanalysis serves Kerouac as a point of reference for artistic techniques aiming at reaching the deep structures of one's mind. For one thing the writer is aware of Neal Cassady's unsuccessful psychoanalysis in 1951 and a year later discourages Ginsberg from reentering psychoanalytic therapy (Nicosia 391), but then again, he appears to draw his spontaneous prose heavily on the quest for self-knowledge and self-disclosure, which might be achieved by tracking down one's unconscious.

In 1950, still working on *On the Road*, Kerouac refuses to finish the novel until he communicates the "incommunicable" (Nicosia 324), which amounts to the following premise:

> I want to fish as deep as possible into my own subconscious in the belief that far down, everyone will understand because they are the same that far down. (Kerouac, quoted by Nicosia, 324)

Kerouac understands the importance of language in the process of self-disclosure and, therefore, often ascribes a special status to his native French, which rekindles his "childhood revelations of the world" (Kerouac, quoted by Nicosia, 324). It is also during his trip to Mexico when he revels that supposedly foreign places seem familiar and bring him back to his childhood.

It is thus at the break of 1940s and 1950s that mapping the unconscious in the course of literary creation becomes Kerouac's trademark theme itself. As claimed by Nicosia, by 1951 Kerouac had already included "the process of writing into the subject of his writing" (359) and on coming up with his idea of literary sketching, he was preoccupied "not so much with *what* he was describing, as with *how* and *why* he was scribbling at all" (359). As a consequence of "[l]ifting the censorship of the conscious self, Kerouac opened the door to the unconscious" (Nicosia 359). Such literary strategies find their way into *On the Road* (1957) and *Visions of Cody* (1972), which both, apart from referencing psychoanalysis directly, turn their attention to the deep structures of mind and language.

On the Road features records of several lengthy face-to-face sittings during which the protagonists, Sal (Kerouac), Dean (Cassady), and Carlo (Ginsberg), make confessions and discuss troubling issues with one another. Significantly, at times they have a tendency either to use the register of psychoanalytic field or to acknowledge psychoanalytic concepts. On one of many trips, Carlo Marx describes and provides a sort of diagnosis for Dean Moriarty using what might be treated as a variation of the psychoanalytic argot. Sal Paradise recollects that:

> [h]e [Carlo] wrote of Dean as a 'child of the rainbow' who bore his torment in his agonized priapus. He referred to him as 'Oedipus Eddie' who had to 'scrape bubble gum off windowpanes'. (OTR 48)

The oedipal simile gets repeated in *Visions of Cody* where a character based on Cassady, Dean Pomeray, "goes ... haunted in the streets of Saturday night in the American city with his eyes torn out like Oedipus who sees all and sees nothing" (VOC 109). On another occasion, going to sleep, Paradise himself keeps his ears open to Dean's actions and concludes:

> I could hear Dean, blissful and blabbering and frantically rocking. Only a guy who's spent five years in jail can go to such maniacal helpless extremes; beseeching at the portals of the soft source, mad with a completely physical realization of the origins of life-bliss; blindly seeking to return the way he came. (OTR 126).

What comes after is Moriarty's analysis conducted by Paradise; importantly, the latter examines his companion's relationship with parents. Additionally, such an image of Dean instantly invites comparison with the Freudian idea of the death drive which is epitomized by one's longing for the return to a female womb as the source of pre-ontological completeness and tranquility; the fact that Cassady seeks it *blindly* is even more evocative — it again brings forward the punishment of Oedipus and, very likely, some kind of castration-loss that has taken place.

Finally, what occasionally lurks behind his literary alter ego is Kerouac's own oedipal, terrifying self-knowledge, such as when an argument breaks out between Dean and Sal. The latter understands clearly:

> [e]verything I had ever secretly held against my brother was coming out: how ugly I was and what filth I was discovering in the depths of my own impure psychologies. (OTR 201)

The figure of brother appears to denote not as much a brotherly character of Dean Moriarty as Kerouac's own brother Gerard, whose premature death inflicted a sense of guilt on the writer.

Additionally, *On the Road* is no different from Kerouac's previous novel in that professional and institutionalized psychoanalysis serves as the target of mockery and criticism. The novel provides some intriguing comments on the practice on the behalf of Old Bull Lee's character (William S. Burroughs's alter ego). On his visit to Lee's apartment in New York, Sal Paradise observes that his friend has:

> a set of chains in his room that he said he used with his psychoanalyst; they were experimenting with narcoanalysis and found that Old Bull had seven separate personalities, each growing worse and worse, till finally he was a raving idiot and had to be restrained with chains. (OTR 137)

Narcoanalysis, "a treatment that uses sodium pentothal to induce an abreaction" (Menand 197), was practiced by some psychiatrists, such as Roy Grinker and John Spiegel, to battle shell-shocks and other war neuroses among the American soldiers in the post-World War II era. It is also said to have had roots in Freud's early use of hypnosis and abreaction, which involves reenacting a traumatic experience. First and foremost, the above passage from *On the Road* and Kerouac's choice for a "psychoanalyst" performing "narcoanalysis" prove yet again that psychiatry was heavily indebted to and frequently interchanged with psychoanalysis in the mid-twentieth century America. Additionally, the fragment adopts a satirical tone demonstrating the practice as ridiculous, which allows the writer to maintain his stance towards professional psychoanalysts.

As regards *Visions of Cody*, another attempt at grasping the phenomenon of Neal Cassady, Kerouac's textual strategies of spontaneity are even more conspicuous, since the novel quits a horizontal, plot-ridden construction for the sake of a vertical, inward and insightful movement into the nature of things. What facilitates the process of creation is a formal novelty of employing a tape recorder, which is to let the flow of thoughts be as well preserved in writing as possible. Again, such a strategy runs in the vein of psychoanalytic free-association as well as of meaningful parapraxes and is a reflection of Kerouac's and Cassady's sessions of 1951:

> They'd get high on wine or pot, Jack would turn on the tape recorder, and they'd talk. Their free-associative, confessional style owed as much to the communal group on 115th Street (whose methodology Neal had absorbed through Jack and Allen) as to the general psychoanalytical climate born of the prodigious insecurity in post-World War II America. ... After each night's talk, Jack would carefully transcribe the tape, and then read aloud portions of the transcription at their next session, so that they could comment on their misapprehensions and verbal dodges. Being at once actor and spectator, they obtained extraordinary new perspectives on the ungraspability of their own lives. (Nicosia 364)

Apart from ascribing to oneself the roles of both the analyst and the analysand, it is especially the attention put to misapprehensions and verbal dodges that accounts for Kerouac's interest in the ideas first laid out in Freud's *Psychopathology of Everyday Life* (1901). What is more, in one of the transcriptions one may come across Jack Duluoz's (Kerouac) and Cody Pomeray's (Neal Cassady) discussion of the winter 1952 issue of psychoanalytical magazine *Neurotica*. As elucidated by James T. Jones, the number was related to the castration complex and included an article by Otto Fenichel on "Castration Anxiety in Boys", an excerpt from Melville's *Pierre*, and F. Scott Fitzgerald's "The Boy Who Killed His Mother" (*The Mythic Form* 110). Also, Jones adds that during Kerouac's meeting with the founder of the magazine, the writer actually put forward his ideas for its future issue (*The Mythic Form* 110). As well as the time of its making, *Visions of Cody* is then perhaps one of the most psychoanalytically-oriented points in Kerouac's career.

Finally, the writer's psychoanalytically imbued methodology of writing brings him to creating the section entitled "Imitation of the Tape," in which he himself makes an attempt at becoming both a performer and a recorder of his own words. At that time, Kerouac "has discovered that there are a multitude of voices in his head apart from his own, ... *they* (whatever they are) are somehow speaking to *him* ... " (Nicosia 373). The stake here is mastering all of them and gaining knowledge of one's thinking process (and providing a comprehensible account of it) without depending on an external recording device, whose material presence occasionally stands in the way. However, in the end, the experiment fails. Analyzing Kerouac's endeavor, Nicosia holds that

> [o]nce he [Kerouac] succeeds in tapping his unconscious, it starts to flow too fast .... The basic problem is that Kerouac the writer can't help becoming conscious of his own act of listening and recording; and once he realizes what he's doing, he begins to direct the flow rather than simply follow it. (Nicosia 373)

The result is thus either an incomprehensible stream of words, signs and sounds Kerouac does not want to accept, or a communicative yet consciousness-ridden flow. There is a deadlock between the writer's need that literature be communicative and simple, which originates in his above-mentioned esteem for American optimism and simplicity of Twain and Whitman (as Kerouac viewed it), and the pursuit of one's unconscious, which does not play by the rules of linearity, communicativeness and straightforwardness common for everyday (American) use of language.

In addition to Kerouac's progress with textual strategies anchored in a psychoanalytical distrust of the Cartesian understanding of consciousness as the core of one's self-knowledge, *Visions of Cody* seems to retain the writer's skepticism about the proponents of Wilhelm Reich. Yet again, suspicion proves to be superficial. Discussing the band he saw, Duluoz thinks of a drummer as of somebody "with soft goofy complacent Reichianalyzed ecstasy, . . . raggedydoll-necked like all Reichians" (VOC 433). Thus, the ground for judgment is nothing but physical appearance and fashion, which again brings one back to Kerouac's putting an equation mark between psychoanalysis and another pretentious, fleeting trend among the Greenwich Village hipsters of the early 1950s. A change is to come no sooner than in 1953 when the writer gets familiar with Reich's theories firsthand.

4.3 1953, the Lure of Wilhelm Reich, and the Vices of Institutional Psychoanalysis

Initially skeptical towards "Orgonists" and "Reichians," just as towards any other passing fashion hyped by his bohemian friends, Kerouac falls for Reich himself on reading his *Function of the Orgasm* in the middle of 1953. As claimed by Nicosia,

> [p]ositing that most mental and psychical maladies are attributable to the electrical disturbance caused by insufficient or inadequate orgasms, Reich believed no person could be happy or fully productive without a full sex life. The book impressed Jack more than anything he had read since *Ulysses* in 1942 …. (441)

Shortly after familiarizing himself with Reich, the writer advises Reichian psychoanalysis to others. In August 1953 Kerouac recommends going to a Reichian doctor to Carolyn Cassady, underscoring the apparent simplicity as a major value of Reich's theories. As he posits, "Reich is as simple as bread, as pornography" (DC 12–13). It seems then that for Kerouac the apparent clarity, directness and vigor of Reichian psychoanalysis, features that perhaps are compatible with "the true optimism of Twain and Whitman," are an alternative to guilt-inducing, unfeeling, downgrading Freud, of whom the writer is still highly critical. What is striking is Kerouac's change of optics (or simply inconsistency of beliefs) as regards psychoanalysis and sexuality. Conversely to depreciating Freudianism as pornography in 1948, the writer does not refrain from comparing the latter with Reich's theories in order to glorify his new discovery five years later.

As well as leaving a mark on Kerouac's life philosophy, Reich's ideas got transposed onto the writer's textual strategies. Nicosia suggests that writing became for him

> a form of sexual expression; and the more feeling it released (like Reich's postulated electrical discharge during orgasm), the more satisfactory the experience for both writer and reader. (446)

An immediate literary aftermath of becoming familiar with Reichian psychoanalysis was a novella entitled *The Subterraneans* (1958), written in three nights during October 1953. Kerouac claimed that writing the work "was a form of sexual activity for him" (Charters, quoted by Jones, *The Mythic Form* 125), which is supported by its sexual explicitness as well as its raw, impulsive and spur-of-the-moment style. It is also thanks to the spontaneity of composition that the work – a first-person perspective record of an affair between Kerouac's alter ego, Leo Percepied, and an Afro-American called Mardou Fox – achieves its confessional mode. Getting over a failed relationship, the narrator of the novella claims that he is rather "talking – perhaps in his head – rather than writing" (Theado 111), which largely resembles the psychoanalytic *talking cure*. What adds to the psychoanalytic flavor of *The Subterraneans* is the name of the protagonist itself. Leo Percepied is an outcome of joining Kerouac's father's name and the French for "pierced foot," a condition Oedipus struggled with. As aptly observed by Nicosia, the affair with Mardou is a remedy for Percepied being the target of his mother's affections, and so the novella gets built upon the Oedipal complex with Leo being Oedipus (449). However, having in mind Kerouac's stance towards psychoanalysis, one is likely to feel that Percepied's Oedipal lament is imbued with the writer's mockery, best typified by the main character's name. Finally, standing in correspondence to the spontaneous and confessional style of the work, Percepied himself acts as a home-bred psychoanalyst for Mardou, who battles mental disorders. Being able to recall some longer passages of her words and then ponder upon them like an analyst, the protagonist at times itemizes symptoms of a mental disorder and ironically admits: "she threw me over a dead hulk that now I am – psychoanalyst, I'm serious!" (TS 76).

Apart from being another exemplary piece of spontaneous writing and an attempt of putting Reich's theories into literary practice, Kerouac's novella is a stance against the omnipresence of psychoanalysis in the 1950s' America. Although not named once in *The Subterraneans*, its institutional model which lurks in the background of the work could have been nothing but that of ego-psychology, New York being its mid-twentieth century center.

Seemingly overwhelmed by life's bends as well as by the ignorance and alienating power of New York, Leo Percepied draws a bitter conclusion about the condition of his country:

> [T]he difference between men, the difference so vast between concerns of executives in skyscrapers and seadogs on harbor and psychoanalysts in stuffy offices in great grim buildings full of dead bodies in the morgue below and madwomen at windows ... . (TS 71)

Uninformative as it may seem, the short passage actually conjures up quite a rich image of what the dominating institution of psychoanalysis could have been those days. Firstly, possessing traits of the oppressive Moloch (to use Ginsberg's term), the psychoanalytic practice takes the shape of an institution which, with its "great grim buildings," prevails over other elements of social and urban scenery.

Its domineering character is boosted by hinting at the vertical dominance of psychoanalysts' offices, which together with the skyscrapers full of executives, rule over all that is low and common. Thus, the American mode of psychoanalysis seems yet again to be equaled with business and it is worth reminding that the ground for making big money out of the treatment was already prepared. It could be surmised that the burgeoning numbers of psychoanalytic institutions had some roots in the theories of Edward Bernays, Freud's nephew, who attempted to combine psychoanalysis with marketing and public relations. Facing big financial success and settling in "great" buildings, American psychoanalysis could only continue its search for yet a wider influence and target.

It is then no wonder that Percepied deems the offices "stuffy," which as well as connoting a massive number of patients (many of them treated unsuccessfully and ending up hopeless or dead, Percepied seems to suggest) hints at narrow-mindedness, conformity and complacency of the institution itself. What this finally points to is a mechanical and large-scale treatment, unreflective of analysands' individual cases. Considering this as well as the aforediscussed institution of ego-psychology, one might feel tempted to presuppose that Kerouac, through the eyes of Leo Percepied, held a low opinion of the institutional form of psychoanalysis in the United States, ego-psychology being its spearhead in the 1950s' America. Also, apart from depicting the life of the New York Bohemia, *The Subterraneans* and its sociocultural background allude to the failure in uniting the American people. What adds to this fiasco is psychoanalysis, whose allegedly pessimistic and derogatory spirit as well as money-driven politics eradicate a sense of community of men. The novella echoes Kerouac's earlier accusations of psychoanalysis having detrimental and disintegrating effects on the States and their society.

The above-mentioned charges against the institutionalized form of American psychoanalysis run much in the vein of Jacques Lacan's critique aimed at ego-psychology, its influence, and mode of functioning in the States. As we have already seen, ego-psychology was largely aimed at establishing a strong ego and its defensive attitudes with a view to adopting one better to society. Conversely, the Lacanian subject, as elucidated by Dany Nobus,

> should not be understood … as the unified, self-conscious being or the integrated personality so dear to many a psychologist, but as the subject of the unconscious – a subject that does not function as the centre of the human thought and action, but which inhabits the mind as an elusive agency, controlling yet uncontrollable (61).

Lacan called ego-psychology, which opted for a Cartesian, will-dependent ego, a real treason of Freudian ideas. According to him and his reading of Freud, such an equipped subject could not exist, and, therefore, ego-psychological practice fully missed the objectives of psychoanalysis. In other words, it was dead with its textbook-like complacency, authoritarian in its quest for bringing adjustment to American society, and it did not go deep into the problems of therapeutical nature. Roudinesco explicates the matter in detail:

> Lacan approaches Freud's second topography with an opposition to any form of ego-psychology. Two choices were possible after the overhaul aimed at by Freud himself in 1920-3. One was to make the ego the product of a gradual differentiation of the id, acting as representative of reality and charged with containing drives (this was ego-psychology); the other turned its back on any idea of an autonomous ego and studied its genesis in terms of identification.
> In other words, if one chose the first option, which was to some extent the path followed by psychoanalysis in the United States, one would try to remove the ego from the id and make it the instrument of the individual's adaptation to eternal reality. If one chose the second option, which was that of … Lacan …, one brought the ego back toward the id to show that it was structured in stages, by means of imagos borrowed from the other through projective identifications. (29)

Kerouac surely did not have a chance either to think about the aptness of "the second option" or to verify it empirically, yet, he must have grasped intuitively and perfectly well the mechanical superficiality of "the first option" and the fulfillment of what Lacan warned against – the complacency of analysts as a result of the lack of constant reflection upon the theory and individual cases. Thus, psychoanalytical offices are "stuffy" since they are occupied by "stuffy" analysts, whose couches are nothing short of being similar to production lines programmed according to a textbook theory. In a greater image, institutional psychoanalysis would fit perfectly well into the American post-war society's obsession with comfort and stability insofar as it became yet another tool for battling idiosyncrasies often deemed as dangerous maladjustments. Willing to oppose the complacency, narrow-mindedness and authoritarianism of the 1950s authorities, Kerouac as well as other Beat Generation writers find an ally in Lacan, who

> is warning his interlocutors that American institutions have an invisible political effect on post-war intellectual life, censoring and policing the translation of texts … . (Liu "Lacan's Afterlife" 258)

Hence, the institutional model of psychoanalysis Leo Percepied appears to be deliberating over is not, in his eyes, an answer to Mardou's nervous disorders. As if that were not enough, the protagonist goes as far as to blame the treatment itself for his lover's state of being:

> Her own little stories and her minor fugues, cutting across boundaries of the city, and smoking too much marijuana, which held so much terror for her (in the light of my own

> absorptions concerning her father the founder of her flesh and predecessor terror-ee of her terrors and knower of much greater flips and madness than she in psychoanalytic-induced anxieties could ever even summon up just to imagine) .... .(TS 19–20)

The gloom of psychoanalysis is thus to strike once again and wreak havoc by filling the analysand with more guilt and sadness than before the therapy. Perceiving psychoanalysis as a pessimistic and imperfect system, throughout the novel Kerouac as well as the central character of his novella seem to have a common goal

> hoping to instill ... recognition of fact it's a big world and psychoanalysis is a small way to explain it since it only scratches the surface, which is, analysis, cause and effect, why instead of what .... (TS 71)

Again, the end of the quote, a brief enumeration, might allude to a mechanical treatment of the analysands. Much as it is aligned with Lacan's aversion towards psychoanalytical unreflectiveness, Percepied's stance also creates a palpable dissonance with the Lacanian practice. If the protagonist's wish for "what" may be interpreted as a demand to "be given cure" for some kind of distortion, with regard to Lacan it should definitely be "why," since his idea of a therapy does not presuppose any kind of "magic solution" for a problem nor does it believe in the fact that what really speaks is a stable, conscious "I." What Lacanian psychoanalysis aims at instead is making the subject aware of certain mechanisms that govern its life, which does not necessarily entail putting things right in view of one's expectations. A major Lacanian scholar, Alenka Zupančič, observes that

> [o]ne should rather say that once things have gone so far (as to produce a neurosis, for instance), they can only go further. In principle, it is easier to go by the law than to find one's own way around desire. But all the malfunctions and dysfunctions that appear in the clinic (as well as in the psychopathology of everyday life) remind us not only that this doesn't always work, but also that it never works perfectly. Psychoanalysis is not here to repair the damage, to help the social machine to function more smoothly and to reconstruct whatever was ill-constructed. It is there to take us further along the path that our "problems" have put us on, it is there as the "guardian" of the other way, the one that consists in finding our own way around our desire. (179)

It appears then that both Kerouac and Lacan wished the institutional model of American psychoanalysis to have been less superficial and disengaged, yet they saw it taking completely divergent trajectories of change. Also, if we accept that Percepied's wish for "what" is to be interpreted as "a cure," then it could be surmised that the protagonist's (and Kerouac's) demand is not as much of psychoanalytical as of psychiatric nature. Having been interspersed with one another in the mid twentieth-century America, both fields were often used interchangeably and, as I have shown, Kerouac was no exception in doing so. Thus, in Percepied's eyes, psychoanalysis is not the answer to Mardou's mental disorders and one can wonder if it is not psychiatric treatment that was necessary in her case. Bringing the topic of relations between psychoanalysis and psychiatry, Kernberg points out that the former

> exaggerated its claims regarding knowledge and therapeutic success. Psychoanalysis focused on symptomatic neurosis, on character pathology, on the relatively milder psychiatric illnesses, while not being of fundamental help to the more severe, chronic psychotic, organic and mentally retarded patients who constituted a large number of inmates in state institutions ("Psychoanalysis in America")

Medical aims of the American psychoanalysis seem to have been often too vast. Consequently, its specific and precipitous combination with psychiatry could not have turned out fully successful. This can be traced in Kerouac's work, where psychoanalytic treatment appears to be taking the blame for not achieving goals of psychiatric nature.

The Subterraneans also echo Kerouac's previous charges against psychoanalysis as a depraved, passing fashion of the high-brow New York. Having been taught of psychoanalysis and psychoanalyzed, Mardou instantly becomes the object of Percepied's criticism. At one time, being anxious about her comments on his mother's vast influence, Leo virulently remarks that "naturally she, she's just jealous, and has no folk herself, and is one of those modern psychoanalyzed people who hate mothers anyway" (TS 47). On another occasion, Percepied's allegations are general:

> But cope that old psychoanalytic cope, she talks like all of em, the city decadent intellectual dead-ended in cause-and-effect analysis and solution of so-called problems instead of the great JOY of being and will and fearlessness – rupture's their rapture – that's her trouble, she's just like Adam [Allen Ginsberg], like Julien [Anton Rosenberg], the lot, afraid of madness, the fear of madness haunts her–not Me Not Me by God. (TS 57–58)

What comes to the rescue for Kerouac at that time is Reich, whose sexually liberating power, in Leo Percepied's words, is a "sudden illuminated glad wondrous discovery ... clarity as I had not seen in a long time" (TS 46). The liberationist strand of psychoanalysis, whose reading of Freud recommended freeing desire from social repression, stems primarily from the work of Reich and Herbert Marcuse, thinkers of whom Lacan, unlike Kerouac, was equally (though differently) critical. Reich and Marcuse were the psychoanalytic architects of the sexual revolution of the 1960s and 70s, a project whose claim provoked ... Lacan's skepticism (Dean 242).

4.4 1953–1969

Becoming familiar with Reich did not elevate Kerouac's further interest in psychoanalysis. In fact, no sooner had the author of *The Function of the Orgasm* started to be a significant source of inspiration for Kerouac than he gradually began to disappear from the American writer's scope of attention. Following the mid-1950s and *The Subterraneans* there are hardly any references to Reich at all, in Kerouac's novels, letters and journals. One of few examples is a 1958 letter to Burroughs, in which Kerouac calls Reich a "serious, benevolent scientist" (SL2 116). The period between the mid-1950s and the writer's death in 1969 indicates that many of Kerouac's fears and frustrations towards psychoanalysis were simply kept sustained. There was hardly any space for the appreciation of psychoanalytic thought; little of it came with the last years of the writer's life.

One of many trends which is retained towards the end of his life is Kerouac's distrust of institutional psychoanalysis. Alike the writer's partner, Bea Franco, who gets criticized by him for going to a psychoanalyst in 1948, another of Kerouac's girlfriends, Helen Weaver, must put up with a similar treatment in 1957. Having been dumped, the writer "blamed the break-up on her analyst, assuming she had passively followed his advice" (Nicosia 542). He also claimed that "psychoanalyst's advice should have made no difference to her, and suggested she would do a lot better by going to confession. Besides, he added, confession is free" (Nicosia 542). The problem is rendered in *Desolation Angels*, a novel written in 1957 and 1961. Asked to move out from his girlfriend's room (Helen Weaver alias Ruth Heaper) on the advice of her psychoanalyst, Duluoz goes as far as to claim that psychoanalysts want to "screw" the patients themselves (DA 297). Later in the novel, Duluoz repeats his point claiming that "Ruth Heaper's psychiatrists [are] trembling for the snowy thighs of young patients" and are "wretched leering thieves of life" (DA 339). What we thus get yet again is Kerouac's rendition of institutional psychoanalysis as a body of specialists whose advice is not to be accepted, by any means passively, at least for the sake of both its ineffectiveness and expensiveness. The very fact of a psychoanalyst offering advice is a highly problematic case itself. It is something Lacanian psychoanalysis has always avoided and has warned against, whereas the then-dominating trend of ego-psychology, which underscored the importance of adaptation, would make use of. Strengthening the ego and achieving harmony, so endeared by ego-psychologists, were for Lacan merely a manifestation of the imaginary, a deceptive delusion. Kerouac might have seen it so as well.

What the above-mentioned fragments also bear evidence to is the writer's continuous obsession with the allegedly overtly sexual basis of the psychoanalytic thought. While in 1948 it made him equate psychoanalysis with pornography, nearly ten years later it leads him to accuse analysts of taking sexual advantage of their analysands. This gets criticized in Kerouac's poetry as well. As observed by James T. Jones, in *Mexico City Blues*, a 242-chorus poem composed in 1955, the singer finds "Gospel" of "Psychoanalysis Sex / Chart of Mad Talk" repugnant (Kerouac, quoted by Jones, *The Mythic Form* 222). Thus, besides depriving one of money and optimism, the "leering thieves of life," to quote Kerouac, perceive aid-seeking women as sexual prey, something Kerouac himself was surely not innocent of. Interestingly enough, Kerouac perceived himself as such prey as well. In 1963 he sneered at the attempt of a Japanese college girl, who was a student of Gary Snyder's, to provide a psychoanalysis of him on the basis of *The Subterraneans*. In a vulgar and misogynist letter to Snyder, intoxicated Kerouac claims that women are only interested in seducing men and "if they're not in your actual presence to be able to do that, why, they do it in the form of Freudian analyses of your writings" (SL2 362). Much as Kerouac might have had his own ideas over applied literary psychoanalysis, it is impossible to treat these alcohol-infused comments as a serious charge.

We can see how complementary to each other psychoanalysis and psychiatry must have been for Kerouac as he kept interchanging one for another smoothly. Duluoz speaks of Ruth Heaper getting treated by psychoanalysts just to switch them for psychiatrists several pages further. In 1965, with his drinking frenzy in full swing, he was taken to see some psychiatrists.[67] As claimed by Nicosia, the writer was "tolerant enough" to talk with them, although he "thought most of them either squares or fascists" (664), a belief that would concur with his earlier contempt for submissiveness to analysts. Interestingly, it would not hold for Adler and Fromm, who get mentioned in *Desolation Angels* in the context of non-conformity (DA 237). During the medical examination the writer lectured the psychiatrists on Harry Stack Sullivan, an American Neo-Freudian analyst, who "left sexual drives and ... transference behind ... [and instead] focused on the pathologies of human relationships" (Makari 121), which again goes along with Kerouac's disdain for alleged sexual content of the psychoanalytic thought. As well as confirming the writer's contemptuous attitude towards the

67 It is also in 1965 that a fragment of *The Dharma Bums* (1958) appears in an anthology entitled *The World of Psychoanalysis*, "which combines essays by Freudian psychologists with works of creative writers (Jones, *The Mythic Form* 146) and Kerouac's work is to go along with psychoanalytic findings of Franz Alexander, a psychoanalyst who facilitated merging Freudianism with social sciences in the States.

institutional forms of mental care, the record of Kerouac's conversations may be taken for another proof of close bonds between psychiatry and psychoanalysis in the mid-twentieth century America. One of Kerouac's interlocutors, who is identified by Nicosia as a psychiatrist, Dr. Roseman touches upon psychoanalytical matters, such as dreams. Also, Dr. Roseman claims mental illnesses to be "a myth" (Nicosia 666), a stance typical for a psychoanalyst who would see mental disorders to be the effect of certain experiences rather than failures of the nervous system. That the American psychiatry of that time derived ideas from a broad range of sources, mainly Freud, is thus clear. Such interceptions contributed to psychoanalysis losing its own claims and being blamed for what it was not, which is well exemplified by Kerouac.

Another trend that kept strong in Kerouac from the mid-1950s until his death was the resent towards academia, Lionel Trilling, and liberalism. In Kerouac's eyes, all these exposed hypocrisy by fostering conservatism, not broadmindedness as they claimed to be doing. In a 1958 letter to Allen Ginsberg, Kerouac sneers at Robert Brustein, a young Columbia lecturer who in the September 1958 issue of *Horizon* accused the Beats of proponing aggressive, inarticulate, norm-violating literature, which in its "style [is] like automatic writing" (SL2 150). For Kerouac, Brustein is naturally "another columbia trilling fink" who "[makes] irresponsible statements from his cloistered position" (SL2 150) and hastily blames the Beats for acts of artistic and non-artistic violence. It would not be an exaggeration to claim that from Kerouac's perspective what academia of those days stood for was nothing more than a stronghold of narrow-minded moderation, reason, and rigor that inconspicuously separated the better America from the low-brow. As we can see from Kerouac's distrust of changing intellectual trends, any theories, such as psychoanalysis, which the academics occasionally embraced to pass judgments on the world and people must have been instant enemies for the writer.[68] Also in 1958, Kerouac did not refrain from showing his disdain for Freudians publicly. David Sterritt mentions a panel discussion held at Hunter College in Manhattan where asked about the people who were baleful for the future of America, Kerouac mocked "big smart know-it-all Marxists and Freudians" (108). As in the previous years, the more disturbingly psychoanalytic theories seemed to speak of human nature, the more hate they engendered in Kerouac. In 1963 Freud is put side by side with Marx and Pavlov as a disturber

68 Kerouac's temporary turn to Buddhism ends up apparently incompatible with Freud as well since "Freudians ... don't understand [that] all comes to Naught" (Kerouac, quoted by Jones, *The Mythic Form* 236).

of one's peace and quiet (SL2 363). A few years later, anticipating his own passing away, Kerouac deepened his Christianity and preferred it to those who had dared to be critical of it. So had Freud, as we learn in *Satori in Paris* (written in 1965), with "his cold depreciation of helpless personalities" (SIP 89). Death is nothing to be feared of, claims Duluoz, if "you've done no harm" (SIP 89) and his giving up on academia, intellectual trends and liberalism is complete as he asks: "Do we need a Definition-of-Harm University to teach this?" (SIP 89).

Kerouac's turning away from the academic circles comes along with his turning away from bohemia, which preyed on passing intellectual fashions in a similar manner, psychoanalysis taking the lead. What pulled an especially sensitive string in Kerouac were his friends' suggestions that the writer suffered from the Oedipus complex. Paul Maher and David Amram go as far as to claim that "Kerouac's resentment toward Freud may have begun when he was blasted with criticism by friends and critics for his devoted and unselfish attachment to his mother" (494). Such a perspective cannot be fully accepted since, in the mid-1940s, the writer, as we have learned, unopposedly acknowledged his Oedipal inclinations himself and occasionally showed his serious concern about them. It is thus rather a general break-off from academia that was responsible for his giving up on Freud. However, Kerouac's later rage at being stigmatized with the Oedipal complex and hatred towards psychoanalysis engendered thereof cannot be underestimated either. Whereas prior to the mid-1950s his bohemian friends get criticized for passively following intellectual trends (the more they question human well-being, the more precarious in Kerouac's eyes these trends are), later on the writer's harsh critique of intellectual fashions is crystalized into the concept of the Oedipus complex. In *Old Angel Midnight*, a long narrative poem written in mid-1950s and imitative of Joyce's *Finnegan's Wake*, the eponymous character lays bohemian circles bare: "Poetry, all these vicious writers and bores & Scriptural Apocraphylizers fucking their own dear mothers because they want ears to sell" (Kerouac, quoted by Jones, *The Mythic Form* 226). This might be complemented with Duluoz observing in *Desolation Angels* that "[t]he trend nowadays is to say that mothers stand in the way of your sex life" (DA 338). The Oedipus complex spearheads Kerouac's criticism, one might infer, since it gets more and more overwhelming for the writer to clear up on his relations with mother. It is the more difficult to do as it gets public: in 1960 John Updike parodied *On the Road* in *The New Yorker* depicting "Kerouac-persona [as] a little boy on a tricycle, afraid to cross the street without his mother's permission" (KLW 22). One of the attempts to elucidate Kerouac's close bonds with his mother comes with a 1966 letter to John Clellon Holmes, in which the writer cries out:

> I'm really bugged about this silly idea that it's abnormal and "wrong" for a man to take care of his old widowed mother ... "wrong" to a bunch of libertine cads ... . What has annoyed me more than anything has been this arrogant assumption on the part of the Freudians that to show companion for your parents, compassion that is, parents who are your only link with the horror of birth anyway ... that to support them in their old age is some kind of feebleminded mistake instead of what it really is: love on the only unselfish level, Caritas.... (SL2 426)

All in all, Kerouac's case proves that the cost of simultaneously living in the heyday of the American psychoanalysis and having a close relationship with one's mother must have been high by stigmatizing one within the psychoanalytic paradigm (or its simplified image that the American masses got familiar with). The Oedipal problem also makes Kerouac turn to less sexually oriented psychologists and psychoanalysts, like Adler or Sullivan. On the other hand, we learn that Kerouac was ceaselessly nagging his friends for advice concerning his problematically close ties with Gabrielle Kerouac (Nicosia 643). It is then not only Kerouac researchers who have been puzzled over the question of validity of the Oedipus complex in his life; the writer himself must have inquired about it.

There appears to be, yet, another side to Kerouac's links with the Oedipal complex. The above-described Oedipal witch-hunt did not stand in the way of the writer adopting it or acknowledging it for the artistic sake. In *Tristessa* (1960), a novella written in 1955 and 1956, Kerouac's humorous attitude towards psychoanalytic concepts gets repeated. Engaged in a love triangle with a Mexican prostitute, Tristessa, and his friend, Old Bull Gaines, Jack Duluoz finds himself to be an obstacle for the love of two, which reminds him of the Oedipal circle:

> I've screwed everything up with the mama again, Oedipus Rex, I'll tear out my eyes in the morning – San Francisco, New York, Padici, Medu, Mantua or anywhere, I'm always the King sucker who was made out to be the positional son in woman and man relationships ... King, bing, I'm always in the way for momma and poppa – When am I gonna be poppa?" (T 93)

James T. Jones suggests that the humor is a proof that Kerouac "triumphed over his obsession [his excessively intense relationship with his mother] to the point of being able to view it ironically (*The Mythic Form* 137). In *Big Sur* (written in 1961) Jack Duluoz acknowledges the Oedipal triangle when his lover, Billie, digs up a garbage pit "exactly the size fit for putting a little dead Elliot [Billie's four year-old son] in it" (BS 163), which prompts the protagonist's comment: "We've all read Freud sufficiently to understand something there" (BS 163). Hence, among the sheer hate and despair triggered by being stigmatized with the Oedipus complex, there lurks in the late Kerouac some ironic understanding and acceptance of the concept.

It is also the writer's artistic methods and textual strategies that remain in the spirit of psychoanalytic free-associating and talking cure. Kerouac continues holding on to the confessional and spontaneous mode of writing for a few reasons. Since the writer's literary agenda is partially aimed at releasing some emotional excess and resolving conflicts within his personality, one feels inclined to perceive his works as an abreation that aids in rectifying the problems of personal life. The evidence is to be found at the end of *The Subterraneans*, when Duluoz exclaims: "And I go home having lost her love. And write this book" (TS 130). This is also in *Desolation Angels* that he will blatantly admit that writing is catharsis (DA 315). Finally, in *Vanity of Duluoz*, going over his Columbia days, Duluoz claims that he had burnt most of what he had written "so that [his] art would not appear to be done for ulterior, or practical motives, but just as a function, a daily duty ... for the sake of purgation" (VOD 257). Near the end of his life Kerouac goes as far as to launch critique towards the literature which is detached from personal experiences. In *Satori in Paris* Jack Duluoz states that

> what would happen IF [stories] are for children and adult cretins who are afraid to read themselves in a book just as they might be afraid to look in the mirror when they're sick or injured or *insane*. (SIP 10)

Once again the writer underscores writing as a therapeutic process. It would not be an exaggeration to claim that Kerouac brought the confessional mode close to its extremes. *Some of the Dharma*, a non-fiction reflections over Buddhism written between 1953 and 1956, brought Kerouac's plan to compose all his writings into "the biggest book in the world" (Kerouac, quoted by Jones, *The Mythic Form* 239) which could be entitled as *Analyzed Versions of Myself* (Kerouac, quoted by Jones, *The Mythic Form* 239). As further observed by Jones, Kerouac explains that the "title means "Psychoextermination /not psychoanalysis" (Kerouac, quoted by Jones, *The Mythic Form* 315). Yet, by "writing from 'memory-mind,' he refutes his own refutation of Freud" (Jones *The Mythic Form* 239) as he is fixated on Freudian ideas. We can therefore conclude that even if the writer himself denied giving his oeuvre psychoanalytic frames, it is impossible not to sense a certain psychoanalytical underpinning to his aims and methods of work. Freud is thus not much significant for Kerouac as a therapist, yet he is an important point of reference as regards language and artistic creation. The writer notes in the first of his columns for a magazine called *Escapade* (June, 1959):

> My position in the current literary scene of American literary scene is simply that I got sick and tired of the conventional English sentence which seemed to me so ironbound in its rules, so inadmissible with reference to the actual format of my mind as I had learned to probe it in the modern spirit of Freud and Jung, that I couldn't express myself through that form anymore. (Kerouac, quoted by Maher and Amram, 395)

Kerouac naturally remained faithful to his goals of mapping the unconscious. As observed by Maffina,

> [i]t is impossible not to notice a certain effort by Kerouac to come up with a personal variation of Freud's concept of the flowing of thoughts and feelings, from someone's subconscious. (144)

Automatic writing at its peak, *Old Angel Midnight*, was conceptualized and created to let the thoughts flow "without the slightest effort to censor or alter . . . expression" (Nicosia 517). The pursuit of the unconscious also finds its way in *Book of Dreams* (1960), a novel version of his dream diary kept between 1952 and 1960. Although the focus of the writer's work, dreams, is the key substance matter in psychoanalysis, Kerouac makes it clear that he is not interested in a Freudian dream analysis. Instead of "Freudianism ... a big stupid mistaken dealing with causes & conditions" (BOD ix), he advocates concentrating on "the mysterious essential, permanent reality of Mind Essence" (BOD ix). Two years before his death, Kerouac bravely admitted to the failure of his efforts. In his last column for *Escapade* the writer confesses:

> But I'd gone so far to the edges of language where the battle of the subconscious begins because words come from the Holy Ghost first in the form of a babble which suddenly by its sound indicates the word truly intended ... .
> [I] began to rely too much on babble in my nervous race away from cantish clichés, chased the proton too close with my microscope, ended up ravingly enslaved to sounds. There's a delicate balancing point between bombast and babble. (KLW 47–48)

Hence, in the end, as Kerouac's Catholic faith intensifies, writing and the unconscious alike achieve the status which is close to some sort of God's grace. The problem of concurrent spontaneity and communicativeness appears to find an answer.

Kerouac's final references to Freud are devoid of either hatred or ignorance characteristic of the previous years. In one of his last novels, *Vanity of Duluoz* (written in 1968), Kerouac reminisces over his Columbia readings mentioning Freud's concept of ego, which "has risen to the surface" (VOD 257) and proved, as we might conjecture from the passage, to have been a useful tool when understanding music and art (demonstrated by the writer's own image of himself as a "conflicting" formation). The end of the writer's life conveys an impression of his reconciliation with all that seemed as detrimental shortcomings of various theories and trends.

5 *The Beat Analyst?* Jack Kerouac, Beat Models of Writing, and Lacanian Psychoanalysis: Textual Strategies and Comparative Perspectives

As I have demonstrated, the relationship between Kerouac's life, his work and psychoanalysis is all but smooth and untroublesome, just as the history of psychoanalysis in the United States has proved itself to be. Yet, despite all the shades of disdain displayed by the American writer towards what would stand for him as the phoniness and danger of psychoanalysis, one cannot overlook the debt Kerouac's textual strategies owe to a psychoanalytic way of thinking about language, literature, and subjectivity. Bearing in mind that it was also Ginsberg and Burroughs who found psychoanalysis a significant point of artistic reference, one feels tempted to test some tenets of the psychoanalytic theory against the Beats' literary tactics. Much as each of them demonstrated a heterogeneous way of thinking about literature, Kerouac, Ginsberg, and Burroughs turned their eyes to spontaneity, irrationality, and subversiveness as remedies for the conservative, stifling and stiff atmosphere of the mid-twentieth century America. Their artistic techniques, Stephenson claims, focused largely on

> circumventing or ... breaking through the rational, logical intelligence, the ego consciousness, to establish contact with the unconscious mind, with the deepest levels of being (180).

In a perpetual and spontaneous reinvention of his life, Kerouac searched for ways to let his hidden mental life emerge and bring together the ambiguities of his personality. Ginsberg, on the other hand, was interested in capturing what might be deemed the objectivity of human experience by unleashing the deepest level of his subjective feelings. Having possibly the deepest distrust for rationality and conventional ways of communicating of all the three writers, Burroughs believed his cut-up method would disclose some new and fresh modes of existence, and by doing so, be a tool of liberation.

In a similar manner, Lacanian psychoanalysis turned its back on the Cartesian *cogito* as well as stuffy, unreflective, and complacent state of psychoanalysis at the half of the century. By placing main emphasis on the medium of language, Lacan reinvigorated Freud and underscored the instability of human subjectivity as being forever lost and estranged within the alienating matrix of signifiers. What could be achieved by analysis, however, was tracking down the traces of the unconscious, disclosing one's desire, and learning to cope with symptoms, all done in the mode of spontaneous and unrestrained free-associating.

5.1 Lacanian Tenets of Free-association

One of the most crucial tenets of psychoanalytic practice established at an early point was the necessity of subjects' free-association as the means of coming across the ambiguities of one's speech among the plentitude of statements made by the analysand. For both Freud and Lacan, free-associated speaking became the most significant way of moving towards the causes of a given symptom in a case. With his implementation of structural linguistics, Lacan underscored the role of speech even more strongly and to a great extent leveled the unconsciousness "structured like a language" with a chain of signifiers, or in other words, to the symbolic knowledge (*savoir*) which the subject does not know he knows and whose gradual revelation every treatment aims at. The French psychoanalyst's stance is less hermeneutical than Freud's; for the latter the final knowledge is the matter of an interpretation of free associations while the former undermines the value of interpretation by noticing that it produces yet another set of signifiers. What is thus proposed by Lacan is the need to evade any predetermined matrix of interpretations and proceed towards the disruption of interpretative signifiers in order to achieve a clear position of the analyzed subject within the symbolical order and determine where he or she really "speaks from." As commented by Evans,

> [f]ar from offering the analysand a new message, the interpretation should serve merely to enable the analysand to hear the message he is unconsciously addressing to himself. … The analyst plays on the ambiguity of the analysand's speech, bringing out its multiple meanings. Often the most effective way for the interpretation to achieve this is for it too to be ambiguous. By interpreting in this way, the analyst sends the analysand's message back to the analysand in its true, inverted form. (90)

Much of Lacan's thinking concerning the aims and the course of psychoanalytic treatment as well as the significance of the speech material and free association starts with his early 1936-essay "Beyond the 'Reality Principle." The French psychoanalyst's distrust of systematization came from his disrespect for the late nineteenth-century psychology which he perceived as a failure due to its erroneous, as he believed, method of classifying phenomena according to a fixed set of rules. In his own words, the criticized practice is

> [a] construction on the basis of knowledge phenomena, the objective of which is to reduce the higher activities to complexes of elementary reactions; it is reduced thereby to seeking differential criteria of elementary reactions in the control of the higher activities. (Écrits 61)

As a result,

> once the phenomena are defined in that psychology as a function of their truth, they are submitted in their very conception to a classification on the basis of value ... [the result is the hierarchy which] impoverishes ... meaning. (Écrits 62)

Accordingly, classifying fosters eliminating certain psychical phenomena which, being not intentional, are perceived as useless to the field of psychology. In his disagreement and return to Freud, Lacan decides to dedicate his attention to all the "psychical phenomena which are ... granted no reality of their own" (Écrits 63). It is perilous, as he claims, when

> [t]he role of psychology is merely to reduce psychical phenomena to ... system and to verify the system by determining through it the very phenomena that constitute our knowledge of it (Écrits 63)

Lacan's departure from the hard objectivism of existing psychology also touches upon the issue of what the nature of truth may be. Asking for the modern ground for the notions of certainty, self-evidence and non-contradiction, he states that "truth is a value that (cor)responds to the uncertainty with which man's lived experience is phenomenologically marked ..." and in this form it "remains foreign to the order of science [which] cannot in any way identify truth as its own end" (Écrits 63).

According to Lacan's model of the proper course of analytical experience,

what therefore has to be enclosed within the rule of "free association" are the interspersing laws of "non-systematization" and "non-omission," which have to characterize the relationship between the analyst and the analysand. The former is anchored in the above-mentioned distrust of interpretative frames. The latter basically denies the right to reject any of the material coming from the patient. Lacan clearly states that

> [i]f we wish to recognize a reality that is proper to psychical reactions, we must not begin by choosing among them; we must begin by no longer choosing. (Écrits 65)

What such an intuitive and non-limiting approach further entails is the focus on interconnectedness and order of elements of the patient's material, as well as the relation between such elements and the whole (Burgoyne 75). As it was believed by Lacan, any disturbance or reordering of the analysand's speech could cause the loss of trace as regards the symptom:

> In order to gauge their [psychical reactions] efficacy, we must respect their succession. Certainly, there is no question of restoring the chain of those reactions through the narrative, but the very moment in which the account is given can constitute a significant fragment of the chain, on condition that we demand that the patient provide the entire text and that we free him from the chains of the narrative. (Écrits 65)

Such understanding of text production and processing aligns with the Beat poetics of spontaneity. The aspect of spontaneous text creation took such a crucial place in the Beat mindset that it was often to attest the general literary value of a given text. As I will try to demonstrate, the tenets of psychoanalytic "free association," "non-systematization" and "non-omission" are reflected in Jack Kerouac's (as well as the other Beats') methods of composing a literary work.

5.2 Jack Kerouac – Towards the Message from the Other

One of Kerouac's main artistic aims oscillated around the search for an unrestrained, vibrant, unalterable and fresh voice glorifying the beauty of the American land and its possibilities. A huge contribution to this vision came with the person of Neal Cassady, a role model embodying the vitality and power of the American man whose actions were described in *On the Road*. The novel itself has been treated as an exemplary outcome of Kerouac's attempts to speak out his mind. In the preliminary stage of its creation *On the Road* was to be yet another conventional story resembling the previous *The Town and the City*; however, a friend of the writer convinced him of adapting a more pictorial mode of work which could rely on verbal, impressionistic sketching and include all normally discarded thoughts (Theado 74). What has also been one of Kerouac's trademarks is his free poetic prose, which, in recognition of writer's admiration for jazz music and improvisation, has been often called "spontaneous bop prosody" (Sterritt 54). Adjusting the flow of speech to a bebop jazz solo allowed the writer to achieve high fluidity, irrepressibility, and sonorousness of lines complementing the technique of verbal sketching. The formal aspect underlying the techniques, both the cause and effect, was the necessity of "first thought – best thought" rule. To be precise, at a certain point Kerouac started to believe that what comes out as the first draft is by all means better than the text with further adjustments and, what is more, reflects best both the mind and reality. In "Essentials of Spontaneous Prose," where he explains his poetics, Kerouac advises one not to "afterthink except for poetic or P. S. reasons. Never afterthink to 'improve' or defray impressions …." (EOSP 2012). In 1952 he writes to a fellow Beat Generation writer, John Clellon Holmes:

> Wild form's the only form holds what I have to say — my mind is exploding to say something about every image and every memory in — I have now an irrational lust to set down everything I know . . . I'm making myself sick to find the wild form that can grow with my wild heart … . (SL1 193)

The "wild form" necessitated the need of continuous flow of sentences that could not be inhibited by technical problems; therefore, Kerouac prepared a scroll of conjoined sheets of paper not to get interrupted with the constraint of changing the sheets. Holmes again recalls the writer's words:

> I'm going to get me a roll of shelf-paper, feed it into the typewriter, and just write it down as fast as I can, exactly like it happened, all in a rush, the hell with these phony architectures and worry about it later. (Kerouac, quoted by Hunt, 110)

Moreover, so strong was Kerouac's urge to see this kind of mental sketch as the final version that he leveraged other fellow writers to exercise this method only; the famous case concerns Ginsberg who having sent Kerouac a draft of "Howl" got it back with a remark that crossed-out words should have remained and was requested for a preliminary version of the poem.

What has to be underscored is the fact that Kerouac's method cannot be equated with an image of unstoppable logorrhea. Many critics suggest that prior to putting the words down and owing to his great memory skills the writer could have relied on some kind of mental outline to be subsequently transposed onto paper. Sterritt observes that

> [t]he spontaneous, improvisatory ... writer is not a raving verbiage-machine hurling out every word that comes to mind. Rather, he resembles a man telling a barroom story — that is, a self-aware narrator with a consciously construed tale ... and a desire to share experience by verbal means for the satisfaction of all who care to participate. ... Spontaneity was ... a carefully considered means for accomplishing such clear-cut goals as recording a greater amount of though ... and tapping deeper levels of thought .... (194–195)

Thus, it can be added that the perception and reception of Kerouac's legendary artistic impulsiveness always needs a closer scrutiny to avoid simple generalizations. This also seems to hold for the clinical situations; spontaneous writing is not about a thoughtless flood of words and neither is the patient's speech at a session.

Kerouac's insights into the matter of writing do not diverge much from what constitutes the principles of psychoanalytic free-associating. Uncorrected and written in the spirit of Whitmanesque richness, the writer's chains of free thoughts and reminiscences appear to be similar to the subject's unrestricted production of speech in the course of psychoanalytic treatment. The inspirations drawn from psychoanalysis are already clear and explicit on the level of the vocabulary employed by the writer:

> If possible write "without consciousness" in semi-trance (as Yeats' later ""trance writing") allowing subconscious to admit in own uninhibited interesting necessary and so 'modern' language what conscious art would censor .... (EOSP 2012)

Kerouac's descriptions very frequently comprise of long chains of elements, colors, noticed oddities which can be linked to one another or, in Lacanian terms, are simply a string of connected signifiers revolving around some kind of a center. Moving along the chain of signifiers with a view to finding final satisfaction, which cannot be eventually gained, resembles much the Lacanian idea of desire for successive objects. The role of Lacanian analyst is to trace the analysand's desire and disclose his position in the symbolic. Similarly, as noted by Nicosia, Kerouac

> believed "the truth" could not be stated in any formula, but that it existed only in the movement *from moment to moment*, incomprehensible, ungraspable, but terribly clear. (279)

What is also common for the sequence of signifiers in the patient's/writer's material is its metonymic inclination towards sonic resemblance or uniformity. Some passages of Kerouac disclose his fascination with the sound of particular words and are often written on the wave of this charm, even at the expense of semantics. Let us consider this excerpt from a narrative poem *Old Angel Midnight*:

> I'd as lief be scoured with a leaf rust as hear this poetizin horseshit everywhere I want to hear the sounds thru the window you promised me when the Midnight bell on 7th St did toll bing bong & Burroughs and Ginsberg were asleep & you lay on the couch in that timeless moment in the little red bulblight bus & saw drapes of eternity parting for your hand to begin & so's you could affect-and eeffect -- the total turningabout & deep revival of world robeflowing literature till it shd be something a man'd put his eyes on & continually read for the sake of reading & for the sake of the Tongue .... (2012)

Here, one can notice that Joyce's *Finnegan's Wake* was Kerouac's inspiration and the aural experience of speech is the key factor in the poem's creation. From a psychoanalytic point of view one can recall the Freudian case of the Rat Man discussed in "Notes Upon a Case of Obsessional Neurosis" (1909) as an example parallel to literary creations. Freud's patient's free-association utterances were built according to the dominance of *rat* phoneme and resulted in its various repetitions, such as *Ratten* (rats), *Spielratte* (gambler), *Rate* (debt installment), *heiraten* (to be married), *Ratenmamsell* (Rat-girl) (Apollon et al. 64).

Moving on further, Kerouac's Whitmanesque inclusiveness also connotes the previously described principle of "non-omission." The American writer shared faith in the value of completeness and non-exclusion of one's experience with Freud and Lacan. Significantly, not only did Kerouac's openness amount to the lavishing of details about subsequent journeys across the States or meticulous descriptions of the surroundings, but it also determined the stylistic and formal variety of his works. An exemplary case is the experimental *Visions of Cody* which had remained unpublished for twenty years until 1972; what formed the novel was a merging of "novelistic descriptions, autobiographical musings, poems and drawings" (Sterritt 54) and a tape transcription of his conversation with Neal Cassady. Such polyphony of styles is naturally not the domain of a single work; it is an integral component of many of Kerouac's novels. As I have demonstrated in my discussion of Kerouac's attitude to psychoanalysis, all the marginal and involuntary outcomes, whether verbal, stylistic or formal, were of special interest to him as well as to other Beat Generation writers. The "non-omission" rule is perhaps most evident and best described in the following fragment from *Visions of Cody*, in which Jack Duluoz pleads with the eponymous character: "there were no images springing up in the brain of Cody Pomeray that were repugnant to him at the outset. They were all beautiful" (VOC 355). It is also one of the laws laid down in "Essentials of Spontaneous Prose": "Not 'selectivity' of expression but following free deviation (association) of mind into limitless blow-on-subject seas of thought …. (EOSP 2012).

Stimulated by such a textual agenda, Kerouac's process of writing was concomitant with searching for something concealed, the possibility of shedding some light on it and learning oneself better, just as, according to Lacan, the function of the talking cure is to unveil the position one's desire is speaking from. John Updike's commentary on *On the Road* seems to endorse the image:

> Kerouac was right in emphasizing a certain flow, a certain ease. Wasn't he saying after all, what he surrealist said? That if you do it very fast without thinking, something will get in that wouldn't ordinarily (Dickstein 185)

Kerouac's motivation partially came from his need to get some understanding of unclear moments from the past. David Sterritt indicates that writer's literary search was focused on all that could have been initially ignored in his past years:

> Kerouac ... used his writing to rediscover in words, memories, and ideas the sort of resonances ... that are never truly dead but only forgotten or overlooked. (54)

Regardless of the reason for his literary quest, the artistic stupor and trance Kerouac was working in were again to bring him closer to some supreme truth in order to comprehend it. In this light it is even easier to understand Kerouac's obstinacy and conflicts with subsequent editors who repeatedly tried to woo the writer into shaping his works so that they could become more accessible.

Since the model of writing offered by Kerouac necessitated a flow of thoughts never to be confined within a previously concocted form ("[b]egin not from preconceived idea of what to say about image" (EOSP 2012)), Lacanian "non-systematization" might be claimed to be its counterpart in the psychoanalytic procedure; what counts the most in both cases is the first appearing sequence of words and paragraphs with no rearrangements to be made. As we have said,

Lacan drew special attention to the interrelations between the elements of free-association and the complete material. We might risk a statement that Kerouac's oeuvre works according to a similar pattern; the units (Kerouac's novels) are highly interwoven as they touch upon the (often the same) events of writer's life and describe his milieu in a varied form depending on the work we take into consideration. What is more, all the units are equally significant and organized in *The Duluoz Legend,* a form of a legend into which the author wanted to fit the story of his life.

The principles of psychoanalytic free-association highlight the necessity of the analyst's play on the ambiguity of the text produced by the analysand. As I have pointed out in the previous chapter, Kerouac's textual strategies were much preoccupied with putting special value to all the uncertainties, verbal dodges, misapprehensions and loose associations on the way of speaking/ spontaneous writing. This is very much the case of *Visions of Cody* (with its imitation of a tape recorder as well as group reading of conversation transcripts) and *On the Road* (with its spontaneous process of creation as well as descriptions of group discussion sessions). Let the atmosphere of it be brought back with a passage from the latter novel, describing a vigorous conversation between the alter-egos of Ginsberg and Cassady:

> Then they got down to business. They sat on the bed cross-legged and looked straight at each other. I slouched in a near-by chair and saw all of it. They began with an abstract thought, discussed it; reminded each other of another abstract point forgotten in the rush of events; Dean [Cassady] apologized but promised he could get back to it and manage it fine, bringing up illustrations.
> Carlo [Ginsberg] said, 'And just as we were crossing Wazee I wanted to tell you about how I felt of your frenzy with the midgets and it was just then, remember, you pointed out that old bum with the baggy pants and said he looked just like your father?'
> 'Yes, yes, of course I remember; and not only that, but it started a train of my own, something real wild that I had to tell you, I'd forgotten it, now you just reminded me of it . . .' and two new points were born. They hashed these over. Then Carlo asked Dean if he was honest and specifically if he was being honest with him in the bottom of his soul. (OTR 48)

Looking at Kerouac's various descriptions of and attempts at spontaneity, one may get the impression that their common and inherent feature is their reliance on feedback. Whether with the aid of Neal Cassady, as depicted in *Visions of Cody*, or by himself, Kerouac seems to be always revisiting his scene/act of writing so as to search for and ponder over the ambiguities arisen thereof with a view to reaching the deep structures of one's psyche. By this token, Kerouac's literary agenda again bears intriguing resemblance to the

Lacanian analyst-analysand contract, in which the analyst revisits the scene of the analysand's speech so as merely to draw on its peculiarities and, not interpreting them, allow the analysand to receive his own message in an inverted, true form. In Lacanian parlance, noticed as ambiguous and unclear by the analyst, the message from the analysand to the analyst goes back and turns into the message from the Other (as the ungraspable and unconscious potential of the symbolic), which is to reveal the subject's true desire. Interestingly, returning to a scene of spontaneity seems to have been similar to the methods of Lacan's seminar teaching. Inventive, spontaneous, and experimenting during his lectures, the French psychoanalyst allowed his seminars to be recorded so as to let one revisit the act of speech by looking at the tape transcripts. As remembered by a media theorist, Friedrich A. Kittler on the occasion of one of Lacan's seminars:

> Only tape heads are capable of inscribing into the real a speech that passes over understanding heads, and all of Lacan's seminars were spoken via microphone onto tape. Lowlier hands need then only play it back and listen, in order to be able to create a media link between the tape recorder, headphones, and typewriter, reporting to the master what he already said. His words, barely spoken, lay before him in typescript, punctually before the beginning of the next seminar. (Kittler, quoted by Liu, 112)

As we thus see, the medium of the tape proved to be of considerable use to both Lacan and Kerouac for the same reason, that of returning to and reconsidering a spontaneous and performative act of speech.

What is also demonstrated by juxtaposing the aforementioned analyst-analysand contract in the Lacanian treatment and Kerouac's return to the scene of writing/speaking is the apparent circularity that is at work in both cases. Lacan implies that at the starting point of the treatment the analyzed subject has already got the knowledge he or she is to be made aware of in the course of the psychoanalytic process. Therefore, what can be inferred is that the end of the analysis (disclosing all the ego identifications and teaching the subject where he or she is speaking from or, to use other words, where he or she *is spoken* from) somehow overlaps with its starting point, in which the subject is yet to perform the talking cure and disguise his or her desire in the symbolical order. One of Kerouac's most famous poems, *Mexico City Blues*, in a Buddhist manner, carries an analogous message in the 113th Chorus:

> You start with the Teaching
> Inscrutable of the Diamond
> And end with it, your goal
> is your starting place (113th Chorus, *Mexico City Blues*, 2012)

Thus, Kerouac and Lacan seem to share the conviction that the goal of acquiring a certain awareness is simply a return to the point of departure, where the knowledge of one's desire has remained all the time; if we identify the knowledge with "the Teaching," then the subject paradoxically ends up with what must have already been taught.

Finally, it seems that Kerouac's textual strategy of what I would call the revisited scene of spontaneity might be both concretized with and enriching for the Lacanian schema L. The latter, being the first of Lacan's efforts at mathematizing psychoanalytic concepts, can be read in various ways, yet for the sake of this argument it might be employed to elucidate the subject as a text-producing being.

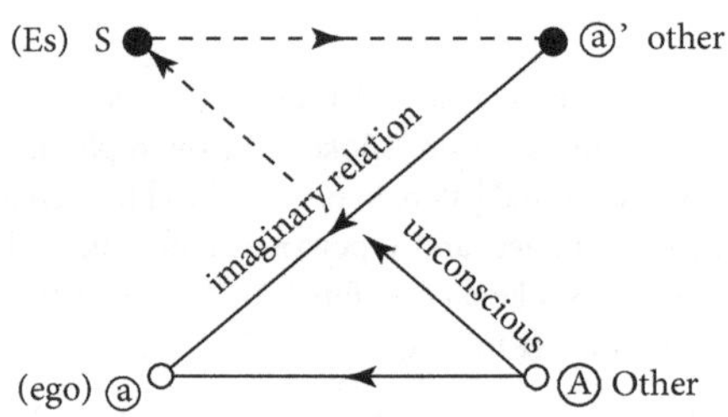

(Schema L, S III 14)

The scheme might be divided into the left and the right side. The former represents the subject consisting of its symbolic representation (S) and its imaginary identifications (a), that is its ego and the ways it wants to be perceived. The latter is the side of the other (a'), another subject, which apart from its own imaginary identifications incorporates the unfathomable universe of the symbolic Other (A). Sending the message to the other, subjects are primarily interwoven in a dual imaginary relation, the one analogous to Lacanian mirror stage (elucidated in further chapters), in which the subjects misrecognize and take one another for what they are not. However, there is the third element that looms over the two, the Other, which holds the knowledge of the true position and desire of the subject in the Symbolic order, yet, whose answers are delivered in the register of the unconscious. The subject is able to sense the message provided that his or her imaginary identifications and expectations are done away with and that he or she recognizes the peculiarity of the text he or she produces.

The above-described scheme seems to overlap with Kerouac's strategy of revisiting the scene of spontaneity. By means of a spontaneous work/text the subject/writer (S) might want to learn the other (be it a Beat companion), which is primarily based on the imaginary representation of him or her (a'). What he gets in return is stimulus which his own imaginary identifications can prey on and which yet offers also a surplus he did not expect. That perplexing feedback, ambiguity, a remainder of an overlooked matter, is the locus of the Other's speech, something Beat writers hoped for to reveal itself and be illuminative. When Jack Duluoz finishes his story in *Tristessa* with the following words: "This is my part of the movie, let's hear yours" (T 96), the call can well be interpreted as longing for the voice of the Other.

Given the recent call of psychoanalytic criticism to reverse the thus-far performed roles and put psychoanalysis as the object investigated by literature, Kerouac's strategies of spontaneity seem to have the potential for raising challenges to psychoanalytic theory. Drawing upon the textual character of the unconscious, they tentatively hint at the possibility of self-analysis through revisiting the scene of one's writing. Consequently, the Lacanian scheme L might be re-shaped so as to recognize this possibility, which is presented in the below structure:

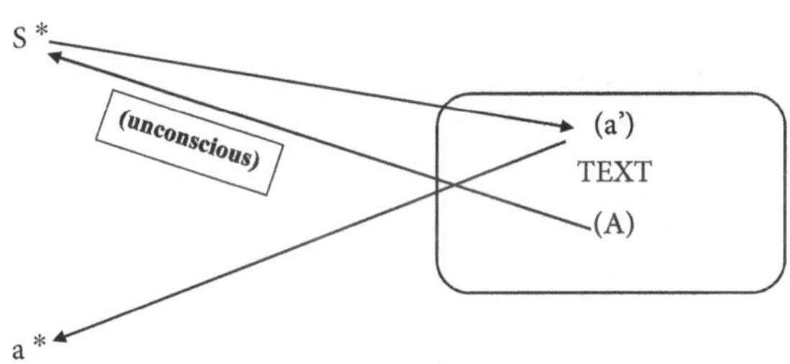

As with the scheme L, the uttering subject /writer expresses him- or herself in the text both in the symbolic (S) and the imaginary (a). The spontaneously produced text incorporates the imaginary (a'), which, so to speak, satisfies the subject's imaginary identifications (a) at the moment of revisiting it. However, what also lurks through the text are the peculiarities of one's utterance, which, in Lacanian terms, estrange the subject of the statement (what the subject thinks he or she said) from the subject of the enunciation (what really happened in the act of speech). This confusion can be identified with the locus of the unconscious and the Other (A), which sends the inverted message back to the subject. As put by Lacan, "the presence of the unconscious, being situated in the locus of the Other, can be found in every discourse, in its enunciation" (Écrits 707) and a spontaneously produced text is not an exception here. Thus, the strategy of revisiting the scene of spontaneity corresponds with the Lacanian model for the analyst-analysand relationship and was meant to help Kerouac in circumventing his imaginary identifications on his way to the voice of the Other.

What is interesting, with his strategies of spontaneity aiming at disclosing latent content of a produced text and, consequently, a self-disclosure, Kerouac in some way anticipated some of the most recent and central demands of psychoanalytic criticism. In view of the currently-postulated reversal of a subject-object relationship in the psychoanalytic approach to literature (psychoanalysis being the former and a literary work the latter), one needs to point to one more transposition which is called for. As posited by Lorelei Caraman-Paşca,

> in the last decades, more and more critics became interested in the two-way exchange between the instances of the critical-analytical process. ... In this more recent phase, the immutability on the critic-as-analyst position gradually shifts to the point of a complete role reversal within the analytic/critical dyad. Under which circumstances can the critic/reader be viewed as the analysand and the literary work as the analyst? ... Through the self-analytical function triggered by literature, is the critic not, simultaneously, both analyst and analysand? These fundamental questions articulated a new field of inquiry which transferred the scope of analysis from how the critic works on the text to how the text works on the critic; from how the text-as-analysand is structured to how the text-as-analyst structures the critic/reader-as-analysand. Drawn closer to the foreground is the act of analysis itself, the process of reading/interpretation, and the ways in which it affects and transforms both the work and the one who approaches it. (88)

Kerouac appears to ask analogous questions by examining the ways in which a spontaneously produced text, the reservoir of the Other, enters the position of the analyst and becomes capable of transforming the one who interacts with it. Naturally, as we have seen, the American writer also studies the possibilities of merging the positions of the analyst and the analysand in a self-analytical process. Having attempted self-analysis, Freud claims that a "genuine self-analysis is impossible" since, as pointed by Lacan, one should understand the limits of self-knowledge in the face of the Other (S II 121). Kerouac appears to be aware of such an obstacle as in his self-inquiry he relies on his own as well as others' observations.

The congruence between Jack Kerouac's literary tactics and Lacan's outlook on the speech material can be better understood when anchored in the context of homologous textual strategies represented by other Beats. The following references to Allen Ginsberg and William S. Burroughs might prove helpful in shedding more light on how Lacanian tenets of free association interact with poetics of spontaneity endeared by many of the Beat Generation writers.

5.3 The All-inclusive Poetry of Allen Ginsberg

Taking into consideration Allen Ginsberg's admiration for Kerouac's work, it is easy to predict that he owes certain techniques associated with spontaneous writing to his friend. Therefore, all the links between Kerouac and the psychoanalytic principles of free-association, non-systematization and non-omission, remain valid, yet open for some divergence, in the case of Ginsberg.

Again, the best vantage point to adapt at the start is the rationale behind the production of a literary text. The best-known poetical face of Ginsberg, the twentieth-century successor of the Whitmanesque democratic prophecy, began when persuaded by Kerouac, he decided not to dedicate too much attention to conventional, aphoristic poems anymore. Owing to this decision, American poetry gained another voice (after Langston Hughes or William Carlos Williams) in the Whitmanesque tradition of free verse. One could argue that up to that point it had not had such an explosive and potent face. Ginsberg chose to praise the topics of body and sexuality with much lesser hindrance than any other American poet; although Whitman's vision was daring enough to be slung mud at for its alleged indecency, it has borne some evidence of fear and secrecy. Whitman's successor retained his master's inclusiveness, vast literary form, and mysticism; still, he grew bold enough to make the sacred and the profane equal. However, the poetical volte of accepting a strong, prophetical stand writing "Howl" in 1955 set off with some doze of intimidation. Sterritt notes that Ginsberg

> wrote the first and lengthiest section of the poem in one sitting, breaking with his usual habit by composing it directly on a typewriter, instead of writing by hand barely because he held a view that this work was merely experimental and would never be published. (105)

Soon, on Friday, October 7, 1955 he was able to see that his fears were ungrounded. Having read out the part of the poem for the first time, he cast a spell on the audience of The Six Gallery in San Francisco and ushered in the hype around the Beat Generation movement.

With regard to psychoanalytic tenets which have been discussed in this chapter, it can be claimed that the poet's mode of work, following Kerouac's, demonstrates some semblance with them. Ginsberg's free verse poetry begins as an unhampered stream of thoughts turned to words. It would not be an exaggeration to claim that free association could serve well as another name for the poet's unplanned writing. Considering the significance of verbal meandering exercised by the subject in the course of the psychoanalytic treatment, Ginsberg's long, repetitive confessions in the first part of "Howl" find their source in a similar will to lose the constraints and let the subject *be spoken* by the language. As it is observed by Sterritt, numerous critics have signalized the affinity of such a literary method with the quest for a greater insight into one's mind. For instance, Schumacher speaks about Ginsberg's poetic manner as of an effort to be presented with one's "graph of the mind." Tytell compares it to André Breton's demand of "subconscious irrationality" achieved by an uninhibited flow of monologue and the mimicry of spoken thought (Sterritt 132). What is also interesting, Ginsberg somehow admitted to a cathartic experience during the creation of the poem, which again keeps him close to the course of analytical treatment:

> I thought I wouldn't write *a poem* but just write what I wanted to, ... let my imagination go, open secrecy and scribble magic lines from my real mind ... writ for my own soul's ear and a few other golden ears. (Ginsberg, quoted by Sterritt, 131)

The poet seems to neglect the concept of the poem itself, and simply transfers the significance to the speech consisting of long, inclusive lines. Each of them forms a single syntactical and semantic entity. Significantly, each one acquires the length of the breath. Perhaps most importantly, Ginsberg underscores the role of secrecy and its unraveling through a literary process; the fact that somewhere there is his "real mind" hints at the poet's awareness of the unconscious and its perplexing form.

At this point one may be tempted to refer to the ending of Ginsberg's reasoning, that is, his notion of poetry being written for "his own soul's ear and a few other golden ears" (Ginsberg, quoted by Sterritt, 131). Here, the paths of psychoanalysis, Ginsberg's and Kerouac's methods of work seem to concur. The Beat Generation writers were engulfed with everlasting conversations over their experiences and the matter of receiving some feedback was of prior importance to them. Ginsberg's words are another hint at this procedure: there is a limited number of people who know the poet well and who are able to listen to his poetry with true attention ("golden ears") so as to provide feedback which goes deep beyond the surface of the poetic utterance. Significantly, the poetry is also written for the poet's "own soul's ear," which can allude to literature as the auto-therapeutical tool that aids in pursuing self-knowledge. The pattern of Kerouac's self-examination seems thus to be eligible for Ginsberg's poetics.

Much as Ginsberg's lack of constraint reminds one of the loose connotations that a psychoanalytic patient is encouraged to present, there is a certain novelty in his process of creation — there remains some space for the elements which are *planned*. Again, "Howl" provides an excellent example; contrary to an utterly improvisatory status of the first part, the two subsequent sections had gone through numerous revisions until the desired effect was reached. Corroborating Schumacher's view, Sterritt notes that:

> Ginsberg tested the "Moloch" section at public readings subsequently adapting its structure to the print medium by rearranging lines, reciting them aloud to assess rhythm and altering phrase lengths; this went on through more than twenty drafts (197).

It is therefore the mimicry of speech that makes Ginsberg's poetry a double agent — it works as much as a link to psychoanalysis as it cuts the ties. If some presence of alterations in Ginsberg's method does not put the entire sense of free association into question, it surely makes the matter more complex. Consequently, the interweaving tenets of "non-omission" and "non-systematization" come into play and make the search for the common ground between psychoanalytic procedures and Beat literary strategies a more multifaceted task. Nonetheless, from a psychoanalytic perspective, it is of utmost importance that the bulk of Ginsberg's work remains in a strong bond with improvisation that cannot do without free association.

If the analysis of stylistic and formal aspects of Ginsberg's production of poetic speech is not always feasible from the perspective of "non-omission" (as a result of poet's corrective tendencies), the semantic capacity of the poems breaks such a deadlock. As it has often been observed, the poet's long, Whitmanesque verses aim at embracing the entire spectrum of the American experience; they bond all the dichotomies, such as nature and culture, body and spirit, low-brow and high-brow, the sacred and the profane. One of the many examples may be found in "Footnote to Howl":

> Holy my mother in the insane asylum! Holy the cocks of the grandfathers of Kansas!
> Holy the groaning saxophone! Holy the bop apocalypse! Holy the jazzbands marijuana hipsters peace peyote pipes & drums!
> Holy the solitudes of skyscrapers and pavements! Holy the cafeterias filled with the millions! Holy the mysterious rivers of tears under the streets! (*Collected Poems* 142)

Real places intersperse with the imaginary ones, particular relatives and friends stand next to classified groups of people, physicality complements spirituality. Plentiful proper nouns serve a crucial role in Ginsberg's poems-confessions as they anchor the poetic speech in real-life experience, which may be said to bring it another step closer to a confession of the analysand.

Whitman's formal method to achieve the complete inclusiveness of experience was strongly anchored in the use of participles, which allowed the poetical "I" to flow through the text. Ginsberg technique relies mainly on the extensive use of anaphora to attain the same effect, not to exclude elements, nor prioritize them. Such perspective echoes Lacan's precaution for the analyst to reject the temptation of selecting the speech material. Ginsberg's "non-omission" finds some common ground with Lacanian ideas as it searches, by the means of a poem, for the above-mentioned secrecy and the self-knowledge one is unaware of until the process of creation ends. What is also sought in the trance of developing Whitmanesque catalogues are the marginalities which would not be registered in the course of carefully-considered thoughts; those marginalities, crucially, are not only the outskirts of social life but also of consciousness.

What is also of utmost importance is that just as Ginsberg does not exclude any of the items when improvising, he keeps guard over various registers of speech and literary styles, which are enumerated by his commentators. According to Sterritt, "Kaddish" is an illustration of a poem

> incorporating an electrifying flow of childhood memory, early-adulthood reflection, religious invocation, and even animal sounds, all within a cascade of long-line verse that manifests a heady influence from jazz. (55)

Jarniewicz highlights the coexistence of the old English, religious language, the argot of immigrants, drug addicts, and homosexuals, the discourse of the media, advertising market, and the world of music (107). As the critic continues, each of these is of key importance as the words function in various registers simultaneously, for example the word *spade* in "In the Baggage Room At Greyhound" which refers to the object, playing card suits, and an offensive slang term for an Afro-American person (Jarniewicz 108). Ginsberg's multi-register poetics seem to comply with the text production taking place in the analytic situation. Just like with the analysand's speech, the ambiguity of a given signifier (in a poem) seems to open the discourse of the Other with its interpretative potential and bestow on the reader the role to call one's attention to the ambiguity of certain words. Finally, Jarniewicz indicates that composing the poem freely, Ginsberg tended to choose some words over the others on the basis of the affinity of sounds. The critic recalls the chain of words which form one of the lines in "Howl"— "battered bleak of brain all drained of brilliance in the drear light of Zoo" — and emphasizes the occurrence of such alliterations as a crucial link between the life and the work of the poet (2008). The phenomenon of alliterations and polysemy, which Ginsberg shared with Kerouac, may be viewed in terms of the relevance of psychoanalysis to the literary techniques of the Beat Generation writers.

Comparably with the rules of "free association" and "non-omission," the Lacanian principle of "non-systematization" is also mirrored in Ginsberg's poetic spontaneity. As it has been pointed out, Ginsberg does not rank his verses accordingly to any preconceived system when "improvising" his poetic speech. The anaphoric lines do not bear any hierarchy; they simply unroll the confession. The exemplification of such a scheme finds support in the fact that some parts of the poem or items from the catalogue were easily added or dropped by the poet during poetry readings. Ginsberg was able to improvise entirely over some time; the first attempt took place in 1971 and was remembered by him as momentous:

> it was so profound…and so liberating when I realized I didn't have to worry if I lost a poem anymore because I was the poet, I could just make it up (Ginsberg, quoted by Sterritt, 197)

Finally, as we remember, the pillar of "non-systematization" is the significance of the given order of elements (which cannot be changed) as well as the interrelations among the elements and the whole. In each part of "Howl" we are presented with a construction which is developed metonymically as subsequent lines unroll the descriptions of "the best minds of generation," "Moloch," and the poet's compassion for Carl Solomon. One is tempted to suggest that the order of the lines could be alternated without the loss of fluency; yet, each line softly hooks up with the next one and their order must be retained to sustain the clarity. Further, as we have mentioned, each catalogue line forms a semantic entity, usually a subordinate clause which refers to the main clause at the beginning of a given poem. Hence, the principle of "non-systematization" could definitely not be applied to the entirety of Ginsberg's poetics; any clause which would be taken out would not stand by its own without the support of the entire structure of the poem.

Although occasionally divergent from Kerouac's textual strategies, the all-inclusive poetry of Ginsberg helps to augment one's understanding of the homogeneity of Beat literary spontaneity and the Lacanian tenets of text processing. Referenced with Ginsberg, Kerouac's literary tactics demonstrate all the more their enduring priority of impulse over a meticulous attention to structure. The artistic revelation that comes thereof – the language harboring the voice of the Other – lends weight to Lacan's ideas on the spontaneity of text production.

5.4 William S. Burroughs – Cutting, Pasting, Curing the Mind

Were the core Beat writers to be juxtaposed with one another as regards the similarities of their artistic techniques, it is highly probable that William S. Burroughs would be an exemplary odd one out. What is shared by many commentators of the Beat Generation movement is a stand that Burroughs served more as a mentor or adviser than a brother in artistic arms for writers like Kerouac and

Ginsberg. Psychoanalytic free association plays a significant role in textual strategies of Kerouac and Ginsberg. It also does so in Burroughs's prose, yet, spontaneity and unrestricted text production are understood and employed differently there. The writer himself claims:

> The best writing seems to be done almost by accident but writers until the cut-up method was made explicit ... had no way to produce the accident of spontaneity. You cannot *will* spontaneity. But you can introduce the unpredictable spontaneous factor with a pair of scissors. (182)

What is striking, unlike Kerouac and Ginsberg, Burroughs does not believe in any spontaneous literary process which could evade human consciousness, habitual reactions or preconceptions. What seems to be assumed by the writer is a total determinism of human thoughts and actions; spontaneity as understood by Kerouac and Ginsberg is not spontaneous enough for Burroughs. Therefore, what the writer opts for is pushing the boundaries of free writing – he decides to eradicate human agency from the act of spontaneity by subjecting the literary work to a radical operation: the much randomized act of cutting and pasting the fragments of a written text, or creating a literary mosaic.

Unusual techniques had to find their way in Burroughs's career. His two first novels, *Junkie* (1953) and *Queer* (first published in 1985), relied on biographical data organized into linear stories about the everyday life of a heroin addict and the quest for a drug named Yage respectively. A revolution came when Burroughs was visited in his apartment by Kerouac and Ginsberg, who found approximately a thousand of scattered and rat-eaten pages of loose manuscripts and helped Burroughs to compose a final draft to meet a short deadline of Olympia Press, which eventually published the novel in 1959. The order of successive vignettes of the final manuscript was "largely arbitrary" (Robinson 34) and was retained in the printed version. Leading through dystopian imageries and places, and adapting the form of a collage composed of texts of various sort and style, *Naked Lunch* does not equip the reader with any stable main character nor does it provide a typically understood plot. What is more, the author himself approved of the idea that the text be read from any point. The appeal of this largely accidental outcome gave him a push with further literary experiments and soon, with the assistance of a fellow writer, Brion Gysin, Burroughs decided to refresh the method of literary collage by cutting and pasting the already written passages and pages in view of achieving new unanticipated senses and reshaping his prose constantly. An exemplary employment of such techniques is the so-called *The Nova Trilogy* comprising of the novels: *The Soft Machine, Nova Express* and *The Ticket That Exploded*. All are based on the same loose manuscripts.

Although Burroughs's associationism is more of a mechanical action than a purely productive activity as it is in the case of Kerouac, Ginsberg, it can be referred to Lacan's concepts of "free association," "non-systematization," and "non-omission." As stated earlier, Lacanian psychoanalysis wishes to pass through all the deceptive representations of the analysand's ego and locate the true position of subject's desire. Free-associating is then an indispensable tool for tracing the ambiguities which come out of one's utterances and identifications during a session with an analyst. Lacan's psychoanalytic approach towards the system of language, which is capable of producing ambiguities in speech despite one's will, is of an utmost (poststructuralist) mistrust. Burroughs's stance is similar and radical. To be precise, he finds the language corrupted in the entirety of its existence. If Lacan sees the deadlock of human impossibility to place language under one's command due to the fracture between the signifier and the signified, and the unconscious emerging thereof, Burroughs perceives language as a tool of command and supervision practiced over people by some kind of a hidden agenda. Speaking in Lacanian terms, Burroughsian stance is that of a paranoiac, who believes there exists the Other of the Other controlling all of the symbolic order. Putting it more bluntly, Burroughs conceptualizes language as a virus. Interestingly, critical response has tended to take such an attitude as an element of Burroughs's poetics; yet, some commentators claim that

> to say that the word is a communicative sickness was not, for Burroughs, metaphoric analysis or poststructuralist platitude but an awareness integral and material to the act of writing, and this is what the toxicity of Burroughs' textual politics insists upon, ad nauseam. (Harris 37–38)

Here enters the writer's literary method: cutting previously written texts and rearranging the pieces serves to a large extent as a sort of weapon against the stagnation of traditional syntax and habitual ways of reasoning and thinking, which were all believed by the writer to be the tools of control (Robinson 39, 40). Dismantling linear narration and existing syntactical and semantic norms allows Burroughs to juxtapose all what is unexpected in thought, language and speech in view of achieving a fresh and free look on previously unsighted possibilities. Such is also the purpose of Kerouac's and Ginsberg's poetics. If Lacan attempted to trace the unconscious governing the subject's speech while free-associating and aimed at the subject's true desire, Burroughs searches similarly for a new, free and "uncorrupted" language by using scissors. Owing to such an approach, the American writer finds a secret partner in Lacan insofar as psychoanalysis also underscores the supremacy of language over the subjects that speak it, or rather, *are spoken* by it. Consequently, both Burroughs and Lacan worked out and shared their deep conviction of language as a treacherous formation.

The act of cutting the textual tissue which could be said to remain confined to the domain of avant-garde literature, film and art, seems to have its equivalent in Lacanian psychoanalysis. Understood as a sharp bringing of the subject's speech to an unexpected end, the clinical alternative to the cut-up method appears to pursue objectives common to those of its artistic counterpart. Apart from his search for the uncorrupted language Burroughs cut pages so as to find new narrative ideas through the juxtaposition of pre-existing samples of his writings. He explained his ideas: "I cut up every page and suddenly got a lot of new ideas that were then incorporated into the structure of the narrative" (Burroughs, quoted by Sterritt, 198). As regards Lacan, in 1951 the French psychoanalyst introduced a novelty into the routine "narrative" of psychoanalytic treatment, sessions of variable length. The practice was condemned by the Société Psychanalytique de Paris the moment it entered the stage. Diana Rabinovich comments on the existing order of matters in the psychoanalytic world:

> Freud fixed the length of a session at forty-five minutes in terms of the attention span that worked best for him, never in relation to the temporality of the unconscious. ... [P]eople forgot that sessions must be of variable length in response to how the analysand's work unfolds. The duration varies according to the opening and closing of the unconscious, which uses standard time to favor resistance so as to counteract the closure which results from fixed time sessions. (210)

Lacan's idea was to defy the resistance of the unconscious by bringing an abrupt stop to the analysand's speech even at the expense of the usual length of a session, which often left his patients in deep bemusement. There were several reasons behind such an action:

> Chronological time and the temporality of the unconscious are different. Doubtlessly this change increases the psychoanalyst's responsibility, his "discretional power," but it also disrupts routine action; it awakens him or her from comfortable naps. ... Cutting the session short emphasizes the simultaneity of several lines in the signifiers of the analysand's free association. Whether or not the cut is timely can be only known afterwards, ... because the effect of the interpretation can only be read in its consequences. This involves a risk, which should be as calculated as possible, although this calculation is no guarantee against erring ... . [T]he analytic act lacks an Other to guarantee it. (Rabinovich 210)

Thus, it can be inferred that varying the length of a session is on the one hand beneficial for psychoanalyst's effectiveness insofar as it necessitates more attention and mistrust to what is heard; it is the point at which the language truly starts to be the primary focus of the therapy. On the other hand, and even more importantly, it gets more beneficial for the patient. As it has been pointed in the passage above, having been faced with an abrupt "cutting" of his/her story or session, one is left perplexed with the ambiguity of uttered words and the immediate actuality of the clinical problem. What should come next is greater awareness and self-reflection (also concerning one's speech), or simply, some new fresh ideas found between the lines over what a given situation might mean.

It can be inferred that Burroughs's struggle against linear and syntactically conventional literature was also aimed at what he believed to be exhausted textual formulae. The language of these fostered "resistance" similar to that of a conventional, fixed-time psychoanalytic session, that is, the tendency of language (safe within its complacency of (over)used forms) to repress and avert any subversive meaning. The juxtapositions resulting from the technique of cut-up make an endeavor similar to the Lacanian idea of an abrupt stop: they bring to light the new meanings, which have already been incorporated in one's speech. Burroughs's performative use of scissors hints at such possibilities as does the Lacanian act of a variable-length session:

> The analyst's interpretation of the analysand's discourse is also in itself a performative use of language. This interpretation, precisely by introducing a "closure" to the analysand's associative discourse brings into existence "something new," namely the signification that was only virtually present in the discourse. ... Of course, it is only by producing something new that interpretation — and the psychoanalytic dialogue as a whole — can be said to have any effect on the analysand and his suffering. ... [W]hat is at stake here is quite literally the production of a new subject. ... Thus, it is the performative dimension of the analyst's contribution to the analytic dialogue that makes this dialogue potentially therapeutic.
>
> Thus, the psychoanalytic dialogue is best construed as a monologue by the analysand, in itself largely indeterminate in meaning, which is given a more determinate meaning by the punctuation that the analyst brings to it. For Lacan, it is primarily session endings that serve as appropriate punctuation marks for this dialogue. (Lee 89–90)

With reference to literary and psychoanalytic strategies, both cutting/pasting and an abrupt textual closure respectively allow one to take a deeper look at the perplexing potentiality of signifiers which bear traces of the subject's desire (Lacan) or a language "uncorrupted" by the discourse (Burroughs). Lee's observations point to another commonality between Lacan and Burroughs, which is that of the agent of the act of closure, since the latter is not random but calculated. According to Lacan, it is the psychoanalyst who is to decide about the "punctuation" of the analysand's speech due to the ambiguities that appear. Naturally, the analysand's subsequent, self-reflective interpretations should not be taken for granted as they remain in close link with the aim of receiving a previously described reverse message from the unconscious. Here, of course, there appears the risk of error in "punctuation," misleading and putting away the successful end of a therapy. Correspondingly, Burroughs's cut-and-paste method is also calculated to a certain extent, and juxtaposing separate elements is, as the writer stated himself,

> not unconscious at all, it's a very definite operation. ... It's quite conscious, there's nothing of automatic writing or unconscious procedure involved here. (Burroughs, quoted by Sterritt, 198)

The decision where to "dissect" and conjoin the text is then again primarily in the hands of the author; secondary interpretations come from the potential readers. Although the writer speaks much about the accidental and spontaneous nature of cut-and-paste technique, in the text "The Cut-up Method of Brion Gysin" he provides the followers with an exemplary, simple set of instructions on how to construct a text:

> The method is quite simple. Here is one way to do it. Take a page. Like this page. Now cut down the middle and across the middle. You have four sections: 1 2 3 4...one two three four. Now rearrange the sections placing section four with section one and section two with section three. And you have a new page. Sometimes it says much the same thing. Sometimes something quite different ... in any case you will find that it says something and something quite definite. (Burroughs 182)

Additionally, in the same text Burroughs also adds some rules for creating a cut-up poem, and again, the first stage depends on choosing out particular passages consciously; cutting and rearranging the lines comes next.

By distorting the cause-and-effect nature of a plot, Burroughs endeavors to break through the thick rationality of our everyday use of language which, as it has been mentioned, forms a defensive mechanism against what is believed to be a subversive, disclosed potentiality of our language and mind. Here again, the insecurity and eeriness of experiencing syntactically and semantically unmatchable fragments might find their equivalent in Lacan's reasons for unconventional behavior during his sessions. Namely, the French psychoanalyst compared the unexpected endings of the session to some procedures of teaching Zen Buddhism. As it is commented by Lee:

> [t]he analyst's sudden ending of sessions is comparable to the Zen master's use in teaching of bizarre questions and apparently irrational responses. The analyst's interventions serve to reduce the analysand's faith in the imaginary and symbolic illusions that have sustained his self-meconnaisance, just as the Zen student's faith in rationality is reduced by the master's behavior. (90)

Thus, although with slightly different aims, complacency and stagnation which came along with rationality were perceived as impediments by both the American writer and the French psychoanalyst, and as both claimed, undermining them required undermining the analysand's/reader's safety within the symbolic order.

Summing up Burroughs's employment of free association, it is now visible that its nature is twofold in relation to its Lacanian equivalent. Namely, it is similar to the latter in the sense that they share acts in which the creation of new senses is not randomized (Burroughs's use of scissors and Lacan's use of "punctuation" in the treatment). In these acts spontaneity is desired as a "natural" phenomenon (Burroughs's afterthoughts on juxtaposed elements and Lacan's idea of the analyst's/analysand's reflection on ambiguous elements, or simply, the general necessity of free association in the therapy).

Also, the rule of "non-omission" of the speech material remains in resemblance to Burroughs's strategies, although to a limited extent. Lacan advised to completely abandon choosing some parts of a text produced by the analysand over the others both in fear of losing the trace of desire and in recognition of all what had been previously apprehended as marginal in therapy. Conversely, for Burroughs the idea of keeping a total record of primary speech production was often of no importance insofar as he dealt with it using a pair of scissors, or simply rejected some parts of literary material while favoring the others. Modifying the content of the outcome, he did not impose the rule of spontaneity on the final draft of his works, as Kerouac and Ginsberg often wished to do. He claimed to do the contrary:

> I may take a page, cut it up, and get a whole new idea for straight narrative, and not use any of the cut-up material at all, or I may use a sentence or two out of the actual cut-up. (Burroughs, quoted by Sterritt, 198)

On the other hand, one can speak of a specifically understood "non-omission" employed by Burroughs as the literary pieces found by Kerouac and Ginsberg in their fellow writer's apartment were later employed as the source material not only for *Naked Lunch* but *The Nova Trilogy* as well. It may be conjectured that such a literary recycling proves the value of basic literary substance in Burroughs's search for what lies underneath the "virus" of language. Once produced, textual material is pressed to its limits.

What is consequently being complicated by the ambivalent status of free association in Burroughs's prose is the third of the discussed psychoanalytic tenets, "non-systematization." The American writer seems to break Lacan's basic rule at the very start — he does not attach any weight to the order of the elements of his (literary) outcome, which remains one of the key laws for the French psychoanalyst. In other words, Burroughs's textual strategies have hardly any relation to what is crucial in the psychoanalytic field and what is the free-associative, metonymic chain of signifiers. As I have demonstrated, disrupting linearity was one of principal matters to Burroughs, who stated that "the wish for perennial present, the linearity of everything enslaves us into systems, limits us, we must disrupt linearity" (Burroughs, quoted by Sterritt, 133). Conversely, even if non-linear, the order of appearing elements in the analysand's speech was crucial for Lacan. On the other hand, what was shared by both of them was non-systematic mistrust in a single and preconceived interpretative system. While Lacan merely hints at certain ambiguities of the analysand's speech and refrains from usurping the right to provide their ultimate meaning, Burroughs allows one to freely interpret his loose vignettes and read them in any order. As a consequence, the distorted plot of a Burroughsian novel is prone to leave open spaces and sensitize the reader for ambiguities of Lacanian sort. The writer must not organize plot events into a preconceived hierarchy. It is also symptomatic that Burroughs's characters do not allow themselves to be classified as main and marginal nor do they succumb to petrification thanks to their fluidity. We might say that Burroughs, just like Lacan, leaves much in the hands of the one who engages with a text; the sense is to be finalized by its addressee.

Finally, Sterritt claims that

> [t]he very form of his [Burroughs's] most characteristic prose reflects his vision of an explosively unfinalized and self-contradictory world inhabited by an equally unfinalized and self-contradictory self … . (61)

Such an attitude bears some resemblance with Kerouac's dominating idea of establishing his life as the central topic of his literary creation and the strategy of constant re-writing of one's own person as a literary character. Here, it is tempting to claim that Lacan's career was accompanied by a similar purpose, an ongoing reevaluation of the psychoanalytic theory. The French psychoanalyst's seminars bear much analogy to Burroughs's prose: they functioned to a great extent merely as an indicator of the audience's emotions and reactions. Lacan often craved for the contact with listeners and used to perform a show at his own expense, in which he expatiated over a number of matters and often contradicted himself. *Écrits* were to serve as a distilled form of his theories; yet, his attitude towards psychoanalytic theory remained that of perennial reevaluation, just as the idea of the world and the self in Burroughs's or Kerouac's prose. Both Lacan and Burroughs were interested in purely practical aims: Lacan helped patients by means of psychoanalysis, Burroughs often claimed that he, extraordinary as it may seem, searched for cures for illnesses (i.e. cancer) by means of literature.

It appears that Burroughs's literary aims are applicable to the model of production/ reception drawn in Kerouac's strategies. One may refer to Sterritt's words which elucidate Burroughs's process of generating literature. The procedure

> provided a way for Burroughs to separate himself from *himself* – providing access to a quasi-Archimedean position outside self-generated consciousness, from which he could observe and manipulate the strips of his own thoughts and behaviors, as well as those that came to him from others via the printed (cuttable and foldable) page. (136)

5.5 Surrealism – A Missing Link?

When thinking about the common ground between the fields of the Beat Generation writings and Lacanian psychoanalysis, one should not overlook the indirect influences. These may appear less obvious, yet are significant in understanding the shape of each field. Such appears the role of Surrealism and its inspiring representatives. As I will argue, many surrealist concepts find their way into Kerouac's and other key Beat writers' works as well as Lacanian way of thinking about reality.

The relationship between Lacan and the surrealist movement can be characterized as that of mutual respect and influence. The French psychoanalyst first came into contact with and started to show his reverence for Surrealism during his medical studies. As noted by Jonathan Paul Eburne, Lacan's doctoral thesis is widely believed to be partially indebted to the surrealist experiments concerning *schizography*[69] and their ideas on paranoia (186). The surrealists valued psychoanalysis as a theoretical frame for their artistic pursuits related to and reaching into the deep structures of human psyche. Lacan's friendship with Breton, Dali, Picasso (whose personal physician he was), made him an influential member of the milieu and a significant contributor to a surrealist-oriented magazine, *Minotaure*. The mutual interest occurs at both general and deeper levels. What was first and foremost shared by both French psychoanalyst and the surrealist milieu was their being at odds with the blanket of silence over stagnation, hypocrisy and corruption of the French bourgeois of the inter-war period. The prominent causes célèbre of that time — the case of Violette Noziere and that

69 A term coined by Lacan to name both written counterparts of *schizophasia* and their field of study. *Schizophasia* was understood by the French psychoanalyst as a display of disturbances and disruptions in speech, such as "elision, denegation, neologism, displacement, and the like" and as "the demonstration on the linguistic order of the disturbance itself." See Anthony Vidler 143.

of the Papin sisters[70] — united the surrealists and Lacan against the dominant trends of what was understood by them as dangerous rationalism and misogyny serving as authoritative tools. Simultaneously, it allowed them to acknowledge the irrational and unconscious nature of human beings and to scrutinize "the ontological and epistemological uncertainties of the self" (Lusty 37) typical for modern(ist) sensibility.[71] The year 1933 witnessed the publications of both "Motives on Paranoid Crime," Lacan's psychoanalytic case study of the Papin sisters, and *Violette Noizieres*, a surrealist pamphlet incorporating their poems and drawings in relation to the case. The latter contained an illustration entitled *L'impromptu de Versailles*, which depicted

> the incestuous relationship between Violette and her father ... made graphic with a young Violette sitting on the lap of her father, his hand disappearing under her dress. Looking on this scene of incestuous desire is a man with a white beard and a bowler hat, who bears a striking likeness to Freud. The facial expression of rapture of both father and daughter seem to gloss any sense of trauma experienced by Noziere. (Lusty 36–37)

Lusty argues that Lacan's essay bears much of the surrealists' fascination with violence (especially its visual aspect) and transgression, namely the apparent lack of a motif in the criminal case of the Papin sisters. Lacan's understanding of the crime — a typical display of paranoid psychosis — concurs at that time with his interest in paranoia as one of the key subjects of his doctoral thesis. This constitutes an important merging point with the pursuits of the surrealists and, as I will claim further, the Beats.

Considering the level of Lacan's affinity with the surrealists, it is perhaps Dali who remained closest to Lacan, both as a friend and a thinker. Lacan endeared "The Rotten Donkey," Dali's essay from 1930, in which the artist introduced a new form of epistemological tool, the concept of *paranoia-criticism*. In the essay Dali proposed that paranoia is neither a passive state of a denied access to reality nor a foreclosed consciousness, but an active state of mind which gives one a sense of certainty and is deprived of logic and rationality. As it is underscored by Thomas Brockelman, "one could speak of paranoid "experience" and thus of phenomenology of paranoia — as Lacan did" (211). Also, with the emergence of *paranoia-criticism* Dali underscored the role of society and the necessity of working out a system that would integrate all possible interpretations of visual

70 See Natalya Lusty.

71 Critics have found more fields of mutual influence. Margaret Iversen argues that Lacan's concept of *object petit a* could not have been developed but for Breton's concept of *trouvaille* — an accidental confrontation with an object. See Margaret Iversen 64–66.

aspects of reality. These contributed to Lacan's better understanding of a subject as an intersubjective construction interwoven into symbolic order. Perhaps the most general lesson to be drawn from Dali is the sign of equation between a hallucinatory reality and a non-hallucinatory one, or in other words, the assumption of the very uncertainty of what reality could ultimately mean. Looking at Dali's famous perception of a woman as a horse and seconding the painter's own words that "our images of reality themselves depend upon the degree of our paranoid faculty" (Dali, quoted by Rabaté, "Lacan's turn to Freud" 18), Jean-Michel Rabaté argues that:

> [i]f paranoia opens a door into other kinds of visual perception, it also turns into a principle that replaces any idea of the material world by simple hallucination — a view leading to Lacan's later distinction between reality and the real. ... [R]eality is just a kind of simulacrum. ("Lacan's turn to Freud" 18)

Rabaté also suggests that Lacan could have experienced himself what he was writing about; namely, the case of Aimée could have brought him to some kind of paranoid clarity:

> by "clinical exhaustion," systematically and exhaustively examining one single case, he [Lacan] had reached a "paranoid knowledge" that finally forced him to take [Aimée's] creativity into account. ("Lacan's turn to Freud" 16)

Although in his later years Lacan was more eager to cut the ties with the surrealists than to find their ideas enlightening, the influence is beyond any doubt; as it is believed by many scholars, Lacan owes Surrealism his crucial turn from traditional psychiatrics to a non-biologically-determined modern psychoanalysis.

To bring back the Beats into the main focus of attention, many commentators share the belief that the American literary movement did not remain out of the scope of the surrealists' influence. A general idea that emerges from a comparative insight is that despite the heterogeneity of both milieux, what united the Beats and the surrealists was their dissatisfaction with societies in which they lived and were artistically active. The inter-war France and America of the 1950s have surprisingly much in common with what could be perceived as the rule of petty bourgeois tastes regarding aesthetics, lifestyle, and politics. If the discourse dominated by materialism, conservatism and conformity had been shared by both nations of their respective time periods, there was also a counterforce, a reactionary way of opposing it.

Alike the surrealists, the Beats advocated turning away from what could be understood as authoritarianism of civilization driven by rationality and fake morality. Despite many a divergence in displaying the repulsion for tastes of the masses (vulgar and obstreperous public acts of the surrealists as opposed to passive disobedience of the Beats) and political activism (the surrealists' likings for Marxist movements contrasting the Beats' general disregard for politics), both groups advocated returning, by the means of art, to one's inner self in search of states of the "naturalness." For Breton this meant being "uncontaminated" by civilization forced upon one, or even letting one's subjectivity melt passively in automatics of thought. For Kerouac and Ginsberg's insights took the form of meditative and spiritual peregrinations enabling spiritual ascension and the sense of unity with the world. Getting liberated from social constraints entailed acknowledging the potential of sexuality for both movements. Again, Breton, prior to his disillusionment with meeting Freud personally and his withdrawal from Freudian theories, perceived and favored psychoanalysis as an eye-opening set of tools admitting one to the true self. As for the Beats, Wilhelm Reich's theories on sexual freedom and Walt Whitman's poetics embracing both the sacred and profane served as a counterpart.

Comparably to the surrealists' fascination with the dark side of human activity, Beats were highly interested in the underworld of the American society of the mid-twentieth century. On the one hand, they displayed solidarity with those who did not fit (according to Kerouac, *beat* meant broke, homeless and maladjusted) or deliberately did not want to toe the line of moral conformity, like petty crooks and drug pushers. On the other hand, some who were regarded as members of the movement constituted the underbelly of the 50's America themselves, John Clellon Holmes and Herbert Huncke among them. The low-life world seemed alluring for it induced a feeling of personal transgression and exceptionalism, and was deemed as a door to deeper self-understanding. The blandness of society engendered the antihero as an offender. Despite victimizing them, the surrealists found criminals a fascinating exemplification for their theories on irrationality and the need of social mutiny. For the Beats, as it is well put by Nicosia, a crook was "a political figure, a revolutionary opposed to an unjust society" (148–149).

As far as artistic strategies are concerned, the Beat literary endeavors owed much to the surrealist formulae. Burroughs's method of cut-ups was in debt of Tristan Tzara's acts of randomized choice of words in the process of poetry writing; a good deal of Lawrence Ferlinghetti's oeuvre was influenced by the surrealist performances and Breton's works; the spontaneous writing Kerouac, Corso, and Ginsberg sought inspiration in the surrealist automatism.

When discussing the influences of Surrealism on Beat writers, critics very often call upon less headlining names than those of Kerouac, Ginsberg, or Burroughs. Wagner underscores Philip Lamantia as a Beat figure probably most influenced by the surrealist aesthetics, and embracing "the discoveries of Surrealism" to its fullest extent. Introduced to Surrealism at the age of 16 and hailed by Breton as "a voice that rises once a hundred years," Lamantia was invited by him to publish his poems in a surrealist magazine *VVV* (Wagner 51). Further, Michael Skau recognizes Gregory Corso as a major example of a poet employing the surrealist poetics, one who "gives conventions ironic twist, situates images in alien environments, and spins language through unfamiliar contortions" (*A Clown in a Grave* 88). What is further emphasized by Skau is the poet's "peculiar strain of surrealism" characterized by an "unsettling combination of humor and threat," the former being a salient feature of the surrealist aesthetics and often, as Skau argues, an unrecognizable aspect of Beat literature (*A Clown in a Grave* 88).

Pertaining to both Lacanian psychoanalysis and Beat sensitivity, Surrealism may be helpful in locating correspondence between the two above-mentioned worlds. Given their wide interest in irrationality, what is common for both is, first of all, the concept of paranoia. For the early Lacan it achieves the status of an epistemological tool in the sense that there is no objective reality but a set of outer projections which obtain the right for such a referent. Paranoia is similarly conceptualized by Kerouac and other key Beat writers.

Lacan's "phenomenology of paranoia" anchored in a state of exhaustion and extensiveness of a given activity, is clearly echoed in what might be called Kerouac's literary exhaustion. Throughout his career, yet especially at its end, Kerouac fell for a particular mode of writing in trance (or, after experiencing visionary trances) with the idea that a certain state of truth could be reached. The level of automatism in the process of creation drags him close to the Lacanian *schizography* and finds correspondence with the Joycean escape from the constraints of meaning into the realm of sign/sound as the Lacanian *jouissance* of the signifier. According to some critics, the concept of automatism may be treated conversely as a point of divergence between the psychoanalysis, the Beats and the surrealists. Anthony Vidler argues that the first advocates an unplanned speech production while Surrealism (and by the same token, Beat Generation writers interested in automatism) deals with certain intentions and self-awareness. Thus, with regard to the second group, he coins the term of "conscious schizography" (144). Furthermore, Kerouac, in a surrealist and Lacanian manner, openly defends the validity of paranoia in his works. In Part Three of *Visions of Cody* Jack Duluoz supports the power of immediacy of an image (opposing T.S. Eliot's stance) and, glorifying Cody's psychic "nakedness" and accuracy of a paranoid mind, he says:

> paranoia's a possibility remotely to be wished or avoided, let it go, till it proves it was right all the time when you die, ... Cody allowed himself the conviction that in the darkness old men lay in wait, which was proved later when he himself lay in the darkness of

> the straw, the paranoia, the vision having been just an expression of the truth of things, not the silly-ass moment! (VOC 356)

Thus, as believed by Kerouac's alter ego, Jack Duluoz, paranoia is a vehicle for the expression of the true nature of things: "paranoia is reality, ... paranoia is the content of things" (Kerouac, quoted by Nicosia, 374). What better vessel can there be than the character of Cody Pomeray (Neal Cassady), a true (anti)hero of the modern society standing against its petty-bourgeois rationality and morality. The above description, in a peculiar way, mirrors Kerouac's own experience of April 12, 1949:

> That night ... he awoke from a dream ..., then slipped into a visionary trance. The house in Ozone Park suddenly became the weird house he had dreamed of many times ... . From Cross Bay Boulevard the house was transported to the edge of the world, and through its open windows he was able to reach out to all things. Down the street stretched continents, and up the street, strange cities. Crowds rushed through the rainy night, shouting – the familiar faces of men and women flashing through the city lights. Even Jesus passed by. At that moment the whole universe was present with Jack, and he was one with it. (Nicosia 279)

The uncanny vision made the writer feel "[e]ach world was but a different sort of dream, and in each we rearranged "the memories of other dreams, other existences, like file-cards" (Nicosia 279). This further had "crucial implications for Jack's art. To realize that such mysteries weren't "exotic or esoteric, but merely the thing we all feel" inspired him to universalize his notions"" (Nicosia 279) and put efforts into "rearranging the elements of life into some sort of pattern that would suggest their link with infinity, their interconnectedness in a cosmic web" (Nicosia 279). Thus, Kerouac does not put any hierarchy to his experiences, treating all of them as equal manifestations of reality in the vein of "phenomenology of paranoia." As noted by Nicosia, Kerouac and Burroughs at one point coined the term "Factualists"

> to refer to ... dealing with all mental data – including perceptions of material objects, fantasies, dreams, and visions – as different levels of a fact. (241)

All the manifestations of reality are closely linked to what the American writer calls "visions." A "vision," according to Kerouac, is:

> a sudden intuitive understanding things triggered by some momentary sight. The fruit of such moments was an acute sensation of space, a panoramic awareness of the infinite universe. (Nicosia 154)

The abundance of the term in Kerouac's oeuvre, whether in the titles of his works or in the works themselves, is by no means accidental; it is strictly connected with his literary strategy of a sudden phenomenological insight into true nature of things, be it material or hallucinatory.

Kerouac's body of work, which may be well inscribed into the tradition of visionary poetics, relies heavily on a specular field, with images being the source and scene of the writer's epiphanies. It might be argued that the scopic experiences in Kerouac's prose are so forceful that they dominate over the subject; he often speaks of his visions as of "a kick in the eye." This brings us close to the aggressiveness and impudence of an image, a phenomenon undertaken by both the surrealists and Lacanian psychoanalysis. Skau recalls Andre Breton's statement that

> it is true of Surrealist images as it is of opium images that man does not evoke them; rather they 'come to him spontaneously, despotically. He cannot chase them away; for the will is powerless now and no longer controls the faculties. (*A Clown in a Grave* 8)

Words of the author of *Nadja* are clearly echoed by ideas on the image and the gaze proposed by Lacan. According to the French psychoanalyst, it is any object in the sensory spectrum (primarily, yet not necessarily, visual) that may take hold of the subject's look through the means of the gaze. In other words, Lacan puts the gaze not on the side of the subject (as Sartre did), but on the side of the object/ Other which looks at the subject. What is inextricably connected with the gaze is its capability of *captation*. The power of this phenomenon, a neologism adopted by Lacan from the French psychoanalysts, Edouard Pichon and Odile Codet, bears striking likeness to Breton's ideas on the image. Dylan Evans comments on *captation* in the following way:

> On the one hand, it has the sense of 'captivation,' thus expressing the fascinating, seductive power of the image. On the other hand, the term also conveys the idea of 'capture,' which evokes the more sinister power of the image to imprison the subject in a disabling fixation. (21)

Such power of the image and the gaze may entail various identificatory consequences for the subject, yet, the always-present effect is the advantage of an image over the one who looks at it.

Kerouac's oeuvre proves to agree with such an understanding of the image and of the gaze. It can be argued that the images/objects hold primacy over the plot for most of Kerouac's body of work. An exemplary case is that of *Visions of Cody*, where, being mesmerized by a given object (thus, experiencing *captation*), the narrator generates extremely detailed, meditative passages of description, the so-called verbal sketches. These dissect the object of interest to its basic elements, which often overshadows the plot and bears witness to a sudden petrification of the subject's look under the insistence of a given object and its gaze. As regards

Visions of Cody, model examples of the above-mentioned depictions can be found in the chapter entitled "Joan Rawshanks in the Fog" and sketches from Part One and Part Three. The former describes Jack Duluoz's accidental captivation and illumination by the scene of shooting a movie with Joan Crawford. Kerouac's eye is doubled by the eye of the camera and the film crew, which strengthens the effect of looking at a fascinating object: "Joan Rawshanks stands alone in the fog and a thousand eyes are fixed on her in all kinds of ways" (VOC 318). The latter are devoted to portrayals of New York and illustrate places like men's room at the railway station, St. Patrick's Cathedral, a B-movie cinema, or an employment agency; the new technique of spontaneous and lengthy, gradually dissective sketching is clearly palpable:

> And over at third avenue and 9th street is a beat employment agency; it's over a music store which (Western Music Co.) has a dirty piss splashed and littered sooty sidewalk in front, ... *Western Music Co.* written in white against green glass with lights behind but so sooty is the white part it makes a dirty sad effect. ... Black with dust planking is hall leading in — sign says (34 is the number) — *chefs, cooks, bakers, waiters, bartenders, etc.* - In the office (brown light) sits a shirtsleeve vest brownsuit boss at desk ... as two beat clients wait in blue leather chairs ... . Building is ancient — 1880 redbrick — three stories — over its roof I can see cosmic Italian oldfashioned eighteen story office block building with ornaments and blueprint lights inside that reminds me of eternity, ... black stairs like fire escapes ... the dungeon of Time underneath just a few feet over the Snake ... (VOC 20).

With regard to Burroughs and Ginsberg, the former, who perceived drugs, irrationality and borderline states as a source of liberation from the oppressiveness of homogenizing social system and language, can be also said to be operating according to "the phenomenology of paranoia." Like Lacan, the writer does not want to deprive hallucinatory reality of its logic and rationality, as he "metaphysically refutes any distinction between reality and fantasy" (Tytell, quoted by Sterritt, 135); he is a "Factualist" just as Kerouac. Looking at Burroughs's prose from another angle, it was also the idea of cut-up which aimed at reaching (though naturally not encapsulating its entirety) language as an objective construction. Having in mind the writer's conviction about the contamination of surrounding speech, which may be understood as a certain overuse of clichés and linguistic inertia that comes as a consequence, Burroughs's goal was to dive into an uncontaminated spot of the very construction and substance of language in order to observe the world from the point where language is still *alive* and *true*. Such approaches and aims, to some extent reminiscent of Gertrude Stein and her *Stanzas in Meditation*, may be compared to Lacan's differentiation between *parole* (speech) and *langage*. The latter is the fundamental structure underlying all languages and the former is a particular realization of *langage* in any given language.[72] Thus, the possibility of a fundamental and objective structure remained in the scope of interest for both Burroughs and Lacan. Ginsberg's strategies of writing can also be argued to be concurrent with the surrealist roots of Lacanian psychoanalysis. His urge for a literal approach towards a text (exactly like Lacan, the poet was calling to mind Freud's texts) and accepting visionary illuminations as a form of reality are based on the premise that anything may be a tool for epistemological sake.

Finally, as it was mentioned before, what emerges as the common "surrealist" root of both Lacanian psychoanalysis and the writings of the Beats is the potential of the figure of a low-life offender, whose transgressions often serve as a weapon against bourgeois sensitivity and stagnancy. Lacan's stance is probably a less glorifying one than the Beats,' yet, both take fascination in the display of unique idiosyncrasies which break the standards of society. The logic of violence, often inseparable from crime and so perplexing for psychoanalytic and surrealist studies could not have remained without the scrutiny from the Beats; it is especially Burroughs's prose whose notorious dystopian visions soak with vulgar interdependence of cruelty, sadism and power. The overtone of his prose is thus similar to Lacan's and the surrealists' critique of hypocrisy which permeates the cliques of decision-makers and standard setters. The writer's outcome clearly hints at the problem of the private, as represented by sexual activity, being gradually overtaken by the domain of the public, a worry characteristic for the inter-war French society in the eyes of Lacan or Breton. Finally, depicting the overpowering absurdity all-round, Burroughs's visions, alike the surrealists' performances, are not deprived of black humor.

72 Here, Lacan is naturally indebted to the Saussurean model; however, de Saussure's division juxtaposed *parole* with *langue* (a particular language).

6 "[C]ome Up to Rivers and Cross Them One Way or Another" – *The Town and the City*

Lacan's theories may shed new light on the intricacies of Kerouac's texts primarily because these revolve heavily around the figure of the father. If, as suggested by many critics, Kerouac failed at his attempt to unify his life in a form of a legend comprising his entire oeuvre, it is the author's stance that the incoherence of the Duluoz Legend is fundamentally the consequence of the problematic deficiency characterizing father figure(s) in the successive installments of Kerouac's project. The insufficiency of the paternal function becomes paradoxically both a recurring theme which haunts the Duluoz legend and prevents it from cohesion as well as the phenomenon which makes the discourse possible at all. Commenting on the narrative foundations of *The Odyssey*, Robert Con Davis observes that

> in terms of narrative function, it is ... clear that Odysseus' absence and Telemakhos' awareness of that absence satisfy what Lacanian theory shows to be need for the inauguration of discourse. This absence ..., a primordial want-to-be – is pre-ontological and, as such, is a theoretical precondition of all structure. Just as in Lacanian theory where the initial absence of the father inaugurates a desire for the father's, and the child thereby becomes the embodiment of knowledge about the father (and the absence associated with him), the oddysean son begins the epic as he gazes toward a fatherless horizon .... (7)

Gazing towards a fatherless horizon is also the stance of what will in the presented work be onwards called the Kerouacian subject, a textual creation and a parallel to Jack Duluoz, Kerouac's alter ego and the protagonist of the Duluoz legend. The Kerouacian subject, I will argue, emerges and operates in consequence of the absence of the father figure; it is equally the factor that generates Kerouac's narrative and that launches the writer's attempt to give it a closed and coherent form of the Duluoz Legend. Regina Weinreich suggests that

> [t]he construction of the entire Duluoz legend is built on a series of repetitions .... Each novel goes over material already expressed, restated at a different level of consciousness or perception, restructured again and again for greater personal as well as aesthetic clarity. (20)

The central position among these reiterations appears to be held by the question of the absent father. The repetitions indicate the Kerouacian subject's trauma of the lack of paternal figure. Insofar as the trauma fails to be completely inscribed into the symbolic, it must undergo reconfigurations of the father figure which attempt at making up for the absence. In Lacanian terms, the trauma "returns with a difference" with the subsequent novels of the legend. As held by the author, the motif of paternal reconfigurations is inaugurated by the very first installment of the Duluoz cycle, which is *The Town and the City*, to be followed by *On the Road* and *Visions of Cody* as characteristic of the next stage, and closed with *Visions of Gerard*, *Satori in Paris*, and *Vanity of Duluoz* all representative of the final stage.

As it has been discussed in Chapter Four, the first and the longest installment of Kerouac's legend takes the form of a conventional and sentimental prose to present the reader with the saga of the Martin family comprising George and Marguerite Martin together with their eight children. Largely autobiographical, the novel spans the period of 1935 to 1946 ending with the funeral of George Martin, which seals the dominant motifs of the novel, the fall of the family and the loss of one's innocence, much in the vein of naturalistic American novel and Dreiserian "American tragedy" (Weinreich 15). The overarching structural aspect of the work which fuels the dynamics of the narrative is the dichotomy between the eponymous town and the city, Lowell, Massachusetts and New York City. The former, epitomizing innocence, simplicity and sincerity, is confronted with the deviance, cynicism, and intellectual pretense of the latter, whose charms eventually contribute to the disintegration of the family. The conflict, as observed by Tim Hunt, is

> expressed in the form of an argument between two of the Martin brothers. The small-town brother, Peter, brings to New York sympathies which are out of place in the city. Francis, tutored by an older, worldly, and (Kerouac implies) homosexual gentleman, professes a brand of aesthetic cynicism that fits him for city life but cuts him off permanently from the town. Both town and city values are presented as permanent and permanently in conflict. (81)

Despite its anchorage in the realist mode imitative of Thomas Wolfe's stylistic method, the novel goes well beyond realist aesthetics. The driving force behind the narrative of *The Town and the City*, the conflict between contradicting principles, can ultimately serve as a metaphor for the conflictual nature of human subjectivity. Such a perspective has been taken up by some critics, most notably Warren French, whose reading of the novel establishes links between diversified agendas of its characters and multifaceted personality of the author.[73] For the scholar the two extreme poles are Peter and Francis, who

73 See Warren French, *Jack Kerouac: Novelist of the Beat Generation*. Boston: Twayne, 1986.

> must have warred constantly for domination over Kerouac's thoughts and actions, and this struggle was to play a major role in the shaping of the Duluoz Legend. (French, quoted by Theado, 46)

Such a reading seems to have been compliant with Kerouac's own intentions. As Nicosia explains, at the early stage of composing the novel, the writer told Allen Ginsberg "that he was splitting his mind into discreet parts and embodying each part in a different person" (303).

Following French's steps, yet not delving into Kerouac's psychobiography, one might suggest another reading of the novel, one that would both take focus on the psychological realm and expand the analysis onto more ontologically- and epistemologically-oriented categories. Jacques Lacan's theory might help to discuss *The Town and the City* as a novel about the emerging subjectivity (which is orchestrated into several voices), its entering the symbolic realm, and the resulting alienation in the world, all the more confusing as the paternal metaphor is out of place.

What seems to be the venture point for a Lacanian reading of *The Town and the City* is noticing the initial common feature of the male members of the Martin family, which is their encapsulation in and submission to the world of dreams. In their fantasies, the Martins hold themselves as magnificent and capable of the highest achievements. The best instances are Peter and Mickey Martin. Peter is presented as somebody immensely fixated on a desired image of himself, especially with regard to his future life:

> he saw his future ... and dreamed and dreamed of greatness. There was never anything else that could hold his dreamy attention: all was the fulfillment of himself, the future, greatness, a heroic struggle and overcoming of all obstacles. (TTATC 120)

Peter appears in the novel as a subject entrapped within the imaginary order and his ideal-ego; the totalizing character of fulfillment he dreams about can be compared with "the total form of ... [infant's] body ... given to him only as a gestalt" (Écrits 76), as a phantasm. Such a mode of functioning is also the case of the youngest of the Martins, Mickey. What stands out, however, is a religiously-oriented variation. Mickey's fantasies revolve around glory-winning martyrdom. During one of his visits to church:

> [T]he boy looked up again at the altar manger and saw that he too must suffer and be crucified like the Child Jesus there, who was crucified for his sake, ... but who also pointed out what was going to happen to him, for he too, Michael Martin, was a child with a holy mother, ... This would be some time after he was a cowboy in Arizona on the Tonto Rim. (TTATC 178)

Fixated on transcendent goals, Mickey's fantasies make thus a spiritual reverse of Peter's conquering attitudes.

The Martins' imaginary engrossment in the fantasies of their greatness parallels their idyllic existence within the completeness and security of the domestic. However, this residence within an untouched, Edenic world precedes the eventual confrontation with the reality of becoming separated from it. What the imaginary gives way to is the symbolic, the realm of law and language, in which one gains his or her subjectivity at the expense of being denied the access to the protective unity with the maternal. As Lacan teaches, the agency which regulates such emergence is the paternal metaphor, which castrates the child of its Oedipal leanings. In consequence, although given subjectivity, one is forever lost in the deficiencies of the symbolic – the incompleteness, infiniteness, and inaccuracy of signifiers that one gets entangled into and is represented by. Lacan's text seems to provide a commentary on the Martins' struggle with their estranging and fantasy-dispelling nature:

> [s]uch is the signifier's answer, beyond all significations: "You believe you are taking action when I am the one making you stir at the bidding of the bonds with which I weave your desires ... ." (Écrits 29)

The fall of the Martin family shall ultimately represent castrating the subject of its maternal realm and getting lost within the estranging nature of the symbolic, epitomized by a world external to that of the homely.[74]

In the novel, the maternal is vividly different from the symbolic realm since it is not of a conflictual nature but rather of a homogeneous and a mythical one. As a mother, Marguerite Martin is in a way prophetic since she senses and anticipates bad events (TTATC 9); she is also depicted as a psychic being able to establish a link between the worlds of the living and of the dead (TTATC 10). What is more, Kerouac draws a sharp distinction between her subjectivity and the subjectivity of all men. We learn that Marguerite

> would notice how each of them burned and raged with a particular loneliness, a special desolate anger and longing that was written in each pair of eyes, and she knew that all men were the same. (TTATC 69)

Marguerite's words mirror Lacan's concept of the phallic *jouissance*, both pleasurable and painful pursuit of the allegedly lost state of bliss that men are confined to due to the castrating power of the phallus.

---

74 In a 1948 letter to Ginsberg, Kerouac explains: "I associate the 'outside world' (you and Neal and Bill and wars and work and hitchhiking and cops and jails and taking my chances making women win-or-lose ...) I associate this outside world with half-of-life-is-death" (Kerouac, quoted by Foxe, 49).

The separation from the motherly and the destruction of the illusion of the imaginary are first represented by a series of revelations experienced by the Martin sons on their leaving home, both literally and symbolically. What might be viewed as the founding gesture is the wish of Joe Martin, the oldest, the most happy-go-lucky and robust of the sons, to go on the road, which, on the one hand, is seconded by Peter and Mickey, and on the other hand, meets strong objections, mostly of their mother (TTATC 96). From that moment on, having parted with home, the Martin brothers shall experience the epiphanies which hint both at the fragility of the imaginary realm and the lurking, unsatisfiable emptiness of the symbolic. Spending his first night at a preparatory school in Maine, New England, Peter Martin experiences

> the final terrible realization that he was only Peter Martin, only Peter Martin – and who was that in the world? Who was he, if not some sort of impostor and stranger and scoundrel, who somehow managed to fool people and even his old family into believing that he was Peter Martin. Who *was* he? (TTATC 126)

Such understandings often come in the form of seeing one's own image in the mirror and feeling estranged to it. It is possible to think of the scene as a representation of a reverse mirror stage, in which one's image is being fragmented and there is the threat of one's falling to pieces. These are exactly Peter Martin's experiences:

> He was no one – looked at himself in the mirror, looked out the window in the dark Maine night, and he was no one. He was a ghostly stranger, he was a dreaming forgotten thing .... (TTATC 127)

Mirrors in *The Town and the City* seem to materialize a Lacanian bar between the signifier and the signified which sets up a barrier disabling any stable meanings and identities. As "a sign that doesn't refer to any object . . . [and] is a sign of absence" (S III 167), the Lacanian signifier embodies Peter's lack of essence. Despite his initial joy of moving to New York and his literal absorption in the new language, the intellectual jargon of its elites, Peter's brother, Francis, experiences a moment of estrangement one night in front of the mirror having returned to his family house:

> Francis stepped out in the hall and paused for a moment in the grey darkness. ... He rubbed his eyes sleepily and leaned back against the wall, as though suddenly he had forgotten where he was and what he was doing ... .
> "What am I doing here?" he suddenly thought. "Who am I?"
> ... In his room he looked vaguely around as though he had never seen the room before, not *this* room, and he ... stopped before a mirror.
> "Francis Martin, Francis Martin, Francis Martin," he kept thinking, ... and gaped at himself in the mirror. (TTATC 194)

Repeating the mantra of his own name is, on the one hand, the experience of how alienating the language may be, and on the other, a way to console himself and restore the unity of his image. The other disillusionment comes when Francis joins the Navy. We learn that on his third day on duty he

> realized in a sudden flash that he could not bear any more of this … . So tremendous was his hatred of his new position in the world that he was literally blind, he bumped into people, … and once when he looked at himself in the mirror and saw the absurd haircut they had given him …, he flew into a rage … .(TTATC 315)

The inconvenience of Francis' "position in the world" is ultimately the inconvenience of a subject's position in the symbolic. His own idea of the signifier he was to occupy (the "master signifier" in Lacanian nomenclature) eventually diverged from what that signifier really did to him. Later on, Francis is being examined by psychiatrists and their conclusion is that he cannot adapt, which again appears to be meaningful in the context of Lacan's theories of (dis)possessing the subject by signifiers.

Self-unrecognizability is also experienced by Joe and Mickey. Despite being a robust and happy-go-lucky person, the former "to himself … was just someone abandoned, lost, really forgotten by something, something beautiful and majestic that he saw in the world" (TTATC 67). The latter, presented in the introductory parts of the novel together with other members of the Martin family, is

> stunned by the sudden discovery that he does not know who he is, where he came from, what he is doing here, remember that all children are first shocked out of the womb of a mother's world before they can know that loneliness is their heritage and their only means of rediscovering men and women. (TTATC 14–15)

Thus, the Martin brothers are evocative of the emergence of the subject, a separate consciousness being born at the expense of experiencing the loss of comforting unity with the motherly. As it was mentioned, from a Lacanian perspective the separation comes from the one in the position of the father, who bears the authority of instilling in the subject the laws and regulations of the symbolic realm. The peculiarity of George Martin occupying that function is that he seems not to stand up to the task of administering the paternal metaphor among his sons. This has a number of significant consequences for both sides.

To look for the roots of George Martin's paternal indolence is to acknowledge that the head of the Martin family has himself been the victim of his ideal ego. His failure to stand up to the paternal function is engendered and sabotaged by the social and financial grandiosity he has been dreaming of. On the brink of losing his printing business, George craves for another life (or, perhaps, even for losing his life):

> But he wished he could leap right out of his life as George Martin ... . [H]e felt like a little boy hanging by his arms from a high tree just to see what it would be like to "risk everything." (TTATC 196)

The father ends up finding himself out of his place, both as regards his symbolic function and the future enforced relocations of the Martin family. It is also the outbreak of the Second World War which shatters the structures of the Martin family in the novel making the sons move away from home. Yet, rather than a historical event, the war might be well-read as the conflict within the father. George Martin's position is neither that of a father who enforces the paternal law in cold blood nor that of a father who clearly admits his failure to stand up to the role of administering his symbolic function. Afraid of losing his authority, he is capable of either cutting the sons off from the domestic when convenient or keeping them close to support his deficiencies in a clandestine way. On the other hand, he is repeatedly consumed with guilt for "castrating" his sons of their dreams and hopes.

In order to cope with the troubling events, George sublimates the predicament of his professional and symbolic inefficiency into martyrdom, which opens him up to perverted pleasure of taking the blame for the decay of the Martins:

> He felt a tremendous desire to become even more sorrowful and lonely than he had ever been, he knew that this was goading him on more than anything else and it was a terrifying unspeakable thing. (TTATC 196)
> "And all on account of my own damn foolishness – ... I should know better than anyone else why this family is falling apart ... .
> "Who says this family is falling apart? ... " cried the boy [Peter], laughing, trying to cheer up his father ... . (TTATC 235)

The ineptitude of his actions and the instability of his status gradually start to account for the ineffectiveness of instilling the paternal metaphor in his sons, as when they become inclined to their mother's rather than their father's suggestions as regards their life choices. Neither of the Martin brothers wishes to yield to the paternal metaphor. Due to his indolence, George eventually tries resorting to perverted ways of getting things his way. One of them is exercising emotional blackmail on his sons and desiring their pity:

> Petey, all the pride I've got left is you, in you, do you understand? ... I want you to go on smiling all your life the way you used to do when you were just a plump little tike with rosy cheeks ... . Listen to me! Do what your old father says, I know best. Study! Study! Work hard and make good. ... Be my good boy, Petey, be my own good boy. (TTATC 236–237)

It is also Francis that undergoes the perverse form of castration when George visits him in the Navy to make him change his mind about joining the army.

Although the tone of the father's words allows to believe in his true concern for Francis, the oppressiveness of the paternal function is emphasized by George's overprotectiveness and ostentatious display of sacrifice. George Martin exclaims:

> I was really worried – I took three days off from work to come and see you, that letter scared me so much. I'm going back tonight right away, I just wanted to see you myself, it's only for these few minutes they allowed. And, gosh, what a trip out here, a thousand miles, Francis, a thousand miles! (TTATC 330)

Once Francis decides to remain persistent in his decision, George shows his understanding ("it's all right with me, don't you worry, ... I'm not the one to judge." (TTATC 330)) yet, in a sly way, does not stop to push his son into his stance:

> Do you realize that this was the longest trip I ever took in all my life? ... I'd travel clear on out west tonight! But the old lady and I have a budget to watch, dammit. (TTATC 330)

Whereas Francis represents the consciousness relatively well detached from the domestic, Peter's relationship with his parents may well be inscribed into the unresolved Oedipal conflict. On his offering to send some money home when away studying, Peter is forbidden by the father to provide for the family:

> " ... I'll have a job on the campus this year and send some money home to Ma whenever I can, see?"
> "No, no, no, don't talk like that!" cried the old man quickly. "I don't want you to be sending any money home, do you hear me? We'll make out, we'll make out. ... You hold up your end of the battle and we'll hold up our end here." (TTATC 236–237)

In Lacanian terms, George bars his son from being the phallus, the provider for the mother's alleged lack and desire, which comes together with shame that he apparently cannot exercise the phallic function himself. Peter's subsequent departure from home bears traces of the symbolic castration. No other scene in the novel contributes as much to the sense of loss of one's innocence and of one's being dispossessed of maternal safety:

> And Peter ... knew that he was no longer the joyful eighteen-year-old boy ... of powerful sensual vigors, ... of life as a delicious loafing laziness ... . He knew that ... something in him was done and finished and departed, strange melancholy forebodings were in him, ... a dark sense of loss and dull ruin, ... And something dark, warlike, mournful and far was suddenly brooding in the air ... . [H]e would never come back here again, this was the last time, ... and then no more, no more. Where was he going? And his father's voice speaking to him in the darkness was still haunting, still heard. (TTATC 238)

The sense of Oedipal longings in Kerouac's novel is strengthened by the character of Mickey Martin. The aforequoted conversation between Peter and his father is directly followed by a short note about the Martins' moving over to the new place and its detrimental effects on the children. There, we encounter Mickey who, coming back from school, gets confused and loses his way home. The most intriguing part of the scene is when Mickey starts

> to walk towards Galloway Road [Martins' old place] again, feeling that this was distinctly wrong, virtually a sin, and at the same time again remembering with an awful painful impact that they did not live there any more. (TTATC 240)

To give the scene a Lacanian reading, the sinful character of the comeback invites the Oedipal metaphor of a subject who cannot fully get over the separation with the maternal. Despite Mickey's young age, his he is preoccupied with

> the thought that perhaps nothing was real, that he was wandering in the world alone, that he had no home actually, and that he himself was an intruder and a ghost in the real world of regular ordinary things. (TTATC 240)

It is in such moments that Kerouac's novel loses its obvious realistic underpinning and acquires a mythical quality which also opens it wider to psychoanalytic interpretations.

George Martin's voice will be haunting his sons throughout the novel wishing to seal the process of castration. The father keeps the pressure on Peter to continue his studies (TTATC 256, 262), the pressure which soon gets escalated as Peter starts to question his father's requests and underscores his past wishes to stay at home (TTATC 269). When it turns out that George Martin's dreams about Peter have been highly narcissistic and have been revolving around the dream of Peter being George's fruit of success and boosting his social image (George's paternal function) (TTATC 269–271), Peter finally fights off his father's wishes, quits college, and plunges into the world as "a free man" (TTATC 263). Speaking of the most fundamental aspect that the Oedipal conflict poses, Régis Durand points to "the merciless war between two narcissisms (that of the father, ... and that of the child in happy symbiosis with his mother)" (48). *The Town and the City* does not only depict the failure of the paternal narcissism, but also the one represented by the child(ren).

On entering the symbolic, the mother-son(s) dyad is substituted with the presence of the Other. In Kerouac's novel just when the Martin sons set out from family home, the third element enters and changes the imaginary relationship with their life at Galloway adding brand new external "world" to it:

> It was the world itself, to which ... he [Peter] was descending for the first time in his life, amazingly as from some unknown previous dreaming existence in dark Galloway .... He was amazed because of life, because of sheer human presence on the earth. (TTATC 251)

For Francis, as we have noted, this means literally the world of (a new) language, which is the intellectual jargon. As for Peter, holding on to the perspective of studying in college and later joining the merchant marine, he welcomes the freedom of possibilities and new opportunities (TTATC 296). However, he soon starts to experience the burden of entering a new world which offers nothing comforting but

> an inexpressible sense of amazement and expectation, full of confoundment that in that direction, to which they slowly pushed, there could be no warm light and comfort and no friend, only the North, the far White North as ruthless and indifferent as the ocean's own overlowering night. (TTATC 302–303)

From a Lacanian perspective, the trajectory of Peter's escapades is that of the imaginary breaking under the pressure of the symbolic, as narcissistic expectations do not stand up to the reality. Kerouac appears to hint at the fact that the realm of the Other does not offer either completeness or satisfaction. The disaffection and disappointment first come at the sea:

> It was all so far from what he had expected of the 'adventure of the sea,' … . It was this instead. He thought of Galloway with a smile. (TTATC 304)

Estranged with and by the new world, Peter tries to sublimate his merchant marine adventure of "unbelievable desolation and final solitude" (TTATC 304) into the beauty of heroism and death, yet this strategy does not console him. Having thought of never coming back home at first, he feels either guilt for leaving his parents (TTATC 299) or a heartwarming sense of nostalgia (TTATC 304). Once again, the mirror plays the function of something that breaks the illusion of the imaginary; it literally breaks together with Peter's high opinion of himself:

> Suddenly his mirror on the locker door fell on the deck. "What am I doing here?" he thought, sitting up." (TTATC 306)

If mirrors could be understood as the bar between the signifier and the signified, they may well serve as the basis for Peter's going through the mirror stage, in which he experiences dissonance between his own subjectivity and the idealized image concocted by his ego. This, I have discussed, is a well-needed turn from the primary narcissism to socialization. Also, Peter's perception of his fellow mariners somehow anticipates his forthcoming troubling status of one not feeling right anywhere. It lets Kerouac launch a question which shall run throughout the Duluoz legend: is (re)finding the solace of one's sense of belonging in the world possible at all, having entered subjectivity (understood in Lacanian terms)?

> For thousand unknown miles away from home, they were all haunted, lost in the premonition of never returning, delivered to the nothingness of the earth, ... as-if-doomed within the gates of a misnamed impossible continent. And where was home? ... and the soft, sweet summerlands they had left behind it seemed forever? They all felt this and none of them could speak of it. (TTATC 306)

As I will try to demonstrate in the further chapters of this work, the nostalgic impression that there was once home which offered an unwavering sense of completeness and belonging can be treated as the very effect of the deficiencies of the symbolic.

Peter's peregrinations continue undermining his fantasies. Even a long-awaited visit home loses its dreamy character:

> Peter Martin was ... coming back from a nostalgic and sad visit to Galloway. Nothing had happened there. He had expected something intensely meaningful, dark, immense, and wonderful. (TTATC 354–355)

Leaving home and coming back to New York, he quickly adopts and acts out another set of phantasmata and visions:

> Out of the sadness of his heart, he began to imagine that he had never been to New York and that he was coming into it for the first time in his life. He even selected an old woman who looked like a farmer's wife, ... as proof human and simple that coming into New York for the first time in one's life was an event of the most wonderful importance. He watched her greedily. (TTATC 355)

It comes thus with no surprise that the city eventually brings him nothing but disappointment. New York with its "horror of endless streets and uncomprehendable sprawl and distance" (TTATC 358–359) leads to Peter's epiphany in which he feels contained within some

> dark mystery and ghostly sorrow as the world itself – the world as it had become to him since the beginning of the war, or since some unnoticed time when he had begun to look around and say to himself: "It is not known, it is not known!" (TTATC 359)

Thus, as much as it displays the modes of shifting from the imaginary to the symbolic, *The Town and the City* touches upon the impossibility of suppressing the imaginary in the symbolic. Since the process of setting phantasms is never-ending, newer and newer mirrors keep emerging just to keep breaking under the pressure of the signifiers. As it is pointed out by Markowski who interprets Gombrowicz's short story "Na kuchennych schodach,"

> Gombrowicz's short story rests on a strong opposition between the imaginary and the symbolic ... . The former ensures the understanding of the world insofar as it relies on clear and lucid signs ... . The latter keeps incessantly undermining the transparence of the former. (365–366)

Kerouac's novel testifies to the perpetual conflict in the subject between the imaginary and the symbolic. It evolves into a kind of a *bildungsroman* inasmuch as Peter, its central figure, gains knowledge of these deceptive processes and begins to speak of his own nature as of something

> vast, false, complex, shifting, treacherous, saddened by the mere sight of life. Something complete, and wise, and brutal too, had dreamed this world into existence, this world in which he wandered haunted. Something silent, beautiful, inscrutable had made all this for sure … . (TTATC 360–361)

This deceptiveness and trickery of human nature is what Lacan calls "ideal unity … [which] escapes [the subject] at every moment" (S II 166); it is the missed encounter between Lacanian *moi* (imaginary "I") and *je* (the symbolic subject). The merchant marine, Galloway, and New York episodes are merely objects founded on Peter's ego, and the spell of each imaginary object always fades away with a direct confrontation.

Another aspect which allows one to read Kerouac's *The Town and the City* as a novel about entering the symbolic is the structural duplicity that emerges in the world of its characters once out of the maternal and into the realm of the Other. As mentioned earlier, the whole set of dialectics that the novel presents the reader with stems from the eponymous segmentation of the world into Galloway and New York City. The divisions that follow make up for the "ghostly" and "lost" quality of the world crafted by Kerouac, the world of the essence which is vanished upon gaining subjectivity and whose trace is experienced merely as some haunting presence:

> Everything that he [Peter] had ever done in his life, … was haunted now by a deep sense of loss, confusion, and strange neargrief. He had known a boy's life in Galloway … . Now all that was lost, vanished, haunted and ghostly – because it was no more. . . . And there had been his mother and father in the old house on Galloway Road: and now, more lost and vanished than anything could ever be, they were in Brooklyn, dark Brooklyn nearby, within a subway's distance from where he was, yet farther and more forlorn than ever. (TTATC 359)

In Peter's eyes the world is thus theoretically the same, yet when he compares the states "before" and "after" it seems to have lost its soul. In a way, the world of "before" haunts him literally as he imagines his New York companions to be those from Galloway. His girlfriend, Judy, is perceived by him as his sister; similarly, his friend, Ken, is imagined by him as his brother (TTATC 388). Peter's way to somehow master the situation is to displace the coordinates of the allegedly lost world onto the new one:

> And if there was no Alexander Panos in the world any more … if not Alex and Danny and the gang, then there were Kenneth Wood, and Leon Levinsky, and Will Dennison,

> his friends "waiting" in the city for him. And if there were not the father and the mother he had known as a boy in Galloway, then there were the father and mother he would know now in the city, and they were "waiting" too. (TTATC 360)

Referring once again to Markowski's reading of Gombrowicz's oeuvre, one of the distinctive features of the Polish writer's literary tactics is the use of inverted commas and brackets for a number of purposes. Among many, as suggested by the critic, is Gombrowicz's wish to demonstrate that humans can merely "cite" their humanity, which, as a consequence of facing a repetition, becomes deprived of its essence. Punctuation marks are also used to mediate feelings, making and proving any authenticity impossible (97–98). One may have the impression that Kerouac's use of inverted commas is analogous to that of Gombrowicz's since it signals a repetition of the subject's reality, a gesture hinting at some alleged loss of essence.

From another perspective, the dialectics of the imaginary and the symbolic find their epitome in the clash between Peter and Francis, setting high spirits and hope against disillusionment and nihilism. The conflict of two perspectives peaks at one of conversations, when, to Peter's utter confusion, Francis admits that being given a consciousness has been the greatest crime of this world since what comes after is only sadness (TTATC 157). As noted by Nicosia, the conflict in the novel also takes the form of "a kind of dialectic between good and bad weather" (308). "Sunny joys of daytime" are confronted with "cold night ... [and] icy blackness" (308) and the light is "a moment of pure being" (Nicosia 312). Thus, the general model that arises out of Kerouac's work is that of Lacan's split subject, a consciousness composed of a fantasized sense of totality and essence and of the sense of void where the real things were substituted (or, as Lacan, would prefer "killed") by their signifiers. Such is Bruce Fink's take on the Lacan's model of the subject presented in Seminar XV: the subject is actually the bar between the signifier and the signified and as such it cannot make itself being at the mercy of signifiers and the unconscious (Fink reads *cogito* as a split between "I am not thinking" (the upper part of the bar, the ego) and "I am not" (the lower part of the bar, the realm of the unconscious)). The unconscious of the subject is perfectly epitomized in Kerouac's novel as the aforementioned "icy blackness" of the night besetting any sense of a fixed subjectivity. However, as it was claimed by both Fink and Žižek, the unconscious has its own logic and thinking which precede any subjectivity and consciousness and make the latter emerge as an offshoot. In his very first description of Galloway in the novel, Kerouac adopts a narrator who is extremely detached from the place and who claims that despite all the visible scenery, there is "[s]omething in the invisible brooding landscape surrounding the town, something [that] ... tells ... a different story" (TTATC 3).

It might then be argued that, like the Lacanian subject, the entire world of Galloway is founded on and emerges from the unknown, ominous realm of the unconscious.

Speaking of the critics' general disappointment with Kerouac's novel, Regina Weinreich observes that the failure of *The Town and the City* comes down to "the predictability of each son's experience," which is unavoidable given the insistence of the theme (25). This seems to be yet another level of looking at the novel in a (post)structuralist way; the story of the Martin family is to exemplify some unchangeable patterns that underpin the human life as a collective experience. One might have the impression that the Martins are merely to fill those patterns in and articulate what must be articulated:

> This is the Martin family, the elders and the young ones, ... the flitting ghost-ends of a brood who will grow and come to attain size and seasons and huge presence like the others, ... and give brooding rare articulation to the poor things of life, and the rich, dark things too. (TTATC 15)

If, as Weinreich wishes, *The Town and the City* is a novel about "the overthrow of the authority of the father" (18), then Kerouac shows that the flexibility of human agency is limited, which adds up to the sadness permeating his work:

> Each brother struggles to free himself from a life-style associated with authority and responsibility (with father, god, and so on). Each Martin represents a variation on the theme of the overthrow of the authority of the father George, the prime exemplar of authority in the family structure. ... Each must undergo the pain of loss as each enters the realms of greater, more experienced consciousness ... . (Weinreich 25)

Although the Martin sons function in the symbolic, their notorious persistence of looking back at the domestic, in a way, can be attributed to the above-mentioned deficiencies of the paternal metaphor and, consequently, not fully-assimilated castration process. Back in the merchant marine, Peter occasionally imagines the topographies of the Arctic Ocean and Greenland to be the features of "a sweet fatherland" (TTATC 306), which emerge as an imaginary phallus in the insufficiency of the symbolic one. Near the end of the novel, the conflict between the father and the son opens up and switches all the indirect persuasiveness on both sides for direct allegations and demands. When Peter finally communicates to his father that New York is his final destination, George does not hesitate anymore to prove his superiority over the son:

> I'm your father and I'm older than you are and I've had ore experience ... . (TTATC 421)
> You don't care for your parents who love you. Something *evil* and awful has happened, there's nothing but unhappiness everywhere. (TTATC 423)

The sense of guilt which was previously inconspicuously inculcated in Peter is now being openly inflicted by his father as when he speaks of his son's alleged viciousness:

> "I'm *proud* of you to have dope friends and crackpots and crooks for friends. It's just what I anticipated from you when you were a little kid, when you ran up to me that day crying and telling me that your little brother had died." (TTATC 420)

The conflict alienates the father and the son not bringing solace to any of them. George's aggressiveness seems to conflate with his feeling of increasing loneliness: "Martin was more alone at this time of his life than he had ever been. He began to have the reveries of an irreparably lonely man" (TTATC 351). Similarly, Peter's feelings revolve around not having a model to follow and a right path to take:

> His father was dying – and his own life was dying, it had come to a dead end in the city, he had nowhere else to go. Peter did not know what to do with his own life but somehow he knew what to do about his father, who was now not only his father, but his brother and his mysterious son too. (TTATC 468)

In the final moments of George's life the father and the son bury the hatchet. Both of them recognize that "the destiny of men is to come up to rivers and cross them one way or another, ... and get over them or turn back in defeat and sarcasm" (TTATC 471). From the Lacanian perspective, the puzzling fragment might hint at either successful or unsuccessful acceptance of the paternal metaphor. In a way, due to George's untimely death, Peter does not learn his place in the world. One feels inclined to refer to Lacan's words that in the Oedipal dilemma the child is "never really there at the place where he is, and ... never completely absent from the place where he is not" (Lacan, quoted by Evans, 152). In a way, Peter stops at the pre-oedipal stage, in which the subject's imaginary fixation "established around the [mother's] imaginary lack of the phallus" (S III 319) does not cease to exist. In a consequence, the subject still longs to be the phallus for the mother because the paternal metaphor has not been fully and properly accepted.

When George Martin eventually dies, Peter's thoughts seem to revolve around a Hamletian dilemma:

> What had killed his father, in God's name? He had not done it himself, it was not true that he had done it himself! A thousand times it seemed he had done it himself, but it was not so! Who could say that he had done it himself! How would he ever learn that he had not done it himself! (TTATC 477)

The way Kerouac depicts Peter's reaction to his father's death seems to be hinting at the classical Freudian interpretation of Shakespeare's play, in which prince

Hamlet is stupefied and unable to act since his repressed desire to overthrow his father has already been satisfied. Such a perspective can be supplemented by Porter:

> There are two sides to the paradox of the Father-Subject. To want to be the father, to occupy his place, is necessarily to want to kill him – how else be Him than displace him? But then, to displace him is, unfortunately, to be Him, and thus to be dead. (103)

In his interpretation of *Hamlet* Lacan shifts the main stress onto the question of what the (m)Other's desire is, which ultimately comes down to the mystery of what the phallus that the (m)Other desires is. Prince Hamlet's frustrating and immobilizing dilemma is elucidated by Lacan in the following way:

> The very source of what makes Hamlet's arm waver at every moment, is the narcissistic connection that Freud tells us about in his text on the decline of the Oedipus complex: one cannot strike the phallus, because the phallus, even the real phallus, is a *ghost*. ("Desire and the Interpretation" 50)

With the death of his father (and due to the paternal deficiencies during his father's lifetime) Peter, alike prince Hamlet and called Hamlet by his girlfriend (TTATC 250), experiences a hole in the Other, the unsteadiness of the symbolic realm.[75] The mystery of the alleged phallus which could cover up for such instabilities and fill the lack in the desiring (m)Other is taken to the grave. George's death becomes a perfect epitome of Lacan's idea that the phallus is elusive since it is a *ghost*, something which operates only as a veiled object (or rather, veiled *nothing*). What is more, the ghostly quality of the book, maintained by a repetitive use of the figures of ghosts, adds up to the general impression of a phallic quality of the male world, enwrapped in burdensome loneliness, a sense of unfulfillment, and ineffective communication. Nicosia points out that one of the most significant themes the novel explores is the "failure to communicate" (309). He is referring to the double death of Charley and George Martin at the end of the novel and the discovery of an unread letter of the former to the latter. As added by the scholar, this is a true "symbol of the futility of language: an unsent letter from the dead to the dead" (310). Consequently, the deficiencies of communication presented by the novel may lead to a conclusion that "the fate of man's consciousness is to remain essentially separate" (Nicosia 312).

---

75 It may be of particular interest to psychoanalytic interpretations of their texts that Shakespeare and Kerouac wrote their above-discussed works soon after their fathers' deaths.

The ill-timed death of the father, the mystery of the phallus and the insufficiency of the Name-of-the-Father resulting thereof trigger Peter's quest for the ideal paternal metaphor, which would be able to rectify the lack in the Other and give life a (stable) meaning:

> "The most beautiful idea on the face of the earth," he [Peter] thought unaccountably, "is the idea the child has that his father knows everything." ... But he recalled sorrowfully that ... when the child sought a way of some sort he only found that his father's way was not enough, and the child was left cold with the realization that nobody, not even his father, really knew what to do. And yet, that children and fathers should have a notion in their souls that there must be a way, an authority, a great knowledge, a vision, a view of life, a proper manner, an order in all the disorder and sadness of the world ... . (TTATC 423–424)

I would argue that such rationale ultimately initiates the discourse of the whole Duluoz legend and becomes its *modus operandi. The Town and the City* is only the first of a series of installments which, as I will try to prove, test various tropes of fatherhood in search of the ideal one. To refer once again to Lacan, the subject fixes on imaginary father(s) when it is impossible to assume "the realization of the signifier *father* at the symbolic level" (S III 204). As a consequence, the subject may have to pursue what he or she imagines to administer the law and

> will have to bear the weight of ... dispossession of the signifier and adopt compensation for it, ... over the course of his life, through a series of purely conformist identifications with the characters who will give him the feeling for what one has to do to be a man. (S III 205)

This is as much the case of Peter (who excurses into the unknown at the end of *The Town and the City*) as the Kerouacian subject in general. Theado calls "the loss of the father's world ... one major theme in *The Town and the City* and in Kerouac's subsequent work" (45).

Peter comes to conclusion that the key things in life are love, work, and hope. He suddenly learns how invaluable they are since

> all the struggles in life were incessant, laborious, painful, that nothing was done quickly, without labor, that it had to undergo a thousand fondlings, revisings, moldings, addings, removings, graftings, tearings, correctings, smoothings, rebuildings, reconsiderings, nailings, tackings, chippings, hammerings, hoistings, connectings – all the poor fumbling uncertain incompletions of human endeavor. They went on forever and were forever incomplete, far from perfect, refined, or smooth, full of terrible memories of failure and fears of failure, yet, in the way of things, somehow noble, complete, and shining in the end. (TTATC 472)

These assumptions come as a project, as much Peter's as Kerouac's, which seems to mirror Lacanian concepts of *tuche* and *automaton*, bringing sense into its place in a laborious series of repetitions and revisions, or as Fink would say, "return[s] with a difference" ("The Real Cause of Repetition" 224). The revisions materialize in the subsequent installments of the Duluoz legend and, in a way, Peter's resolutions protrude into further characters of that legend. Also, if Kerouac seeks "redemption" and "cleansing" with *The Town and the City* (Nicosia 164), then they do not necessarily come since the trauma of the dead father will return belated and retroacted in the subsequent works, making them *Vorstellungpresentanz* against *Vorstellung*, taking a heroic effort to represent what is unrepresentable.

7 "Somewhere Behind Us or In Front of Us in the Huge Night His Father Lay" – *On the Road* and *Visions of Cody*

Peter Martin's departure into the unknown of the American land at the end of *The Town and the City* smoothly transits into Kerouac's second novel, whose formal and thematic fixation over the motif of movement finds a fresh literary idiom and makes it a brand new opening for the writer. *On the Road* (1957), together with its derivative *Visions of Cody* (published posthumously in 1972) mark a pivotal change in both Kerouac's diction and his understanding of literature as they exemplify the writer's turn to the poetics of spontaneity, whose major strategies and features have been delineated in the previous chapters. Hailed by Gilbert Millstein from *New York Times* as *The Sun Also Rises* of its generation and often considered the Bible of the Beat Generation, *On the* Road, originally a 120-foot one-paragraph scroll, is an autobiographically-inspired, cross-country itinerary of Kerouac's alter ego, Sal Paradise. Taking place between 1947 and 1950, the novel channels and interrogates many of the fears and hopes of the post-war youth, among them "[t]he yearning for personal relevance, the awkward infatuation with cultures other than his own, that restless desire to get up and *move*," (Holladay ix). Whether he liked it or not, Kerouac became the voice of both the American youth and of a bulk of thinking-alike artists who struggled for finding a fresh literary idiolect as well as a sense of spirituality and who came to be known as the Beat Generation. As noted by Joseph Boskin, *On the Road* "captured the nub of [the Beats'] quest in the single image of the road, the metaphoric American highway that runs toward new possibilities" (96). Crucially, the person to act and be immortalized as a spearhead of the quest was Neal Cassady, a frenetic 20-year daredevil and a homegrown philosopher personified in the character of Dean Moriarty. To a prevailing extent, *On the Road* is an account of Sal's fixation over the mystifying and captivating persona of Dean, the embodiment of a new American hero.

Visions of Cody, an immediate consequence of Kerouac's dissatisfaction with the results achieved with *On the Road*, goes a step further and attempts at reevaluating Cassady's essence without any artistic compromise whatsoever. If Kerouac's sophomore novel formed a bridge between the conventional and the experimental, then its successor abandons any pretense at literary orthodoxy. Retaking Neal Cassady into its scope and overwriting some of the events presented in *On the Road*, *Visions of Cody* makes a daring endeavor at capturing the essence of a gone friend, who is considered to be "an archetypal American man" (Kerouac, quoted by Hrebeniak, 232). Its formal bravado reflects the author's uncompromising attitude and relentlessness in fathoming the enigma of Neal Cassady; as observed by Gregory Stephenson, the non-linear novel is "most boldly experimental, combining stream-of-consciousness narrative, mythopoeic portraiture, realism, and surrealism" (25). Letting the subject matter adopt its own form, Kerouac wishes not to talk about Cassady but simply, in a performative attempt, *make* Cassady out of his text.

What is crucial for this analysis, both *On the Road* and *Visions of Cody* emerge as the next stage of the Kerouacian subject's proceedings with the figure of the father, just as the Kerouacian subject himself begins a new chapter of his life. As we learn in the beginning of the novel, Sal Paradise, the main hero and first-person narrator decides to give up his previous life and plunge into the vastness of the American land. His articulates his rationale in the first paragraph of the novel:

> I first met Dean not long after my wife and I split up. I had just gotten over from a serious illness that I won't bother to talk about, except that it had something to do with the miserably weary split-up and my feeling that everything was dead. With the coming of Dean Moriarty began the part of my life you could call my life on the road. (OTR 7)

Dean's irresistible charm, potency and high spirits buoy Sal up and allure him into following his new companion across the land. Moriarty becomes a route marker for his devotee's life priorities, and he sets up the coordinates of Sal's desires; not least is he a prophet, whose words and actions may be not always clear in meaning, yet which are a promise of spiritual fulfillment. It is perhaps this last aspect of Dean Moriarty, a mystery possessing the secret of life and death, that plays a dominant role in Sal's becoming his disciple. Paradise can hardly resist learning that secret as observed on the occasion of his second coupling up with Moriarty:

> I had been spending a quiet Christmas in the country, ..., but now the bug was on me again, and the bug's name was Dean Moriarty and I was off on another spurt around the road. (OTR 110)

The novel abounds with moments of the protagonist's fixation on his companion's spellbinding quality. Sal is after Dean since "there's thoughts in that mind that [the former] would give [his] last arm to know" (OTR 109), which often leads it up to a point where he is blinded to his friend's misdemeanors and defends him: "I'll bet you want to know what he does next and that's because he' got the secret we're all busting to find" (OTR 184). In the final trip to Mexico, Dean is bestowed with nothing short of divinity: "[i]n myriad pricklings of heavenly radiation I had to struggle to see Dean's figure, and he looked like God" (OTR 268). The ambiguity of what constitutes Moriarty's greatness has not escaped critics' attention. Gregory Stephenson notes that "Dean is an ambiguous figure, ... a hedonist and a mystic, an embodiment of the irrational energies of the unconscious, both destructive and regenerative" (21), who nevertheless promises some "potential [which] is immensely sexual, spiritual and transcendent" (Swartz 91).

As an emanation of some mystifying knowledge, Dean brings to one's mind the image of an ideal father projected by Peter Martin close to the end of *The Town and the City*. Peter's yearning for a sense of guidance, "an authority, a great knowledge, a vision, a view of life" (TTATC 424) extends beyond Kerouac's debut novel and resurges as praxis in *On the Road*. If Sal Paradise's directionless peregrinations across the States are a protraction and a natural consequence of Peter Martin's sense of loss and regret over the untimely death of his father, then Dean Moriarty emerges as a father figure expected to fill in the missing space of the paternal signifier. In the original manuscript of *On the Road*, the devastating experience which initially haunts the protagonist and triggers his escapades is not the break-up of the relationship but exactly the death of Sal's father:

> I first met Neal not long after my father died ... I had just gotten over a serious illness that I won't bother to talk about except that it really had something to do with my father's death and my awful feeling that everything was dead. With the coming of Neal there really began for me that part of my life that you could call my life on the road. (OTR: OS 109)

The quest to rectify the dispossession of the paternal signifier pertains not only to Neal Cassady's literary alter ego, but is also repeated in subsequent works of Kerouac's, which provides more perspectives on a Lacanian reading of the writer's oeuvre. In a general view, Sal Paradise's companion inaugurates a series of displacements of the missing father figure that will run metonymically through the entire Duluoz legend. They will aim at anchoring a stable signified in the signifier of the father, which comes down to ascribing a fixed meaning (or, we should rather say, an illusion of a fixed meaning) to what it means to have a father and who is meant to be a father. In Lacanian parlance, such an action goes by the name of *point de capiton* (often referred to as the "button tie" or the "quilting point") and in the psychoanalyst's own words describes the moment when "the signifier stops the otherwise indefinite sliding of signification" (Écrits 681), which comes down to "the precise point at which meaning is produced in nonmeaning" (Écrits 423). Thus, the Kerouacian subject's search for a father works in accordance with Lacan's understanding of metonymy and metaphor – the former aims at substituting and testing successive father figures in a continual displacement while the latter attempts at building up a condensed and fixed meaning of fatherhood in case a given father figure attracts the subject. Metonymy, as argued by the French psychoanalyst, is a prerequisite for any metaphor to emerge:

> The coordination of signifiers has to be possible before the transferences of the signified are able to take place. The formal articulation of the signifier predominates with respect to transference of the signified. (S III 229)

Being the vessel for operations of the unconscious, the mutual work of metonymy and metaphor is recognized by Lacan as

> the heart of Freud's thought. His [Freud's] work begins with a dream, its mechanisms of condensation and displacement, of figuration – these are all of the order of metonymic articulation, and it's on this foundation that metaphor is able to intervene. (S III 228)

Not only is *On the Road* the first (metonymic) step on the road to restoring the metaphor of the father in the Duluoz legend but also an exercise in (paternal) dialectics of metonymy and metaphor in its own right. Unsurprisingly, the dominant father figure of the novel, yet not the only one, is Dean Moriarty. It is very early in the novel that Sal's fixation on father figures starts to be conspicuous. He claims that his road companion reminds him "of some long-lost brother" (OTR 13) as well as of his childhood years, which emerge through Dean's "excited way of speaking" bringing to his mind "the voices of old companions and brothers under the bridge" (OTR 13).[76] Moriarty is thus endowed with fatherly and brotherly qualities, which occasionally leads Sal to hold such strong identifications with his friend that the latter becomes internalized by the former. During a brief argument with Dean in Part Three, Sal feels that each sentence against his companion

> was a knife at [himself]. Everything [he] had ever secretly held against [his] brother was coming out: how ugly [he] was and what filth [he] was discovering in the depths of [his] own impure psychologies. (OTR 201)

Apart from the above-mentioned internalization, it is interesting to notice the unclear referent of the signifier "brother". This may well designate Dean as well as

76 Naturally, as it happens with the vast majority of Kerouac's works, *On the Road* is highly autobiographical and it hints at the deaths of the writer's father Leo, who died in May 1946, and his older brother Gerard, who passed away in 1926 at the age of nine (Kerouac was four at that time). The figure of the older brother in the novel can thus be treated as another rendition of the father figure.

Sal's long-lost brother, which makes the attempt at a metaphoric matching more evident. All things considered, as pointed out by Omar Swartz,

> Kerouac's vision ... is both metonymic and metaphoric. His vision is transcendent and thus something that cannot easily be expressed in words. It needs to be reduced and embodied and represented by what people commonly know. Thus, Kerouac grounds his vision in Cassady who, as Dean Moriarty, becomes a symbol of a new value system. (85)

As explained by Gregory Stephenson, this "psychological and spiritual reorientation, a new pattern of conduct ... [includes] spontaneity, sensuality, energy, intuition, and instinct" (156).

The process of identifying with Moriarty with a view to assume the Name-of-the-Father works on yet another level. Sal accompanies Dean in his quest to find his father, Old Dean Moriarty the Tinsmith, a drunkard who stays in an unknown place. Matt Theado observes that Dean's father, being referenced several times, "looms invisibly over the story, presenting warning of an ominous possible future for Dean himself" (64) and is equivalent to "Hamlet's father's ghost, ... always distant and hazy, his meaning unclear" (64). In Part Three, while staying alone in Denver and thinking of Dean, Sal realizes that his yearning for a father figure has already become extrapolated to his companion's missing father:

> At dusk I walked. I felt like a speck on the surface of the sad red earth. I passed the Windsor Hotel, where Dean Moriarty had lived with his father in the depression thirties, and as of yore I looked everywhere for the sad and fabled tinsmith of my mind. Either you find someone who looks like your father in places like Montana or you look for a friend's father where he is no more. (OTR 169)

What the passage proves is that in Sal's predicament there might not be any final displacement of the father figure since Dean leads metonymically to another paternal character that allegedly embodies the lacking signified. Also, developing the reader's awareness that Paradise's journey across the States is largely about missing paternal metaphor is all the more easier as Moriarty's situation is the exact mirror image of the narrator's quandary. In Lacanian terms, Sal is after Dean because he is after something that Dean desires, and, according to Lacan's argumentation, a "[m]an's desire is the desire of the Other" (S XI 235).

A symptomatic example of Sal's longing for the answer of what the Other desires and what it means to fully internalize the Name of the Father comes with Sal and Dean's bus trip to Detroit at the end of Part Three. Onboard, apparently with the aim of making advances at a female traveler, Paradise besieges a young girl with loads of questions about her life and her dreams. The interrogation smoothly slides into the following queries:

> 'What does your father do on a summer's night?' He works, he has an all-night shift at the boiler factory, … . 'What does your brother do on a summer's night?' He rides around on his bicycle, he hangs out in front of the soda fountain. 'What is he aching to do? What are we all aching to do? What do we want?' She didn't know … . It was too much. Nobody could tell. It was all over. (OTR 229)

All the above-mentioned questions fired away at the young girl ultimately come together as one inquiry aimed at the Other and referred to by Lacan as "*Che vuoi*?" ("What do you want (me to be)?"). Sal preys on the illusion of the Other as the depositor of knowledge, as the one bearing what Lacan calls the phallus and what is capable of filling the lack he experiences. Dean happens to be put in the position of the Other and as such he is treated as the holder of "the secret … [Sal] is busting to find" since it is only through the desire of the Other that one can gain access to their own desire. Thus, the two peregrinators penetrate the American land with the same goal and in the same, metonymic manner. On the road, they anticipate subsequent father figures and leave behind the insufficient ones, just like the logic of the Lacanian chain of signifiers would suggest. Leaving Denver to find Dean's father in Part Three, Sal's companion slows down the car to conclude:

> ' … But hey, look down there in the night thar, hup, hup, a buncha old bums by a fire by the rail, damn me.' He almost slowed down. 'You see, I never know whether my father's there or not.' … 'I never know whether to ask. He might be anywhere.' We drove on. Somewhere behind us or in front of us in the huge night his father lay drunk under the bush … . (OTR 219)

The father figure is not exclusively ascribed to Dean and resurges in many other characters of the novel. Among others, the paternal metaphor is bestowed on Chicanos, a horse named Big Pop (Kerouac's father was extremely fond of horse racing) and, as demonstrated by James T. Jones, numerous people acquiring the name "Slim" (*The Mythic Form* 93). What is interesting, Jones also suggests that in *On the Road* there exists a "pattern of two brothers looking for love on their way to find the father" (*The Mythic Form* 93), which is frequently repeated. Paternal quality is also discernable in the Ghost of the Susquehanna,

> a shriveled little old man with a paper satchel who claimed he was headed for 'Canady'. He walked very fast, commanding me to follow, and said there was a bridge up ahead we could cross. (OTR 100)

The stranger met in Harrisburg, Pennsylvania promises Sal to take him to a bridge over the Susquehanna which would help the protagonist make his way home. Yet Paradise is lead astray. The bridge is never found. After being informed about taking the wrong road, Sal is given a ride back to Harrisburg by another stranger and watches the Ghost of Susquehanna "dissolving in the darkness of the mournful Alleghenies" (OTR 101). The episode brings to mind the conversation between Peter Martin and his father from *The Town and the City* in which they both conclude that "the destiny of men is to come up to rivers and cross them one way or another" (TTATC 471). In the light of that scene, the Susquehanna Ghost experience emerges as another act of miscommunication between the father and the son, a recurring and failed attempt to fully align with the paternal metaphor. As posited by James T. Jones, the Ghost of the Susquehanna is "the ghost of the father who makes a ghost of the son" (*The Mythic Form* 97), a disturbance in the process of accepting the phallus (or, in the vein of Lacan's interpretation of *Hamlet*, mourning the phallus) that shall haunt the subject with an unresolved oedipal dilemma. Just like Prince Hamlet, for whom the desire of his mother remains a mystery, the Kerouacian subject does not know who he should be to fulfill the desire of the (m) Other. Sal's mother is scarcely referenced in the text (perhaps one could even speak of a repressed mother since her place is taken by the protagonist's aunt), yet there is a single, ominous emergence of her emanation in Part Two. After reaching his final destination, San Francisco, Sal spends some time all by himself. Wandering aimlessly through the streets, he suddenly goes through a haunting experience:

> I passed a fish-'n-chips joint on Market Street, and suddenly the woman in there gave me a terrified look as I passed; she was the proprietress, … . I walked on a few feet. It suddenly occurred to me this was my mother of about two hundred years ago in England, and that I was her footpad son, returning from gaol to haunt her honest labours in the hashery. I stopped, frozen with ecstasy on the sidewalk … . 'No,' that woman seemed to say with that terrified glance, 'don't come back and plague your honest, hard-working mother. You are no longer like a son to me – and like your father, my first husband. … O son! did you not ever go on your knees and pray for deliverance for all your sins an scoundrel's acts? Lost boy! Depart! Do not haunt my soul; I have done well forgetting you. Reopen no old wounds, be as if you had never returned and looked in to me … '. (OTR 163)

Projecting the desire of the m(Other) as impenetrable and embittered, Sal inflicts a sense of guilt and reluctance on himself since he cannot act as the phallus. This constitutes the germ of his self-alienation and occasionally destabilizes his sense of identity together with his self-esteem throughout the novel:

> I woke up as the sun was reddening; and that was the one distinct time in my life, the strangest moment of all, when I didn't know who I was – I was far away from home, haunted and tired with travel, … . I wasn't scared; I was just somebody else, some stranger, and my whole life was a haunted life, the life of a ghost. I was halfway across America, at the dividing line between the East of my youth and the West of my future … . (OTR 19–20)

> At lilac evening I walked with every muscle aching ... in the Denver coloured section, wishing I were a Negro, feeling that the best the white world could had offered was not enough ecstasy, not enough life, joy, kicks, darkness, music, not enough night. ... I wished I were a Denver Mexican, or even a poor overworked Jap, anything but what I was so drearily, a 'white man' disillusioned. ... I was only myself. (OTR 169–170)

At times, yearning for the phallus, which would give Kerouac's characters' a sense of fullness and bliss in the motherly, comes along with referencing, be it intentional or not, what Freud called fixation in secondary narcissism and what amounts to the wish of returning to the mother's womb. One such instance is when Dean unsuccessfully encourages Sal to make love to Marylou, the former's wife. Paradise ponders Moriarty's wild nature:

> I could hear Dean ... blindly seeking to return the way he came. This is the result of years looking at sexy pictures behind the bars; ... evaluating ... the softness of the woman who is not there. Dean had never seen his mother's face. Every new girl, every new wife ... was an addition to his bleak impoverishment. Where was his father? – old bum Dean Moriarty the Tinsmith .... Dean had every right to die the sweet deaths of complete love to his Marylou. I didn't want to interfere, I just wanted to follow. (OTR 126)

It might be thus well surmised that Sal and Dean's peregrinations across the country parallel their erotic conquests and emblematize their calling for an undifferentiated stasis of the motherly womb. The desire to find the Lacanian phallus brings about yearnings for incestuous and impossible jouissance:

> In certain text he [Lacan] says that it is the signifier of desire; in others he says that it is the signifier of jouissance .... You can say the phallus is the signifier of desire to the extent that desire implies a lack of jouissance .... (Soler 261)

Circling around the States is ultimately a pronouncement of the signifiers revolving metonymically around the empty center of the maternal sphere, the vaginal object of the Heideggerian vase.

With the end of the novel comes the ultimate failure to rectify the lack of the paternal metaphor. In "a motheaten overcoat" (OTR 290), Dean makes three thousand miles allegedly just to see Sal in New York and is eventually rejected by his companion, who chooses to look for settlement. In the last paragraph we are presented with the image of a night that comes throughout the American land and triggers Sal's reminiscences over Dean Moriarty: "I think of Dean Moriarty, I even think of Old Dean Moriarty, the father we never found, I think of Dean Moriarty" (OTR 291). The image of Paradise's companion gives a closing to the book, just like it began the work, and, in Gladys Foxe's argumentation, signals the "ultimate futility of Sal's yearnings" for a father figure (55). The view is corroborated by Mary Paniccia Carden:

> This ending emphasis on a traveling son's fatal relation to a lost and powerless father recasts the trope of travel as a "rite of passage to manhood" (Van den Abbeele xxvi) by offering an empty line of male identifications, a missing patrilineal connection that fails to convey dominance and authority. (94)

On the Road, thus, emerges as a novel about a metaphor that has failed. Taking a more general perspective, it might be deemed a novel about arbitrariness and instability of metaphors as such, and it illustrates the Lacanian thesis of the illusion of knowledge that comes with the making of a metaphor. This failure finds its epitome in one more father figure of the novel, a meta-level paternal symbol which is that of the Shrouded Traveler. Never referred to by any name, the figure haunts the protagonist's dreams and perplexes him with its impenetrable obscurity. Sal discusses its manifestations with Carlo Marx in Part Two:

> I told him [Carlo] a dream I had about a strange Arabian figure that was pursuing me across the desert; that I tried to avoid; that finally overtook me just before I reached the Protective City. "Who is this?" said Carlo. We pondered it. I proposed it was myself, wearing a shroud. That wasn't it. Something, someone, some spirit was pursuing all of us across the desert of life and was bound to catch us before we reached heaven. Naturally, now that I look back on it, this is only death: death will overtake us before heaven. (OTR 118–119)

Not having a clue what the Shrouded Traveler might represent, Sal finally reduces it to death as the passage to heaven, the ultimate *jouissance*. The exegesis changes in Part Four, where, preparing for a journey to Mexico, Paradise unexpectedly learns that Dean is coming to join and envisions him as an intruder,

> a burning shuddering frightful Angel, palpitating toward me across the road, approaching like a cloud, with enormous speed, pursuing me like the Shrouded Traveler on the plain, bearing down on me. (OTR 244)

Not having a fixed referent, or rather, persistently hiding its referent under the shroud, the Shrouded Traveler emerges as the very signifier of the lack in the symbolic. This is exactly what the Lacanian phallus is: a reminder of loss that instigates the subject's wish to redeem that loss and, as such, "can play its role only when veiled" (Écrits 581). Just like Hamlet, Sal is given to see that the phallus is a ghost, that it only denotes the empty space of the paternal. Unlike Hamlet, he does not appear to comprehend the menacing figure as the nightmare of the impossibility of filling the gap in the Other, of the futility of accessing the knowledge that the father allegedly possesses. Transposing Lacan's exegesis of *Hamlet* further onto *On the Road*, one could claim that the ghostly character emerges in Sal's projections since the father's death was ill-timed and has not been mourned properly. The fatherly figure is shrouded insofar as the real trauma of the dead father is never presented but only represented. As posited by Régis Durand, "what had been forecluded – owing to the partial failure of the paternal metaphor – returns under the form of hallucinations or regressive fantasies" (51). Concluding, with the figure of the Shrouded Traveler *On the Road* seems to offer a metaphor of the lack and impossibility of paternal metaphor *par excellence*; it is with this metaphor that the Kerouacian subject's subsequent failures at internalizing the Name-of-the-Father are anticipated.[77]

It is also interesting to see how fatherlessness expresses itself in the novel on the level of the narrative. If, as posited by Robert Con Davis, "[i]nstituted by the discovery of absence, the desire for the father [is] articulated in what is essentially a narrative" (9), then this claim finds a perfect epitome in Kerouac's novel, where Sal's regret of having lost his father coincides with his going on the road and his wish to write a book (he considers himself a writer). According to James T. Jones's argumentation, "the absence of the father ... causes and perpetuates the compulsive behavior in both brothers [Sal and Dean]" (*The Mythic Form* 98). In Lacan's parlance, the lack of Sal's real father comes along with the fundamental lack in the symbolic; both of these, instigating desire, propel the subject out of his stasis and make him embark on a journey. What is further linked to the absence of the father and the origins of the narrative, Davis claims, is the passivity of the son's figure. Pointing to "how Telemakhos depends on Odysseus and cannot act without his help, and how Odysseus cannot act without Zeus' aid" (9), the scholar notes:

> [T]he passivity that Telemakhos and Odysseus are forced into by the fact of paternal absence tells something further about narrative structure: just as they are passive in relation to an absent father, the development of narrative, likewise, is fully dependent on the structural absence that initiates it. (8)

As concluded by Davis, "the castration threat, the central event of the Oedipal crisis, must be resolved in acceptance of passivity in regard to the father's authority for the crisis to be ended" (8). Sal seems to attempt passivity along the entire story; he "shambles after those who interest him" (Theado 30). As we learn in Part Two, he engages in journeys with Dean supposedly for no reason. Reuniting with his friend after a yearly break-off, Paradise admits: "It was a completely meaningless

77 James T. Jones points out that the Shrouded Traveler was "a shared dream and then a shared image in literature" by both Kerouac and Ginsberg, which, as believed by the scholar, makes it "perfectly suited for Jungian analysis" ("Sharing a Shadow" 233). Such examination is offered by him in: James T. Jones, "Sharing a Shadow: The Image of the Shrouded Stranger in the Works of Jack Kerouac and Allen Ginsberg." It is also Gregory Stephenson who sees the potential in a Jungian analysis of *On the Road*, pointing to Dean as "a parallel to the shadow figure of Jungian psychology" (158).

set of circumstances that made Dean come, and similarly I went off with him for no reason" (OTR 111). Similarly, on arriving in New York, he says: "I was never scared when Dean drove; he could handle a car under any circumstances. ... I didn't know where all this was leading; I didn't care" (OTR 118). As Lacan's theory tells us, the protagonist's act is not meaningless as it can be well circumscribed in the quest for redeeming the dispossessed father. According to Davis, the son must eventually align with the father in that the former sees the latter as lacking, which is the final stage of acquiring fatherly knowledge. The Kerouacian subject seems to seek that final stage, full symbolic castration. It might also be argued that *On the Road* corroborates Lacanian concept of desire as a phallic construct since the narrative of the novel conflates the metonymic desire of two male characters with the act of travelling as a typically male (and, what is more, American) mode of self-fulfillment. As noted by Mary Paniccia Carden,

> [w]hile women obviously do travel, popular Anglo-European notions of journeying tend to come structured in male-oriented tropes of exploration, conquest, and sexual adventure. (78)

Thus, travelling, which has "long been the medium of peculiarly male fantasies of transformation and self-realization" (Leed, quoted by Carden, 78), is Lacanian desire at work, also on the level of the male narrative discourse. The emergent desire for the father which initiates narration finds its emblem in the "journeyism" of the novel; new places "unreel with dreamlike rapidity" (OTR 216) just like Kerouac's manuscript scroll, "[t]he magnificent car ... [makes] the plains unfold like a roll of paper" (OTR 219).

The fatherlessness becomes the function of the text in one more respect, which is the loose formal structure of *On the Road* and *Visions of Cody*. Originating thematically and structurally in the absence of father, both texts acquire the quality much different from the preceding *The Town and the City*, which demonstrates fairly conventional patterns of storytelling. The dissolution of father-son relationship at the end of Kerouac's debut novel triggers the loosening of the textual tissue of his further works; once the father vanishes and stops presiding over the text of the Duluoz legend, its subsequent installments start to acquire fluidity and a non-restrictive armature. The phenomenon of textual suspension of the fatherly has been investigated by many literary critics. Régis Durand observes that "[the] flow, [the] narrative momentum and shape, are closely dependent on the strategy adopted in connection with [the father] figure" (49). Commenting on Melville's prose, the scholar distinguishes between the paternal rigor of *Redburn* and *White-Jacket* and "a distortion, a perversion of the narrative vehicle" (53) in *Moby Dick* and *The Confidence-Man*. Michał Paweł Markowski comments that the realist prose and the oedipal conflict are both anchored in sexual repression initiated by the father figure (85). It is this breaking out of the confines of the paternal metaphor that gives Kerouac's texts (*On the Road* together with *Visions of Cody* being exemplary) irregular, frenzied rhythm, perpetuating the lineage of "fatherless" classics of literature.

Sal's quest for the paternal metaphor or, in other words, the knowledge of the phallus which is capable of filling the lack in the m(Other), is that of groping in the dark in the world he has been given to live in. Not knowing what the m(Other) wants (him to be), the protagonist of *On the Road* is tossed between various alternatives of self-realization, none of which can provide a permanent anchor. Sal's madness of cross-country journeys and a lack of household constrains are intertwined with a wish for stasis. Paradise experiences domestic felicity with a Mexican named Terry and her son, Johnny:

> Johnny and I played all the time; he liked me to throw him up in the air and down in the bed. Terry sat mending clothes. I was a man of the earth, precisely as I had dreamed I would be, in Paterson. (OTR 94)

Leaving Old Bull Lee's house in New Orleans he senses the loss he is about to incur:

> Then we were off, the three of us – Dean, Marylou, me. ... I realized I hated to leave Bull's wonderful house so suddenly, but Dean was all energies and ready to do. (OTR 147)

Such farewells often instill in him a sense of guilt just as in Part Two, when, during a trip with Dean, Sal is troubled by pangs of conscience:

> At one point I moaned about life's troubles – how poor my family was, how much I wanted to help Lucille, who was also poor and had a daughter. (OTR 115)

Fluctuating between stability and unsteadiness, balance and a caprice, dependability and undependability, or, in his own words, "between the East of [his] youth and the West of [his] future" (OTR 20), Sal does not cease to search for the optimal coordinates for his well-being.

Dwelling on the sailing instructions given to Odysseus by Kirke, Robert Con Davis observes that the strait of Skylla and Kharybdis, which Odysseus must pass through, acquires the features of opposing forces that attempt to acquire an exclusive control over the subject. The rock of Skylla "incorporates several aspects of the rigidity and the authority of paternal prohibition" which renders "[a]n image of an irresistible demand" (Davis 22). Conversely, the maelstrom of Kharybdis, "lacking in rigidity, ... [presenting itself as] an incessant cycle of sucking and spewing, ... takes in everything to satisfy its insatiable need" (23). The Lacanian concepts of need and demand, referred to by Davis, bring us back to Lacan and his idea of desire as a remainder resulting from subtracting the former from the latter:

> [Desire] is ... the margin, the result of the subtraction as one might say, of the exigency of need with respect to the demand for love. (S V 348)

What Lacan means by his mathematical metaphor is that one's needs have to be articulated in the form of demand, which happens to filter and distort them, leaving some residual space of lacking satisfaction that runs metonymically and can be understood as desire. Davis finds the Lacanian pattern reflected in Odysseus' crossing the strait:

> [i]n Kharybdis is an unbound need (corresponding to the biological needs of the body) – insatiable in themselves and situated always outside of articulation. In Skylla is an absolute demand, unfillable in its inscrutability, which is nonetheless a precursor of the law. Only in the possibility of traversing the passage between need and demand does desire (whose object is the father's law) come into being as a mediation of the two sides. (23)

Such a pattern appears to hold well for Kerouac's *On the Road* insofar as Sal's peregrinations are ruled by either the incessant need of intense sensory gratifications or his longings for stability and love.[78] Out of these two interspersing forces emerges desire, a metonymic articulation of the inerasable leftover which pushes one forward. The desire for the phallus is thus inextricably linked with a quest for the optimal position in the symbolic; the never-ending, always-already failed grasp towards the never-to-be-attained sense of bliss and undifferentiation. The relentlessness of desire and the pressure it fosters is often accentuated by Sal and Dean's comments on the compulsion to move forward. Having gone through a moment of self-alienation in Des Moines, the former exclaims: "But I had to get going and stop moaning" (OTR 20). On another occasion, asked by Sal: "Where we going, man?" the latter responds: "I don't know but we gotta go" (OTR 225). As it has been pointed out, the insatiability of desire finds its articulation in metonymy, which results in Kerouac's use of Whitmanesque catalogues of places, objects and people that proliferate along Sal's way without a halt.

> That was Frisco; and beautiful women standing in white doorways, waiting for their men; and Coit Tower, and the Embarcadero, and Market Street, and the eleven teeming hills.

---

78 Some critics have pointed to the affinities between *On the Road* and Homer's epic. Gregory Stephenson finds the archetypical circular journey of *The Odyssey* to be manifesting in Kerouac's novel (18). Omar Swartz compares the central motif of the latter, the life on the road, as "an odyssey; ... a drama" which emblematizes some sort of "wilderness; [and] not the most direct path between two cities" (66). In Part One of the book Sal Paradise speaks himself of logs on the Mississippi river as of "grand Oddysean logs of our continental dream" (OTR 99).

> I spun around till I was dizzy; I thought I'd fall down as in a dream, clear off the precipice. (OTR 76)

Desire is like a perpetual journey coming along with the ever-unrolling scroll of *On the Road*. As observed by Swartz, "destinations are not important" (66) just as "[t]he objects of the quest (selfhood, love, God, community) [are not]. [They] are elusive; they are grails that appear and vanish, are recovered and lost again" (Stephenson 22). On reaching one of his (seemingly) final destinations, San Francisco, Sal declares without any solace in his voice: "Here I was at the end of America – no more land – and now there was nowhere to go but back" (OTR 75). Kerouac's claim that the truth "exist[s] only in the movement from moment to moment" (Nicosia 279) seems then to second Lacan's idea of desire as an endless circulation of signifiers not depending on stable referents. The Lacanian unconscious takes the subject along a chain of signifiers. In Mexico, Dean will admit: "I want to get on and on – this road drives *me*!!'" (OTR 263) just as Lacan posits that language *speaks us*. Being at the mercy of the metonymy of desire, Sal and Dean might be regarded as passive and deprived of agency contrary to what their frenetic peregrinations and potency might suggest.

On the margins of Lacanian desire there operates a force preying on its insatiability, and this constitutes a drive. Elucidating the dialectic relation between the two, Adrian Johnston notes that "[t]here where desire is frustrated, drive is gratified. Drive gains its satisfaction through vampirically feeding off of the dissatisfaction of desire" (Johnston, "Jacques Lacan"). As a relentless, libidinal and excessive circuit around a given object, drive is a concept carrying the destructive and dangerous potency of going beyond the pleasure principle and annihilating the subject. Offering an approach other than the paternal one, one might see Dean as the perfect epitome of an unyielding and disruptive craving for some cathexed objects and places, which come and go. His restless "response to continual disillusionment is to forsake the destination for the journey: "Move!"" (Vopat 8). As we may remember, in Sal's eyes Dean's reckless behavior and unyielding potency account for his search "to return the way he came" (OTR 126). This is exactly the logic of the drive, which

> as it is understood and taken up by Lacan ..., [is] a constant force, an unending requirement imposed on the psyche due to its link with the body ... . [It is] a factor that, on finding closed the regressive path to the encounter with the lost object – the object of desire – is left with no alternative but to press forward, ... without perspectives of ever ... reaching the goal. (Braunstein 105)

What is more, Dean's excessive nature is reflected in his leisure pursuits. As observed by Foxe, "Dean is the ultimate automobile-obsessed sidekick, a tireless and superbly coordinated driver, a god-like celebrant of the new postwar plenitude of cars and gasoline" (49–50). In *On the Road* the word "drive" smoothly conflates the psychoanalytic term together with the ability of operating a motor vehicle, which could not have escaped Kerouac's attention since Dean's "driving skills are often described in overtly sexual terms" (92). Moriarty and the Lacanian drive take power from exploiting and abandoning places, objects and people. Stephenson writes:

> There is, from the beginning, an element of the con artist in him [Dean], as Sal recognizes, something of the self-seeking trickster, the amoral hipster looking for kicks, the young man on the make. His treatment of people often parallels his treatment of cars: using them, breaking them under the strains of his demands, and then abandoning them. (Stephenson 157)

Desire then, as postulated by Žižek, might be treated well as a metonymic escape from the intrusive and obstinate drive, a movement onward against something which drains life. Perhaps this then is the true subtext of Sal Paradise's claim that the road is "protective" (OTR 210).

As it has been said, when compared with *On the Road*, *Visions of Cody* acquires much more uncompromising formal and linguistic quality, yet it also maintains continuity. Nonlinear, based on mind associations, and apparently incoherent, the book gives the impression of a daring and final stab at solving the mystery of Neal Cassady, and, I have demonstrated, at reinvigorating with this discovery the deficiencies of paternal metaphor in the Kerouacian subject. In this respect, *Visions of Cody* thrives on many recurrent patterns present in *On the Road*. Another rendition of Neal Cassady, Cody Pomeray, is put against the figures of brother and father (the first of which is of paternal quality) just like Dean Moriarty was. The fraternal longings come out when Cody confides in Jack Duluoz, the narrator: "[Y]ou ... said, that, Cody is the brother I lost – not that sense as senses, but a gap in the air along by me in the road ... ." (VOC 363). The words about the lost brother are repeated like a mantra in "Joan Rawshanks in the Fog" in Part Three of the novel (VOC 370–372). No less often do direct identifications with the father figure come out:

> I thought he was insulting my age warning me about my kidneys and right there in men's room I yelled angry words at hum, buttoning my fly ('Don't stop and aim at other urinals, for your beat park days as old man it will be bad for your kidneys, there's nothing worse') just like when Pa and me took a leak in the Chinese restaurant john and he was always an angry, a *hating* man ... . (VOC 428–429)
>
> [L]ike me, he [Cody] sinned against his father; he left him flat in Ogden, I left my father flat in New Haven. (VOC 443–444)
>
> [T]here he smiles in his youth, my father, my Cody. (VOC 454)

In Nicosia's view, Cody and Jack "draw upon the same joint stock of knowledge and wisdom, they effectively become one mind" (372). Writing to Allen Ginsberg and Peter Orlovsky in 1961, Kerouac goes as far as to coin the name "Kerouassady" (SL2 317).

It could be argued that the absence of father figure gets more conspicuous and acute in the second of Kerouac's novels on Neal Cassady; it is as if the text itself adopted the formula of the jeremiad over the paternal deficiency and performed a mournful cry over the loss. As suggested by Matt Theado,

> [o]ne may observe that *On the Road* ... was primarily "about it," while *Visions of Cody is* it: writing is performance. (77)

Given the vast performative literary tactics of the novel, the text of *Visions of Cody* is not only in the mourning but also in the making of a fresh and rectifying paternal metaphor; it is entirely focused on performing and quilting the signified, the emblem of which is Duluoz's companion. However, as a signifier in his own right Cody does not have a fixed referent; in fact, it is quite the opposite since for Duluoz anything may refer to Cody:

> He [Duluoz] is reminded of him [Cody] by various places and ambiences, from subway toilets to church interiors; he sees him in other people and he dreams of him. Cody is for him the ultimate referent of all data. Duluoz then relates/creates Cody's history: his boyhood and his young manhood, his adventures, his feats, his humiliations, his sufferings, and his aspirations. (Stephenson 25)

When confined merely to human figures, Cody is already "a cowboy, a "hanging judge," an "Oklahoma posseman pursuer," an "Assistant D.A.," Clark Gable, ... Franklin D. Roosevelt" (Nicosia 380). Thus, the emergence of *Visions of Cody* epitomizes the Lacanian impasse of language which moves around the object with a view to render it accurately and reach its essence. It does not meet its goals since some of the meaning is, in a Derridean manner, always deferred, always missed. Kerouac's experimental novel, more than *On the Road*, is an attempt to break the distance between the subject and the object, albeit an abortive one. Words revolve around Cody, yet they are short of potency to represent him fully:

> What is the truth? You can't communicate with any other being, forever. Cody is so lost in his private – being – ..., Cody is my friend and he is doomed as I am doomed. (VOC 433)

Hanjo Berressem aptly observes that

> [a]s the experience of the object is always already filtered and distorted by the perceptual apparatus and any object is an inevitably anthropomorphic and anamorphic one, there always remains infinitesimal distance between subject and object. (Berressem 20)

Kerouac seems to be gaining awareness of the anamorphism and the inerasable distance in the process of writing the novel; the more angles he takes to portray Cody (such tactics gets condensed in the Joan Rawshank episode), the more he learns that Cody is already lost as a (paternal) object:

> I've had several visions of Cody, ... (this is all like bop, we're getting to it indirectly and too late but completely from every angle except the angle we all don't know) ... . (VOC 342–343)

Nicosia points to the limitation of knowledge as "one of the book's main themes" (374). It gets manifested in the protagonist's words when Duluoz reminisces over the time spent together with Cody in 1947:

> [W]e [Jack and Cody] ... were frightened by the darkness in the house, in fact the creaking mystery, philosophical void, the missing of the point, the obvious sadness of having to die never having to know something about everything and ourselves ... . (VOC 396)

The monologic and litanic passages of *Visions of Cody* might remind one of the late Beckett and his motif of "the ultimate isolation of mind" (Nicosia 376). Jack Duluoz, like the writer himself, realizes that he will not breach the subject-object dualism and that "each retelling is an additional loss" (Nicosia 380). We witness the anticipation of such a subtraction of essence in Part One of the novel, where Duluoz muses over the nightly views from a Manhattan cafeteria:

> [t]here is a huge plate-glass through which the narrator can see the street outside, and in the reflections of which he can also see the interior of the cafeteria. Additionally, there is a mirrored column inside the cafeteria, and the shiny fender of a car parked on the street, which multiply the reflections. Kerouac reports every image and reflected image and re-reflected image until he has woven a web so hallucinatory that it defies definition in terms of conventional reality. (Nicosia 385)

This allows Nicosia to claim that Kerouac's work is to

> examine the way reality is perceived as a rainbow body of light, reflected and refracted so many times that the percipient is prevented from tracing its origin. (310)

The futility of both language and a worn-off reality built up on it occasionally lurk through Kerouac's prose. We read in Part Two:

> people ... in a gnashing map of earth pronounce vowels and consonants around a nothing, they bite the air, there's nothing to say because you can't say what you know, it's a void, a Demosthenes pebble would have to drop way long down to hit that kind of bottom. (VOC 109)
>
> (but I've *known* the world it's all happened before, why do I kid myself with these artificial *newnesses*). (VOC 141)

All one can do, Kerouac seems to be saying, is to admire "a sense of the preciousness of things perceived but once, never to be recaptured in the same configuration" (Nicosia 345). This seems to account for *Visions of Cody* as the subject's momentary delight with a chance for the paternal metaphor, with a fleeing-in-a-minute taste of a perfect configuration of the signifier and the signified that is bound to go.

As with Dean Moriarty, "a symbol of lost possibilities" (Carden 93), the Kerouacian subject eventually farewells with Cody ("Adios, King" (VOC 463) being the final words of the novel) once he runs out of visions of his companion. Just before the end of the book, Cody is being pronounced free, dead, "blanked at last" (VOC 462), which again empties the signifier of the paternal metaphor. Yet, the emptiness the reader is left with seems to continue to speak and mean. Not far from the end of the novel Jack Duluoz, or rather the author himself, pronounces what is perhaps the most significant statement of the entire novel and what gives his rationale for the creation of *Visions of Cody*: "I wrote this book because we're all going to die" (VOC 427). This somewhat obscure declaration might be elucidated by the prism of what Alenka Zupančič writes about the death of Antigone:

> Death can enter the symbolic order as a kind of an absolute signifier, as a "negative" signifier of everything that the subject *is* .... The list of things that she [Antigone] will be deprived of by her early death (not only the things that she has and will lose, but also the things that she does not have but could have had, had she continued to live) does not have the function of expressing a regret. It has a very precise function of making a "whole" out of the inconclusive metonymy of her existence and of her desire. By accepting the death and speaking of it in the above-mentioned terms, Antigone puts an end to the metonymy of desire by realizing, in one go, the in(de)finite potential of this metonymy. Precisely because of its being in(de)finite, this potential can only be realized (constituted as an accomplished, "whole" entity) *as lost*, that is, cast in the negative form. Here, the realization equals representation of the subject's being that is by definition non-representable. (186)

Written in the event of the real death of all who live and interpreted from the point of view of Zupančič's commentary, Kerouac's novel becomes an exercise in performing an accomplished entity out of incongruity of life. Lamenting over what is impossible, what is lost, and what could have been, the writer casts negativity into a potent and positive signifying value. In this respect, both Cody Pomeray and the novel are turned into "*symbols* of lost possibilities." As such they express the true tenor of Kerouac's book, which is the celebration of life as unfulfillable. They are victorious over the ontological and epistemological chaos and death when Jack Duluoz states: "I not only accept loss forever, I am made of loss" (VOC 462).

Finally, both *On the Road* and *Visions of Cody* feed on nostalgia to channel the out-of-placeness and confusion of their characters. Notwithstanding a nostalgic aura permeating his body of work, Kerouac made hardly any attempt at pondering the phenomenon or even merely acknowledging the feeling. The same holds for Lacan, who never examined the notion of nostalgia thoroughly, nor did he address it directly as a theoretical entity. However, when confronted, psychoanalytic theory and literature once again unleash their potential to complement one another in the field of *nóstos* and *álgos*, which makes it possible to read both Lacan and Kerouac "nostalgically." Deconstructing nostalgia into its characteristic traits, one will easily notice how integral for psychoanalytic theory its components prove to be. This is particularly true in the case of Lacan who, in his return to Freud, shifted emphasis to lack, loss, and unsatisfiable desire as constitutive for human subjectivity. In this part of my analysis I will outline what Lacanian nostalgia might mean in order to subsequently confront it with the literary worlds of *On the Road* and *Visions of Cody*.

Due to the lack of Lacan's own clarification over the notion of nostalgia, it may be worth turning to other commentators on the topic as a possible source of mediation and anchorage for some Lacanian ideas. In *The Future of Nostalgia* Svetlana Boym observes that

> [m]odern nostalgia is a mourning for the impossibility of mythical return, for the loss of an enchanted world with clear borders and values; it could be a secular expression of a spiritual longing, a nostalgia for an absolute, a home that is both physical and spiritual, the edenic unity of time and space before entry into history. (8)

Fernando Pessoa seems to second Boym's words in a passsage from *The Book of Disquiet*:

> The feelings that hurt most, the emotions that sting most, are those that are absurd: the longing for impossible things, precisely because they are impossible; nostalgia for what never was; the desire for what could have been; regret over not being someone else. ... All these half-tones of the soul's consciousness create in us a painful landscape, an eternal sunset of what we are. ... I don't know if we weren't in fact other beings, whose greater completeness we can sense today, incompletely, forming at best a sketchy notion of their lost solidity in the two dimensions of our present lives, mere shadows of what they were. (484–486)

Similar in overtone, both of these commentaries on nostalgia share a certain Lacanian underpinning, which can be verified by looking at particular concepts of the French analyst. As emphasized before, one of the key terms here is that of object a (also known as "object petit a"). *L'objet petit a* is closely linked to the subject's fantasy. It might even be viewed as the cause of human fantasy since it emerges as the object-cause of the desire to redeem some assumed and undefined loss that one experiences having entered the symbolic. Once again, one should bear in mind that object a is not a goal but the cause of the search for a redeeming factor, which takes the forms of numerous real-life objects being desired by the subject and never standing up to the task of satisfying that desire. Although not overtly manifested, *l'objet petit a* can be epitomized as a void infinitely filled with hopes for final fulfilment. As explained earlier, such a void is simply the effect of every subject's symbolic existence, whose deficiency demands something beyond signifiers. Thus, object little a proves to be something which actually never was; it is always-already lost the moment one enters into language, and it is the effect of language. What is present is the subject's repetitive and endless revolving around the emptiness of the lost object. All this proves that the nostalgic in a Lacanian perspective takes nothing short of an ontological value.

Further consideration of the notions of return and repetition may serve as a commentary to what Lacanian nostalgia might be. It finds its embodiment in the two Lacanian terms of *tuche* and *automaton*, the missed encounters with the trauma of the real and the subsequent urges of language to give it a meaningful shape. Being always too late at the scene and being denied the real, the network of signifiers is forced to return again and again. These returns are ultimately nostalgic returns to a given object (which, in the end, is always object a), and they are representative of nostalgia insofar as they are impossible encounters. Due to deficiencies of language, they seem to be always too late and always too far from what they revolve around.

Not less important for what might be termed as Lacanian nostalgia is Lacan's theory of the gaze. The concept has been widely addressed by many thinkers, including Sartre or Foucault. According to Lacan, while the eye is located on the side of the subject, the gaze is something located on the side of the object; it belongs to the Other. Elaborating it further, it is some spot in the latter that captivates the viewer by gazing at him or her, or in Slavoj Žižek's words, it is "the point at which the observer is already included, inscribed in the observed scene" (Žižek, quoted by Schreiber, "Reader, Text, and Subjectivity"). This means that the emergence of the gaze blurs the line of division between the subject and the object, or in other words, it "undermines our position as "neutral," "objective" observer" (Žižek, quoted by Schreiber, "Reader, Text, and Subjectivity"). Jennifer Friedlander adds that the gaze is

> the unsettling, but enthralling, object around which the scopic drive revolves, alternately positioning the subject as viewer and viewed, creating both "unrealistic anxiety" and a sense of self-scrutiny. (12)

Žižek argues that such a sense of self-scrutiny and self-awareness is characteristic of nostalgia; namely, the nostalgic subject "sees in the object (in the image it views) its own gaze [and experiences an] illusion of self-mirroring" (Žižek, *Looking Awry* 114). By this he means, "the function of the nostalgic object [and the nostalgic subject, we might argue] is precisely to conceal the antinomy between eye and gaze" (Žižek, quoted by Schreiber, "Reader, Text, and Subjectivity"). In Lacan's cryptic description: I am captured by the gaze as "I see myself seeing myself" (S XI 80). This is basically nothing else than the nostalgic subject's wish to merge with the object since "[n]ostalgia represents a momentary fulfilment of an imaginary completeness or synthesis" (Schreiber, *Subversive Voices* 17).

The aforementioned aspects of what Lacanian nostalgia is may be found in many of Kerouac's novels. The hollow presence of object a finds its most notable rendition in *On the Road* and its characters' mad search for the unfathomable "IT," "the moment when you know all and everything is decided forever" (OTR 123), which is supposed to grant them some undefined sense of completion and bliss. As we remember, prompted by the sense of loss, Sal becomes enthralled by Dean and both engage in a series of peregrinations, which are the paragon of a metonymic, item-filled desire to find fulfilment. According to the concept of *automaton*, there is no end to the chain of signifiers, nor to Sal's metonymical revolving around that which is missing, since the lack and insufficiency are inscribed in the realm of the symbolic. This is what Jacques Lacan means when he claims that metonymy serves nostalgia (Écrits 430). Sal Paradise finds no final solace in any of his destinations. Similarly, in *Visions of Cody* Pomeray dares to claim that "[r]oads never end" (VOC 430). The phantasmatic object-cause of (the peregrinations and) desire, "IT," cannot be pinpointed in any signifier, it does not succumb to words, just as when Dean talks with Sal:

> 'Now, man, that alto man last night had IT – he held it once he found it; I've never seen a guy who could hold so long.' I wanted to know what 'IT' meant. 'Ah well' – Dean laughed – 'now you're asking me impon-de-rables – ahem! (OTR 194)

The lack of mutual understanding results from the hollow (and anamorphic) nature of object a. Signifying lack, it can be occupied by many signifiers, and consequently the idea of "IT" is bound to differ from person to person. Using Lacanian metaphors, Sal and Dean are the troubadours exercising the impossible love to the Lady; they sublimate a number of themes into "IT" which "couldn't have any real concrete equivalent" (S VII 148).

Although object a is as ungraspable as it is a hollow, some lost filler for the empty space is tangible to the protagonists all the way. Leaving New York, Sal senses the vanity of all yearnings and ponders:

> The one thing that we yearn for in our living days, that makes us sigh and groan and undergo sweet nauseas of all kinds, is the remembrance of some lost bliss that was

> probably experienced in the womb and can only be reproduced (though we hate to admit it) in death. (OTR 118–119)

Later in the novel Sal speaks of stars as of the lonely "Prince of Dharma who's lost his ancestral grove and journeys across spaces ... trying to find it again" (OTR 210). Examples of the Freudian fixation in secondary narcissism, Sal's statements might be complemented by Michael Skau's argument that one

> manifestation of the identity problem in Kerouac's novels involves the idealization of childhood and the reluctance to surrender the innocence and imaginative liberty of childhood. ("The Makings of Paradise" 159)

Looking through the prism of nostalgia, one may now hypothesize that Sal and Dean's living at breakneck speed paradoxically performs the stillness of the pre-subjective existence. As observed by Jean Baudrillard in *America*,

> [s]peed is simply the rite that initiates us into emptiness: a nostalgic desire for forms to revert to immobility, concealed beneath the very intensification of their mobility. (7)

Undergirded with nostalgia, Sal and Dean's America of the mid-twentieth century can thus be seen as a specific mental topography; a metonymic network of routes taken and retraced to experience inactivity.

Visions of Cody might finally be read as a perfect exposure of the nostalgic gaze. The peculiar character of Jack Duluoz's approach lies in his attempt to merge with the object of focus that is simultaneously the object of his nostalgia (as I have already demonstrated, a failed attempt). As concluded by Matt Theado, "Duluoz manages a sympathetic perception and for a time sees the world as Cody must have seen it ... He has acquired Cody's vision" (76). The perception of the subject's own act of seeing in the gaze of the object is conspicuous, as Duluoz declares: "I'll look on the world like he does" (Kerouac, quoted by Theado, 298). The line of division between the captivated subject and the captivating object gets blurred when the narrator harmonizes his own psychological coordinates with the eyes of the nostalgic object in the following two ekphrastic comments:

> In this Clark Gable mustachio old Civil War photo Cody would sit there, ... mighty-hands a-rest, with his high cheekbones mystifying back his eyes and deeply glinting with Indian mysteries and the past: this is the enigmatic Cody, the sad one, the one who said hello to tragedy in a womb, and heads now for his raving grave and greedy sleep. (VOC 418)
>
> This is the picture of Cody in the first days of his reformed marriage. ... Our, his children will look at that and say 'My daddy was a strapping young man in 1950, he strutted down the street as cute as can be ... . (VOC 454)

What calls for particular attention is the way Jack Duluoz confuses the pronouns "our" and "his" in the second fragment, making the internalization of the object's gaze evident. At the end of the novel he will blatantly admit: "I'm made of Cody" (VOC 464).

"Roads never end" nor does the Duluozian subject's quest for the paternal signifier. Out of *On the Road* and *Visions of Cody* the "fondlings, revisings, [and] moldings" protrude into the successive instalments of the Duluoz legend.

8 "If I Were God I'd Have the Word" – *Visions of Gerard, Satori in Paris* and *Vanity of Duluoz*

Compared to *On the Road* and *Visions of Cody*, both emerging from the deficiencies of the paternal metaphor and being first to articulate these (both in form and content of the novel), many of the successive installments of the Duluoz legend reinvigorate the tropes of the missing father figure and thus maintain Duluoz's metonymic quest for the paternal. These tropes are governed by what both novels on Neal Cassady already tried to do to the fatherly. They set up a paradigm of a predominantly sturdy, domineering, courageous, prophet-like figure, offering its knowledge and guidance to the inert and stupefied Kerouacian subject. The further installments of the legend are no different; repetitive in the act of reinstalling the paradigmatic paternal metaphor, they sustain the relentless Lacanian desire to know what it means to possess the phallus.[79] In Kerouac's next novel, *Doctor Sax: Faust Part Three* (1959), we are presented with the mysterious Dr. Sax figure. A blend of a pulp fiction superhero (based on the protagonist of *The Shadow* radio program) and an ethereal, menacing figure looming over the adolescent Jackie Duluoz, the character is a residue of secret knowledge which can help the Kerouacian subject to overcome his fears of growing up and introduce him into maturity. *The Dharma Bums* (1958) offers another incarnation of an active brotherly/fatherly hero followed by the passive narrator and protagonist of the novel (Ray Smith). Japhy Ryder, a Buddhist rendition of Dean Moriarty/Cody Pomeray (Kerouac himself regarded *The Dharma Bums* as the sequel to *On the Road*), modelled on the poet Gary Snyder, provides the first-person narrator with his (Buddhist) guidance through the uncertainties of the modern world. As suggested by Theado, more responsible, pensive and reliable than Dean Moriarty, Ryder is "the healthy alternative" to Neal Cassady-based characters (155). It is also Neal Cassady that reenters the stage of the Duluoz legend a few more times, most notably in *Big Sur* (1962), as a menacing figure of Cody Pomeray, coming back to the wretched Jack Duluoz as a reminder of the wild past.

---

79 Michael Skau provides a number of examples on how real figures happened to make up for Kerouac's fatherlessness. See Skau 163.

Continually displaced throughout the entire Duluoz legend, the paternal metaphor is an inherent feature that repeatedly intervenes into the structure and content of Kerouac's novels. Its paradigm, however, changes in the late works of the American writer. As Kerouac's prose starts to acquire a more visceral take (mainly as the result of fame and success), so does the process of making up for the paternal insufficiency. One might claim that the ultimate instance accountable for holding the (imaginary) phallus and positing a chance for the completion of the symbolic castration is the figure of God. Also, with turning to God comes the Kerouacian subject's corresponding quest of retracing one's origins. The circular return of Jack Duluoz has not escaped critical evaluation. Commenting on the presence of the Campbellian monomyth in the Duluoz legend, Gregory Stephenson names the last stage of the Kerouacian subject's journey as relating to the return to God:

> The hero finally attains a vision or achieves atonement with God and then returns home, reintegrated into the community bringing a regenerating power or message to society and to the entire world. (18)

A psychoanalytic reading of Kerouac's work appears to anticipate and corroborate the possibility of such a paternal trajectory, which for Lacan takes the form of perversion. In *On the Names-of-the-Father* Lacan writes:

> Here we see the value of the stress I allowed to be placed on the function of perversion as regards its relationship to the Other's desire as such. It represents the backing into a corner and the taking literally of the function of the Father or supreme Being. The eternal God taken to the letter, not of his jouissance that is always veiled and unfathomable, but of his desire as involved in the larger scheme of things – this is the core where, petrifying his anxiety, the pervert instates himself as such. (76–77)

Hyldgaard elucidates the complex links between Lacanian perversion and the figure of God: "the pervert is submitted to the Other's desire" and since both the father and God might be fantasized as the not-lacking Other, who has the knowledge of what and how to desire, ""The Lord's will be done" could be the motto of perversion" ("The Conformity of Perversion"). This has tangible implications for the Duluoz legend as the Kerouacian subject (re)turns to the figures of God and home as the alleged, not-lacking holders of the phallus. Such a turn might be said to be prefigured as early as in *Visions of Cody*, where Jack Duluoz's pronouncement: "If I were God I'd have the word" (VOC 433) articulates and discloses the above-mentioned phantasm (the character of Dean Moriarty/Cody Pomeray is endowed with godly features to a substantial extent). The actual "fondlings, revisings, moldings, addings, removings, graftings, tearings, correctings," to use Peter Martin's formulations, help the Kerouacian subject to establish the final correspondence to the signifier of the father in the late installments of the Duluoz legend, *Visons of Gerard* (1963), *Satori in Paris* (1966), and *Vanity of Duluoz* (1968).[80]

The first of the aforementioned novels is a venture to immortalize Gerard, Kerouac's older brother, who died at the age of nine of rheumatic fever. Suspended between an eulogy and a hagiography, *Visions of Gerard* is a projection of a child, young Jack Duluoz (referred to in the book as Ti Jean Duluoz), who perceives the brief life of his brother as that of a martyr and a saint. Kerouac's Christian and Buddhist leanings find their way into the novel to a large extent since the story of Gerard is for Jack Duluoz "a dream that ended, life is a dream that ends" (VOG 14). Significantly for the purpose of this analysis, exalting Gerard's life and death is yet another attempt of the Kerouacian subject to set up an ideal configuration of the (paternal) signifier and the signified so as to win the fatherly knowledge. As observed by Nicosia, "what Gerard gave Jack was what Jack made of Gerard: the symbol of a process in himself" (502). With *Visions of Gerard* the current stage of this process is a prefiguration of an altered paradigm of the paternal metaphor, the one that shall, first and foremost, hold tight to divinity and sanctity. Additionally, the already-discussed argument that the absence of the father necessitates the narrative allows one to treat Gerard as another father figure who initiates the discourse; as pointed by Nicosia, "Kerouac intimates that the depth of his writing is due to the *loss* of Gerard" (503).

An alcohol-fuelled travelogue, *Satori in Paris* is an account of Kerouac's 10-day trip to Paris and Brittany with the aim of self-inquiry through genealogical research of his family name. As indicated by title, the narrator (here, Jack Kerouac) experiences several illuminating epiphanies that go under the Japanese name of "satori." According to Nicosia, "[t]he actual terms of ... narrator's journey are profoundly Christian" and with his quest for origins "Jack is seeking the Grail" (661). The nature of this "Grail" can be again well referred to the paternal metaphor insofar as the experience the Kerouacian subject goes through is "a reaffirmation of his father's heritage and values" (Foster, quoted by Jones, *The Mythic Form* 205). The mood of the novel might be therefore described as optimistic; establishing links with the past offers Kerouac an opportunity to test

80 Composed in 1956, *Visions of Gerard* may well be negated as a late work of the American writer, yet, as I believe, with its fixation on the theme of sanctity, it thematically fits the choice of novels. *Pic* (1971), published posthumously, is considered more of "an amalgam of [Kerouac's] early writing" (Theado 171) and has not been considered thereof.

the possibility of the forgotten (com)union with other people. Nicosia speaks of Kerouac's rationale behind the novel: "If life is *not* a dream, there is then the possibility of reaching others – communicating with and helping them" (661). The secret thread and an innate propensity that binds this experience is the Kerouacian subject's search for the (com)union with the symbolic father, which, in Hrebeniak's view, comes down to "the poisonous urge for conquest, dogma, and hierarchy" (123).

As Kerouac's final work, *Vanity of Duluoz* is often referred to by critics as a tie to the American writer's literary universe and a circular close to the Duluoz legend. In Stephenson's view, "*Vanity of Duluoz* serves both as a conclusion and as a coda to The Duluoz legend, bringing the quest to the final ending, returning the traveler home" (47). Covering to a large extent the years and events of *The Town and the City* and given the subtitle "an adventurous education," the work overlays one of the major themes of Kerouac's debut novel and is another account of "the American need to clear out of claustrophobic small-town settlement ... and seek 'adventurous education' on the road" (Hrebeniak 16). As a paraphrase of *The Town and the City* it also "ends with the death of his father" (Nicosia 678). With the final installment, however, "Kerouac slows down into a negative epiphany of compulsive stasis" (Hrebeniak 128) since the overbearing feeling permeating the work is the eponymous vanity, which makes all endeavors look insignificant. Yet, one would be mistaken to estimate this as the sign of Kerouac's final defeat; on the contrary, despite its subject matter, the work "emerg[es] from misery and mortification to realize an affirmative tone and beatific vision" (Giamo 204) and as such makes the "attainment of the peace beyond vanity ... [one] of the book's themes" (Nicosia 674). Humorous and sarcastic, *Vanity of Duluoz* actually tries to convey how tragic life is in its triviality and offer some consoling word of advice in a lose-lose situation; as Nicosia puts it, "Kerouac would make a fool out of himself and everybody else, to reveal how serious life is" (673). A positive outcome is the sudden realization that the earthly troubles and desires do not matter in the end. Jack Duluoz attempts at "detach[ing] him[self] from the vanity of ego" (Nicosia 678) and "affirms the nobility of silence; it is more honest than talk, and the only cure for vanity" (Nicosia 681). A part of this retreat involves turning to God ("vanitas vanitatum, et omnia vanitas") and family lineage as instances offering a promise of and an anchor in an omniscient and omnipotent father, dreamt of by the Kerouacian subject as early as in *The Town and the City*. Thus, interlinking God, family heritage, as well as the authorial comeback to the beginnings of the Duluoz legend, *Vanity of Duluoz* posits the space where various emanations of the return and the father trope intersperse for the last time.

In his ponderings over the absent father figure in Melville's prose, Régis Durand suggests the possible logics of the textual return of the symbolic father. One of the postulated operations regulates the paternal lack by translating

> the image of the father into a conventional or institutional figure, say a captain, a hero, or a god. All of those figures go with a hierarchic, linear, and "discursive" vision of time and narrative, which is evidence that what is at stake is a reassertion of the authority of conventional models. (54)

Kerouac's "fatherless" prose seems to align to the above-mentioned model seeking to reinstate the missing father. After the heroic and captain-like commanding figures, such as the ones modelled on Neal Cassady (Dean Moriarty is referred to by Sal Paradise as "that mad Ahab at the wheel" (OTR 221)), the dispossessed paternal signifier becomes attracted to the image of God. If, as observed by Hrebeniak, in the late Kerouac "the freedom asserted through wild acts ... disintegrates into dependency and nostalgia for the hegemonies of Church and State" (127), then the hegemony of God sought after by the Kerouacian subject is yet another possibility for it to arrange its union with the missing symbolic father. Similarly to the beginnings of the Duluoz legend, the lack of the fatherly is experienced by the Kerouacian subject as the pre-oedipal stage, the imaginary preoccupation with "the [mother's] ... lack of the phallus" (S III 319). This is nothing less than the unyielding fixation on the undifferentiated, homogenous space of the motherly, which makes one experience the atomized, opposition-driven consciousness as something acute and distressful. Consequently, Kerouac's late novels are a mirror of the author, who "sees separateness as the cause of suffering ... [a]nd the flaw that makes him vulnerable is consciousness" (Nicosia 503). Daydreaming about his college years, sporting and literary successes, Jack Duluoz suddenly perceives all of these as achieved in vain and turns to Heaven as greater, undifferentiated space:

> [Waking up] I suddenly realized that all my ambitions, no matter how they came out, they just came out fairly ordinary ... .
> It just didn't matter what I did, anytime, anywhere, with anyone, life is funny like I said.
> I suddenly realized we were all crazy and had nothing to work for except the next meal and the next good sleep.
> O God in the Heavens, what a fumbling, hand-hanging, goof world it is, that people actually think they can gain anything from either this, or that, or thissa and thatta, and in so doing, corrupt their sacred graves in the name of sacred-grave corruption. (VOD 87)

The (imaginary) holder of the key (the imaginary phallus) to regaining peace with oneself (whether by attaining undifferentiation, or coming to terms with the impossibility of undifferentiation), is the authority of God, which is projected onto a number of characters in the final installments of the Duluoz legend. First and foremost, this is the case of Gerard, attributed with many godly features. In Ti Jean's hagiographic projections, his prematurely dead brother reminds one of an angel-like figure, a pure and innocent infant:

> Saintly Gerard, his pure and tranquil face, the mournful look of him, the piteousness of his little soft shroud of hair failing down his brow and swept aside by the hand over blue serious eyes. (VOG 7)

We also learn that the father "explain[s] moralities to his angels" (VOG 21). As a little saint, Gerard is said to be granted a prophetic insight into the mysteries of God's kingdom, which finds him numerous followers:

> [T]he nuns of St. Louis de France Parochial School were at his bedside to take down his dying words because they'd heard his astonishing revelations of heaven delivered in catechism class on no more encouragement that it was his turn to speak (VOG 7)
> ""Heaven is all white" ... he'd tell me" (VOG 11)

Ti Jean's brother is capable of communicating with animals, especially birds (VOG 26). Significantly, as a paternal figure, he offers protection and advice on conduct to his younger sister (VOG 24) as well as Ti Jean, who has the following fantasy of Gerard's daydreaming during a lesson:

> Gerard dreams that he is sitting in a yard, on some house steps with me, his little brother, in the dream he's thinking sorrowfully: "Since the beginning of time I've been charged to take care of this little brother, my Ti Jean, my poor Ti Jean who cries he's afraid –" and he is about to stroke me on the head, as I sit there drawing a stick around in the sand ... . (VOG 64)

Looked at through the prism of the fatherly, *Visions of Gerard* presents the reader with a peculiar phantasmatic network, a scene of interidentifications between the father (Emil Duluoz), Gerard, and Ti Jean, where differentiating between the subject and the object ceases to operate. In the beginning of the novel the Kerouacian subject speaks of himself and his brother as one, which might remind us of the nostalgic gaze operating in *Visions of Cody*:

> For the first four years of my life, while he lived, I was not Ti Jean Duluoz, I was Gerard, the world was his face, ... the heartbreakingness and the holiness and his teachings of tenderness to me, and my mother constantly reminding me to pay attention to his goodness and advice. (VOG 7–8)
> For me the first four years of my life are permeant and gray with the memory of a kindly serious face bending over me and being me and blessing me ... . (VOG 10)
> When the little kitty is given his milk, I imitate Gerard and get down on my stomach and watch him greedily licking up his milk with pink tongue and chup chup jowls – ...

> They see me in the parlor imitating Gerard with imaginary talks back and forth concerning lambs, kitties, clouds. (VOG 127)

At times, Gerard is fantasized as somebody representing the affirmative side of the paternal authority, as opposed to Emil Duluoz strongly objecting to Ti Jean's plans. *Visions of Gerard* contains another rendition of the father-son conflict already present in *The Town and the City*. As Lacanian theory would suggest, its purpose is to overwrite the disturbing encounter with the father by "returning (to the scene) with a difference:"

> "Arguments that raged ... between my father and myself about my refusal to go to work – "I wanta *write* – I'm an *artist*" – "Artist shmartist, ya can't be supported all ya life –" ... And I wonder what Gerard would have done had he lived, sickly, artistic ... .
> "Me when I'm big, I'm gonna be a painter of beautiful pictures and I'm gonna build beautiful bridges" (VOG 62)

Despite being at times positioned at opposite poles, Gerard and his father's ways often converge; in Ti Jean's vision, they show a high degree of mutual commonality. Emil is described as "a reverend, sensitive man, apt-to-understand man, ... the way he shook his head (that little Gerard imitated)" (VOG 95–96). On another occasion Ti Jean's brother ponders the status of reality: ""Maybe there's nothing at all," he divines in his lucid pureness – "Just like the smoke that comes out of Papa's pipe"" (VOG 34). It is also the father who appears to imitate Gerard as during the former's conversation with his friend, Old Bull Balloon:

> His head is held slightly to one side, as I say a little like Gerard, but in this case, the father's sadness is held inside a manly grace, or rather, a manly brace, the philosophicalness abides higher in the cranium here than it can in the recentness-film of the angel child ... .(VOG 116)

Finally, Emil Duluoz's habits are emulated by Ti Jean. Reminiscing over his father's practices, the narrator admits:

> He had a habit I can't forget, even now I just imitated it, lightning a small fire in the ashtray, out of cigarette pack paper or tobacco wrapping – Sitting in his chair he'd watch the little Nirvana fire consume the paper and render it black crisp void" (VOG 25)

Yet, as it becomes evident, the major point of convergence between all three characters is the death and absence of the fatherly. Nicosia believes that although "the father's death is not portrayed in this novel [*Visions of Gerard*], ... it is amply foreshadowed" (503) by what happens to Gerard. After the latter's death, Ti Jean's projections bear much resemblance to these of Sal Paradise envisioning the Shrouded Traveler, the ghostly reminder of the empty space of the paternal:

> An old dream too I had of me glooping, that night, in the parlor, by Gerard's coffin, I don't see him in the coffin but he's there, his ghost, his brown ghost, and I'm grown sick in my papers (my writing papers, my bloody 'literary career' ladies and gentlemen) and the whole reason why I ever wrote at all and drew breath to bite in vain with pen of ink, great gad with indefensible Usable pencil, because of Gerard, the idealism, Gerard the religious hero – *"Write in honor of his death" (Ecrivez pour l'amour de son mort)* (as one would say, write for the love of God) – (VOG 131–132)

As it can be seen, writing in the honor of a protective, paternal figure transits into writing for the love of God, who, in the Kerouacian subject's act of a hopeless and desperate hypostasis, is begged to be the reality itself:

> What you learn the first time you get drunk at sixteen, tugging at old urinaters in Moody Street saloons and yelling "Don't you realize you are God?" is what you learn when you understand the meaning that's here before you on this heavy earth: living but to die... look at the sky, stars; look at the tomb, dead – In invoking the help, Transcendental help from other spheres of this Imaginary Blossom, invoke at least, by plea, for the learning of the lesson: – help me understand that I am God – that it's all God – (VOG 137–138)

Interestingly, after Gerard's death, the (textual) reality of *Visions of Gerard* appears to be losing its coherence as if the paternal stopped securing the rules upholding its organization and the symbolic register revealed its own conventionality. During Gerard's funeral Ti Jean experiences the reality as "the scene behind the scene" (VOG 131); people, things and language reveal themselves as imitative and dispossessed of essence, which entails a loose, free-associating, catalogue-like manner:

> [T]he scene behind the scene ... shows itself compounded be, of emptiness, of pure light, of imagination, of mind, mind-only, madness, mental woe, ... the working-at-thinking which is all this imagined death & false life, phantasmal beings, phantoms finagling in the gloom, goopy poor figures haranguing and failing with lack-hands in a fallen-angel world of shadows and glore, ... the unbelievable Truth that cracks open in my head like an oyster and I see it, the house disappears in her Swarm of Snow, Gerard is dead and the soul is dead and the world is dead and dead is dead. (VOG 131)

For the late Kerouac the sense of living in the world full of misery and vanity seems to run accordantly with the need and acceptance of suffering. In *Visions of Gerard* Emil Duluoz's pointing to the misery of his son appears to go beyond the personal and make a statement about the human condition in general:

> [B]ig scowling Emil Pop Duluoz our father ... [p]atting his sickly little Gerard on the head, *"Mon pauvre ti Loup*, me poor little Wolf, you were born to suffer ... . (VOG 10)

In Ti Jean's eyes, suffering nurtures decency and sanctity since struggling with it allows one to surpass the limitations and deficiencies of the earthly kind and become a supreme being:

> With my little hands clasped behind me I stand at the kitchen window, ... watching the inky snowflakes descend from infinity and hit the ground where they become miraculous white, whereby I understand why Gerard was so white and because of man came such black sources – It was by virtue of his pain-on-earth, that his black was turned to white. (VOG 32–33)

In *Vanity of Duluoz* the apologetics of pain-on-earth go as far as to be turned into a methodology or a textbook of suffering when Jack Duluoz states that what he tells the reader is "the story of the techniques of suffering in the working world, which includes football and war" (VOD 100). As observed by James T. Jones,

> [i]n Kerouac's mind, representing the sufferings of friends and family ... resulted in a passion play in which the artist redeemed the sins of others by his own suffering. (*The Mythic Form* 84)

Accordingly, the late works of the American writer perform a textual passion play and Kerouac, or rather the Kerouacian subject, "comes to see himself as the type of figure of Christ, suffering the repeated pain of self-examination in his writing" (*The Mythic Form* 212). Significant for a Lacanian perspective on Kerouac's late oeuvre is an inextricable interdependence between the suffering and the possible access to the paternal metaphor. What Robert Con Davis notes about Odysseus, Christ and suffering:

> [W]e can wonder whether passivity as a state may not be a prerequisite of action. Using the term "passivity" in this way, we draw on its original meaning, "being capable of suffering" (*passivus* in Latin), the sense in which Christ undergoes the "passion" of crucifixion. In this sense, Odysseus, who was initially incapable of suffering the discipline of restraint in Troy, ... undergoes an education by suffering exile – one like Christ's exile on Earth – as he waits for Zeus' intervention. Once he can properly sustain the son's passion, he has been educated and can proceed toward home. Passivity in *The Odyssey*, then, is a total surrender, a suffering in relationship with the father, "so that," as John T. Irwin notes for the Christian context, "the Son's will becomes one with, is wed to, that of the Father" – suffering being an avenue to the knowledge about the father. (8)

In light of the above, turning to the figure of God in the final stage of the Kerouacian subject's search for paternal metaphor becomes only more logical and justified. Duluoz's "adventurous education" might well be read as education in suffering (on his earthly exile) and passivity, which will ultimately lead to the acceptance of the paternal castration. One of the premises for the latter to operate is learning and accepting the fact that the father is also lacking. Jack Duluoz seems to sense such a gap in God/the paternal when he speculates that being like Jesus would not be effortless since "there's a hole even in Jesus' bag" (VOD 264). It seems, however, that the Kerouacian subject does not (want to) assume the lacking father figure.

Most notable cases of a self-subsumed passion and Christ-like suffering are discernible in the fragments depicting the death of Jack Duluoz's father. Spending time in Queens General Hospital, Duluoz notices the utter atrocity of life:

> It is, face it, a mean heartless creation emanated by a God of Wrath, Jehovah, Yaweh, No-Name, who will pat you kindly on your head and say 'Now you're being good' when you pray, but when you're begging for mercy ..., when Yaweh's really got you out in the back of the barn even in ordinary torture of fatal illness like my Pa's then, he won't listen, he will whack away at your lil behind with the long stick of what they called 'Original Sin' in the Theological Christian dogmatic sects but what I call 'Original Sacrifice'. That's not even worse, for God's sake, than watching your own human father Pop die in real life, when you really realize 'Father, Father, why has thou forsaken me?' for real, the man who gave you hopeful birth is copping out right before your eyes and leaves you flat with the whole problem and burden (your self) of his own foolishness in ever believing that 'life' was worth anything .... Your human father sits there in death before you almost satisfied. That's what's so sad and horrible about the 'God is Dead' movement in contemporary religion, it's the most tearful and forlorn philosophical idea of all time. (VOD 263)

Duluoz's culminating connotation of the absence of God with the untimely death of the father figure is clear; in the event of both the Kerouacian subject suffers hopelessness and indolence since it is left "flat with the whole problem" of inability to assume the signifier of "father" in the symbolic realm. The biblical call "Father, Father, why has Thou forsaken me?" is thus a call to the empty space of the Name-of-the-Father, which can only adopt a myriad of imaginary and always-unsatisfactory paternal figures. The call is repeated at the end of the novel:

> [S]lowly he [the father] withered before my eyes. ... [H]e just died in front of my eyes and I looked at his face in pouting repose and thought 'You have forsaken me, my father. You have left me alone to take care of the "rest" whatever the rest is.' He'd said: 'Take care of your mother whatever you do. Promise me.' I promised I would, and have. (VOD 267)

Although the late Kerouac touches upon many areas, its underlying aim is to reawaken the symbolic father in the figure of God in the belief that, as claimed by the narrator in *Satori in Paris*, "[i]t's only the Son who knows the Father" (SIP 64). From Duluoz's perspective, it is only the Christ-like Kerouacian subject who knows the father/God.

Apart from the final effort to rediscover the father in the image of God, the second major predilection of the late Kerouacian subject is to reassert the paternal authority with the family lineage. If the figure of Sal Paradise indicated that the missing father lay somewhere behind or in front of him and Dean Moriarty on their journey through the States, then it might be argued that the narrators of *Visions of Gerard*, *Satori in Paris*, and *Vanity of Duluoz* choose to look behind themselves with the aim of tracing back their ancestry and the source of their present-day condition. The narrator of *Satori in Paris* plainly delineates the aim of his trip to Paris and Brittany:

> I search blindly for that old Breton name Daoulas, of which "Duluoz" was a variation I invented just for fun in my writerly youth (to use as my name in my novels). (SIP 101)

Accordingly, learning the Lacanian Name-of-the-Father becomes for the Kerouacian subject an objective to be taken literally as the metonymic way back unwinds.

As the installment of the Duluoz legend which covers the earliest days of Jack Duluoz's life, *Visions of Gerard* takes a special place in retracing one's origins; unlike other of the above-mentioned novels, it speaks of the most remote events of the legend by assuming the perspective of little Ti Jean. Reminiscing over his brother Gerard, the narrator offers an ekphrasis of a family photo:

> [V]arious pictures of him [Gerard] we had, one in particular in front of me now, ... on the porch of the Lupine Road house the which, when I recently visited it, revealed to me (to my infant's old gaze) the ancient form of Earth-Beginnings in the form of a fluted porch-ceiling-light-globe that I had studied and studies with infant eyes long afternoons .... (VOG 14)

After many years, Duluoz's family house reveals to the Kerouacian subject its Edenic quality, (so does Paris in *Satori in Paris* when the narrator confirms: "[b]ut I'm home, there's no doubt about it ... ." (SIP 100)), which, as one might argue, calls for further explorations of genealogical nature. However, symptomatic for the entirety of late Kerouac, the above-mentioned revelation comes into being as a nostalgic offshoot of the Lacanian object a, the already-discussed peculiar failure of the symbolic. Its phantasmatic and myth-making nature instigates a series of what-would-be-if scenarios, which often entail the return of something which never really existed:

> [S]ometimes I'd just look out the window of the mad ward and watch a little dirt road that wound westward into the woods of Maryland leading to Kentucky and the rest, on misty days it had a particularly nostalgic look that reminded me of boyhood dream of being a real 'Arkansas Railbird' with father and brothers on a horse ranch, myself a jockey ... I saw that little winding dirt road going west to my lost dream of being a real American Man ....(VOD 167)

Additionally, the textual strategy of *Visions of Gerard*, where the narrating writer assumes the perspective of himself as an infant, invites the nostalgic gaze, as in the previously quoted fragment. Paraphrasing Lacan, the adult Kerouac sees himself seeing himself; he perceives his infant's gaze to be revealing his adult gaze and his present-day condition.

Also, in order to reassert his ancestry and links with the forefathers, the Kerouacian subject does not refrain from ascribing a mythical status to his allegedly Breton and Cornish origins. This may be said to grant Duluoz a compensation for a sense of lack and unfulfillment experienced in the symbolic:

> At least the early Duluozes had fields of green ..., horses and mutton chops, barks and rigging and salt spray, shields and lances and saddles, and trees to look at. Whoever they were, them Duluozes (Kerouac'hs), their name meant 'Language of the House' .... (VOD 249)

In view of all the misfortunes that he and his beloved ones are subjected to, Duluoz (again, in the nostalgic, mythical way resulting from the work of the phantasmatic *objet a*) occasionally asserts that his family must have been cursed a long time ago:

> O when will the troubles of this *cursed* family end, why were we all made to totter in the dark ... why were the wild dark Duluozes cursed .... (VOC 121)
>
> The house is chilled. Aunt Louise sits at the kitchen table shaking her head – "*La peine, la peine*, pain, pain, always pain for the Duluozes – I knew it when he was born – his father, his aunt, all his uncles, all invalids – all in pain – Suffering and pain – I tell you, Emil, we haven't been blessed by Chance." (VOG 69–70)

Nevertheless, even if allegedly cursed, the family name exposes itself for Duluoz as a prospect of a fixed identity, as both a source of pride and a supposed source of paternal knowledge, the lacking and deficient element of his symbolic constitution:

> Well, why do people change their names? Have they done anything bad, are they criminals, are they ashamed of their real names? Are they afraid of something? Is there any law in America against using your own real name?
>
> I had come to France and Brittany just to look up this old name of mine which is just about three thousand years old and was never changed in all that time, as who would change a name that simply means House (Ker), in the Field (Ouac) – (SIP 72)

In the late Kerouac the emphasis put on the native language is not accidental and remains a vital component of the subject's strategy to reinstate the paternal figure. Whether Breton or native French (used by Duluoz in his childhood), the mother tongue appears to the Kerouacian subject as key in filling the symbolic lack and firm anchoring in tradition and identity, which gets articulated as a sense of belonging:

> The amazing long sincere conversations in French with hundreds of people everywhere, was what I really liked .... (SIP 46)

On a deeper level, the native language might be regarded as the component of the (imaginary) phallus, a code fantasized as the language of stable and undifferentiated meaning. It is the language of Gerard, the depositor of godly knowledge, whose teachings need an exegete in the person of Ti Jean:

> "What's the color of God? –"
> *"Blanc d'or rouge noir pi toute* – White of gold red black and everything – " is the translation. (VOG 11)

Again, due to the arrest at pre-oedipal stage, the Kerouacian subject occasionally increases his leanings towards the maternal state of homogeneity and indistinction as when he fixates on some lines of Gerard's prayer:

> *"Et Jesus le fruit de vos entrailles"* – "entrailles" the powerful French word for Womb, *entrails*, none of us had any idea what it meant, some strange interior secret of Mary and Womanhood, little dreaming the whole universe was one great Womb … . (VOG 43)

Yet another instance of the Freudian secondary narcissism, the recognition of Heaven as the womb interweaves in the late Kerouac with his "origin worship … [leading to] the confusion of individuality with identity" (Hrebeniak 127), which might be read as a propensity for the imaginary state of bliss.

Finally, it is Duluoz's very own father who is inscribed into the process of reasserting his son's hereditary identity. Alike the remote forefathers, the figure of the father seems to be interweaving with the phantasmatic and myth-provoking work of *objet a*, helping the Kerouacian subject to establish a nostalgic link with one's heritage and rectify paternal deficiencies. Perhaps the convergence of the two comes best to the surface in *Visions of Gerard*, when Ti Jean fantasizes about the baptism of his father:

> Emil Alcide Duluoz, born in upriver St. Hubert Canada in 1889, I can picture the scene of his baptism at some wind whipped country crossing Catholic church … a little fold of honey enfleshed is being presented to the holy water for life – I can see all the kinds of Duluozes that must have been there that 1889 day, Sunday most likely, when Emil Alcide was anointed for his grave, for the earth's an intrinsic grave … . The mystery there for me, of Montreal the Capital and all French Canada the culture, out of which came the original potato paternity that rioted and wrought us the present family-kids of Emil … . (VOG 95)

Solemn and biblical-like, the scene combines in its mythical dimension all the previously discernible motifs – the father, God, and ancestors – giving the Kerouacian subject a sense of communal experience, even if a phantasmatic one. The mythical status of the family line was apparently purported by Duluoz's male ancestors themselves. We learn the following of the Duluozian origins in *Vanity of Duluoz*:

> And lo! one morning … the ships come into a bright part of sea cliffs of Scotland, on the right the flat green meadows of Ireland … . I stood there crying, my eyes were

> pouring tears, I said to myself 'Ireland? Can it be? James Joyce's country? But also way back I remembered what my father and my uncles had always told me, that we were descendants of Cornish Celts who had come to Cornwall from Ireland in the olden days long before Jesus and the calendar they start Him from, Kerouac'h ('Duluoz') being, they said, an ancient Gaelic name. ...
> Still tears in my eyes, I worked on, but can anybody tell me why? (VOD 179–180)

Duluoz's conjectures about his father(s) fit into what might be speculated as the Lacanian theory of nostalgia; owing to the phenomenon of *objet a*, the subject leans towards the (paternally oriented) past which is deeply phantasmatic and retroactively constructed.

Similarly to the hope-driven, future-oriented search for the paternal in *On the Road*, the nostalgic, past-oriented peregrinations of the late Kerouacian subject abound in encounters with the ghostly, uncanny and hallucinatory reminders of the paternal metaphor as an always-veiled, impossible-to-be-realized phenomenon. In *Satori in Paris* the allegedly familiar and homely surroundings of Brittany spark and stimulate the return of the father materializing in the face of a bartender on Rue de Siam:

> The owner of the bar is behind his cash register doping out the horses at Longchamps ... he lets me sit and goof and drink there all I want – Meanwhile the young bartender is also glad to talk to me, has apparently heard of my books, but after awhile ... he suddenly stiffens, I guess from a sign from the boss, too much work to do, wash your glasses in the sink, I've outworn me welcome in another bar –
> I've seen that expression on my father's face, a kind of disgusted lip-on-lip WHAT'S-THE-USE phooey, or ploof, (dédain) or plah, as he either walked away a loser from a racetrack or out of a bar where he didn't like what happened, and elsetimes, especially when thinking of history and the world, but that's when I walked out of that bar when that expression came over my own face – (SIP 69–70)

Not a long time after another ghostlike father figure reemerges on the narrator's way:

> Now I'm getting scared, I suspect some of ... guys crisscrossing the streets in front of my wandering path are fixing to mug me for my two or three hundred bucks left – ... I get mad and go up to an apparent elderly printer hurrying home from work or cardgame, maybe my father's ghost, as surely my father musta looked down on me that night in Brittany at last where he and all his brothers and uncles and their fathers had all longed to go, and only poor Ti Jean [Duluoz/Kerouac] finally made it .... (SIP 74)

Looking at the late Duluoz's musings over the paternal figures, one may get the impression that many of them posit the spectral nature of fatherhood, which finds its emblem in the ephemerality of subsequent items attempting to occupy the paternal signifier. It is, by instance, tangible in Jack Duluoz's repeated cry over losing touch with some of his close friends. In *Vanity of Duluoz* we learn of the protagonist's grief over the character named Big Slim: "Last I heard he was punching cows in East Texas, probably not true. Where is he tonight? Where am I? Where are you? (VOD 171)" as well as his nostalgic memories of Will [William Burroughs]:

> So Will sits by me on the bench in that irrecoverable night with mild amazement going 'hm hm hm' and ... he's instructing me seriously, looking with blank and bling interested eyes for the first time into mine. ...
> Where is he tonight? Where am I? Where are you?" (VOD 205)

Like none before them, the final installments of the legend focus on the Kerouacian subject's awareness of the fleeting nature of the once dispossessed paternal. The process of repossession seems to offer no end if, as hinted by the narrator of *Visions of Gerard*, "[b]rothers that were saints that died on me, that too's happened a million times in a million repetitudes and reincarnations" (VOG 116–119).

As regards the phenomenon of repetitions, Kerouac's final work offers yet another rendition of the father-son conflict with Jack Duluoz's career path as the bone of contention. Disagreements arise before his picking a college:

> My father wanted me to go to Boston College because his employers, Callahan Printers, of Lowell, were promising him a promotion if he could persuade me to go there and play under Francis Fahey. They also hinted he'd be fired if I went to any other college. ... There were big arguments in the kitchen. My father was fired. ... His only happiness in life now, in a way, . . . was that I make good and justify him anyway.
> That he was fired is of course a scandal ... and is another black plume in my hat of 'success.' (VOD 28–29)

As before, the conflict peaks at the clashing visions of Duluoz's line of work; Jack Duluoz's wish to become a writer pesters the father's wish of a stable job for his son. (VOD 94–95). The novelty brought by the last attempt at depicting the scene is Kerouac's peppering Duluoz's father's words with genealogical references. Jack Duluoz announces that he drops Columbia to "study America," which makes his father laugh:

> 'Poor kid, ha ha ha, you don't even know what you're up against, and the trouble with Duluozes is that we're Bretons and Cornishmen and it's that we can't get along with people, maybe we were descended from pirates, or cowards, who knows, because we can't stand rats, that coach was a rat [?]. You shoulda socked him on the banana nose instead of sneaking out like a coward.' (VOD 109)

One feels tempted to conjecture that the scene of argument between Jack Duluoz and his father reemerges once in a while throughout the Duluoz legend so as to assuage the Kerouacian subject's feeling of guilt over not having followed the way envisioned for him by the fatherly. If its variant in *Visions of Gerard* was to absolve the blame of Duluoz by means of Gerard (who, as claimed by Ti Jean, would also have an artistic vocation, had he lived), then its rendition in *Vanity of Duluoz* attributes the guilt to unfavorable hereditary features (by positing a father who claims the existence of such). It is also the oedipal tension between the family members, previously depicted in Kerouac's debut novel, which acquires a more daring authorial evocation in the late works of the American writer:

> Ma broke in: 'Why don't you two stop fighting all the time? ... [W]hy don't you leave him alone Emil [the father], he knows what he wants to do, he's old enough to know what he wants.'
> Pa rose quickly from the table and began to leave the room: 'Sure, sure' ... 'stick up for him, he's the only thing you got, go ahead and believe in him, but you believe me, you'll starve plenty if you do, let him have his way, but don't come crying to me when you starve. Dammit!' Pa yelled on.
> 'Dammit!' I yelled. 'She won't starve, maybe I'm not paying her back now but I'll pay her back some day, a million times over ...'
> ...
> Ma looks at me and shakes her head gravely:
> 'I never saw such a man. ... he's jealous that you'll go out and make something of yourself, don't listen to him, don't talk to him, he'll only make you mad .... (VOD 110)

If, as claimed by Lacanian psychoanalysis, repetition is an always-missed encounter with the real, then the above-mentioned reinterpretations of a few key scenes are the Kerouacian subject's continuous attempts to inscribe the traumatic disparity between the father and the son into the symbolic realm. Consequently, the eponymous vanity of Kerouac's last novel might be read as the unproductive outcome of such operations – signifiers will always yield to the traumatic gap between the absent symbolic father and the son; their mutual relations will remain deficient and undecidable, making the father figures proliferate further. Hassan Melehy corroborates such a view, examining the late Kerouac's quest for identity:

> The end result of the quest Kerouac portrays, then, is that he is required to continue the vagabondage that has marked his life and literary career ... . There is certainly value in learning one's ancestral roots, but the lesson of a quest that seeks them for the sake of fixity is that fixity will be ever more elusive: searching for grounding in the fathers only turns out to displace them further and require a reconfiguration of identity that stems from the very motion of the quest. (69)

When looked at through the prism of Lacan, the failure of tracing one's roots depicted in *Satori in Paris* equals the hopelessness of paternal fixity. Melehy continues:

> Neither God nor the fathers will provide fixity—but the act of looking for fixity can lead to fulfillment in the realization of the permeations between languages, cultures, territories, and persons that takes place in vagabondage, and thus to a diminishment of the need for the fathers. That is the conclusion of Kerouac's quest for identity: it is an invitation to more vagabond writing that explores the fluidity and unsettlement of the array of North American identities—that is, to a continually shifting literature that traverses them. (70)

While a failed quest for a stable identity could well, as wished by Melehy, be turned into an incentive to explore the identitarian fluidity, from the perspective of the following analysis the learned lesson of the final novels lies rather elsewhere. In the light of the epistemological suspiciousness that it represents ("[t]he whole world has no reality, it's only imaginary, and what are we to do?" (VOG 123)), the late Kerouacian subject starts to relax the perfection previously attached to reinstating the paternal metaphor. This decompression of the Duluozian ambitions has been anticipated as early as in *Visions of Cody* with its celebration of life as unfulfillable and perhaps even earlier, in *The Town and the City*, where Peter Martin describes life struggles as

> forever incomplete, far from perfect, refined, or smooth, full of terrible memories of failure and fears of failure, yet, in the way of things, somehow noble, complete, and shining in the end. (TTATC 472)

Perhaps seeing more clearly the vanity of all human wishes and thus attempting at dismantling his ego so as to reach final indifference towards all that life brings, Jack Duluoz gets to realize the imaginary nature of his pursuit of the paternal. Perhaps his endeavors to learn the paternal knowledge are "forever incomplete" and "far from perfect" but "somehow noble" because he learns that the father, his symptom, is but a metaphor since "the symptom is a metaphor" (E: AS 133). And still, supposedly aware of all of this, the late Kerouac sees the sense in writing when he turns to recipients of his works:

> ... and let me ask you but one more question, reader: – Where else but in a book can you go back and catch what you missed, and not only that but savor it and keep it up and shove it? (SIP 98)

In a 1948 letter to Allen Ginsberg, Kerouac confesses: "It's terrible never to find a father in a world chock full of fathers of all sorts" (Kerouac, quoted by Jones, *The Mythic Form* 58). At the end of his final novel he emphasizes, for the last time, the redemptive function of his prose, his ambition to be redeemed by writing, and he eventually admits: "But nothing ever came of it" (VOD 268). In light of their objectives and the above-mentioned statements, neither Kerouac-the person nor Kerouac-the writer gain the desired gratification. Imagined as one vast book, the entire Duluoz legend collapses under the un-reinstated paternal metaphor and, in the vein of Lacanian *automaton*, becomes "a homage to the missed reality, ... [reality] repeating itself ... [and never gaining] awakening" (S XI 58). Various figures reappearing in most of the installments under one signifier, that of the father, "a misnomer, consisting in the return, not of the same, but of the different" (Fink "The Real Cause of Repetition" 223), prove an unavoidable failure to equate the imaginary fathers with the symbolic one. If, as believed by Nicosia, Kerouac's work is to "examine the way reality is perceived as a rainbow body of light, reflected and refracted so many times that the percipient is prevented from tracing its origin" (310), then a part of such reality is the symbolic father, lost in a thousand of refractions. Kerouac must have been aware of this, yet, apparently he never stopped thinking about the father as one of the central preoccupations of his work. The final, never-to-be-realized project was to be a book on his father and his printing business in Lowell, Massachusetts.

Conclusion

As this study attempted to demonstrate, despite the diversities in their idioms, discourses, and milieux, Kerouac and Lacan might be considered silent partners in a number of ways. They share commonalities at a few levels and reveal to be illuminating for one another.

As observed in Chapter Four, Lacan proves useful when considering Kerouac's relations with Freud and psychoanalysis, undoubtedly troubling and multifaceted ones. Freud's immensurable influence on American health care, intellectual elites, and everyday life made his name something of a trademark on the American soil, a name that splintered into dozens of schools, as we have seen, often not having much in common with the root. All things considered, one might get the impression that although well-read, Kerouac became a bit of a victim of falling into the trap of identifying all the shortcomings of psychoanalysis with the Austrian doctor. Also, for Kerouac, Freud would occasionally become a straw man synonymous with the deficiencies of psychiatry and institutional psychoanalysis, which proved ineffective with either him or his friends. It is also the ego-psychology, a child of European and American psychoanalytic thought which dominated the American clinic in the middle of the twentieth century, which was perceived by Kerouac as an oppressive element (unreflective on its own matter, money-striven and aiming at eradicating idiosyncrasies, it also remained under the heavy critique of Jacques Lacan, who considered ego-psychology a tragic misapprehension of the Freudian thought). What further complicates Kerouac's way of thinking about psychoanalysis are the writer's personal animosities against academia (Lionel Trilling), liberalism and the New York bohemia, entangling the psychoanalytic thought into a private conflict. Kerouac turned away from psychoanalysis since it represented all those who were, according to him, pretentious, hypocritical, superior and intolerant to the weaker ones. What added to Kerouac's image of psychoanalysis was its alleged guilt-infliction, pessimism, disdain for religion, and finally, the supposed pansexuality permeating the theory. The last feature, as elucidated by Eagleton,

> is certainly untenable: Freud was a radically dualistic thinker, no doubt excessively so, and always counterposed to the sexual drives such non-sexual forces as the 'ego-instincts' of self-preservation. The seed of truth in the pan-sexualist charge is that Freud regarded sexuality as central enough to human life to provide a *component* of all our activities; but that is not a sexual reductionism. (*Literary Theory* 141)

The alleged overload of sexual content in Freud seems to have been yet again the effect of superfluous and selective approach of theorists who found it convenient and sufficient to confine psychoanalytic theory to a few resounding tags. This could partially explain Kerouac's disdain for the image of psychoanalysis he got since textbooks have spent and still

> spend as much time warning you about his [Freud's] "penis envy" and reactionary Victorian views as they spend explicating his uncanny insight into unconscious functioning. (Malone 11–12)

As demonstrated in both Chapter Four and Five, despite his unfavorable commentaries towards what seemed to him as the Freudian theory, Kerouac did not refrain from treating the psychoanalytic body of thought as a long-term reservoir of inspiration, be it rather an inconspicuous one. His artistic methods, textual strategies and psychoanalytically-imbued metaphors all reveal the lure that pulled the writer towards the area which was shared with psychoanalysis which could be broadly identified as one's fascination with the subversiveness of human consciousness. Jacques Lacan's reflections on spontaneous free-association – the key to the unconscious desire and identifications – prove its correspondence to Kerouac's (as well as other Beats') literary tactics. Kerouac's model of revisiting the scene of spontaneous writing finds its equivalent in the analyst's play on the ambiguity of analysand's speech (and might be a valuable complement to Lacanian theory). Ginsberg's uninhibited, all-inclusive, democratic poetics resemble to a considerable extent Lacan's call for the non-omission and non-systematization of what the analysand wishes to say. Finally, the Burroughsian cut-up method aims at raising one's mistrust to language and bringing out new semantical possibilities just like the Lacanian idea of varied-length sessions did. The aforementioned indirect correspondences seem all the more reinforced by Surrealism, endeared and respected by both the Beats and the French psychoanalyst.

As demonstrated in the three final chapters attempting a Lacanian reading of selected novels by Kerouac, the French psychoanalyst's theories might offer new perspectives on the meaning and structure of the Duluoz legend. First and foremost, as it was hopefully evidenced by the study, the Lacanian thought helps one to notice and highlight the problematic status of the (symbolic) father figure, and by doing so, suggests an answer to why Kerouac embraced the project of the Duluoz legend and ultimately failed to give it coherence. Kaleidoscopic in its nature, Kerouac's prose reinvents, refracts and recirculates reality by gliding along a never-ending promenade of signifiers, as Lacan might have said, and the central piece of that reality is occupied by the dispossessed father, hopelessly reimagined in a myriad of replacements.

It is believed by the author that the presented study does not derive full benefit from confronting Kerouac and Lacan just like the literary criticism has not yet made full use of the French psychoanalyst's oeuvre. Though still not unanimous about the shape of Lacanian literary criticism, literary scholars and theorists appear to hold Lacan tight in the field of their interest, which gives a promise of newer critical perspectives. It has now been some time since Lacanian literary criticism, alike Lacan in the 1970s, shifted its scope of interest from the symbolic to the real as well as to the late Lacan's theories directly pertaining to literature and particular writers. The concepts of *jouissance*, *sinthome*, *lituraterre*, *lalangue*, and the ponderings on the *letter* as *litter* are still to reveal its potential for Kerouac as well as for other Beat writers. It is also the hope of the present study that the critical calls for reinvigorating and evaluating psychoanalytic thought with literary works shall not remain unanswered in the Beat studies.

Bibliography

Primary Sources

Jack Kerouac

Kerouac, Jack. *Visions of Gerard*. New York: McGraw-Hill, 1976. Print.

Kerouac, Jack. *Desolation Angels*. London: Granada, 1982. Print.

Kerouac, Jack. *Dear Carolyn: Letters to Carolyn Cassady*. Eds. Arthur W. Knight and Kit Knight. California: A. and K. Knight, 1983. Print.

Kerouac, Jack. *Kerouac's Last Word: Jack Kerouac in Escapade*. Ed. Tom Clark. Sudbury: Water Row Press, 1986. Print.

Kerouac, Jack. *Satori in Paris and Pic: Two Novels*. New York: Grove Press, 1988. Print.

Kerouac, Jack. *Vanity of Duluoz*. London: Paladin, 1990. Print.

Kerouac, Jack. *Tristessa*. New York: Penguin Books, 1992. Print.

Kerouac, Jack. *Selected Letters, 1940–1956*. Ed. Ann Charters. New York: Viking, 1995. Print.

Kerouac, Jack. *Visions of Cody*. London: Flamingo/HarperCollins, 1995. Print.

Kerouac, Jack. *On the Road*. London: Penguin Books, 1998. Print.

Kerouac, Jack. *Selected Letters, 1957–1969*. Ed. Ann Charters. New York: Viking, 1999. Print.

Kerouac, Jack. *The Town and the City*. London: Penguin books, 2000. Print.

Kerouac, Jack. *Book of Dreams*. San Francisco: City Lights Books, 2001. Print.

Kerouac, Jack. *Windblown World: The Journals of Jack Kerouac, 1947–1954*. Ed. Douglas Brinkley. New York: Viking, 2004. Print.

Kerouac, Jack. *Big Sur*. London: Harper Perennial, 2006. Print.

Kerouac, Jack. *On the Road: The Original Scroll*. New York: Viking, 2007. Print.

Kerouac, Jack. *The Subterraneans*. New York: Grove Press, 2007. Print.

Kerouac, Jack. "Old Angel Midnight." *The Center for Programs in Contemporary Writing*. The University of Pennsylvania, n.d. Web. 29 March 2012.

Kerouac, Jack. "Essentials of Spontaneous Prose." *The Center for Programs in Contemporary Writing*. The University of Pennsylvania, n.d. Web. 5 April 2012.

Kerouac, Jack. "Mexico City Blues.poets.org." *Academy of American Poets*, n.d. Web. 6 April 2012.

Jacques Lacan

Lacan, Jacques. "Desire and the Interpretation of Desire in *Hamlet*." *Yale French Studies*.

55/56 (1977): 11–52. Print.

Lacan, Jacques. *The Seminar of Jacques Lacan: Book II: the Ego in Freud's Theory and in the Technique of Psychoanalysis, 1954–1955*. Ed. Jacques-Alain Miller. Trans. John Forrester. New York: Norton, 1988. Print.

Lacan, Jacques. *The Seminar of Jacques Lacan: Book I*. Ed. Jacques-Alain Miller. Trans. John Forrester. New York: W.W. Norton, 1991. Print.

Lacan, Jacques. *The Seminar of Jacques Lacan: Book III: the Psychoses, 1955–1956*. Ed. Jacques-Alain Miller. Trans. Russell Grigg. London: Routledge, 1993. Print.

Lacan, Jacques. *The Seminar of Jacques Lacan, Book VII*. Ed. Jacques-Alain Miller. Trans. Dennis Porter. New York: W.W. Norton, 1997. Print.

Lacan, Jacques. *The Seminar of Jacques Lacan Book XI: The Four Fundamental Concepts of Psychoanalysis*. Ed. Jacques-Alain Miller. Trans. Alan Sheridan. New York: Norton and Company, 1998. Print.

Lacan, Jacques. *The Seminar of Jacques Lacan Book XX: On Feminine Sexuality, The Limits of Love and Knowledge: Encore 1972–1973*. Ed. Jacques-Alain Miller. Trans. Bruce Fink. New York: Norton, 1999. Print.

Lacan, Jacques. *Écrits: A Selection*. Trans. Alan Sheridan. London: Routledge, 2005. Print.

Lacan, Jacques. *Écrits: The First Complete Edition in English*. Trans. Bruce Fink. New York: W.W. Norton & Co, 2006. Print.

Lacan, Jacques-. *The Seminar of Jacques Lacan Book XVII: The Other Side of Psychoanalysis 1969–1970*. Ed. Jacques-Alain Miller. Trans. Russell Grigg. New York: Norton, 2007. Print.

Lacan, Jacques. *On the Names-of-the-Father*. Trans. Bruce Fink. Cambridge: Polity Press, 2013. Print.

Lacan, Jacques. "Of Structure as the Inmixing of an Otherness Prerequisite to Any Subject Whatever." *Lacan Dot Com*. N.p, n.d. Web. 8 March 2014.

Lacan, Jacques. *Lituraterre*. Trans. Jack W. Stone. University of Missouri, 2016. Web. 20 May 2015.

Lacan, Jacques. *The Seminar of Jacques Lacan Book V: The Formations of the Unconscious 1957–1958*, unpublished translation by Cormac Gallagher. Web. 21 May 2015.

Lacan, Jacques. *The Seminar of Jacques Lacan Book X: Anxiety 1962–1963*, unpublished translation by Cormac Gallagher. Web. 22 May 2015.

Lacan, Jacques. *The Seminar of Jacques Lacan Book XIV: The Logic of Fantasy, 1966–1967*, unpublished translation by Cormac Gallagher. Web. 22 May 2015.

Lacan, Jacques. *The Seminar of Jacques Lacan: Seminar XXII, R. S. I., 1974 – 1975*, unpublished translation by Cormac Gallagher. Web. 23 May 2015.

Secondary Sources

Jack Kerouac

Amburn, Ellis. *Subterranean Kerouac: The Hidden Life of Jack Kerouac*. New York: St. Martin's Press, 1998. Print.

Bierowski, Thomas R. *Kerouac in Ecstasy: Shamanic Expression in the Writings*. Jefferson: McFarland, 2011. Print.

Carden, Mary Paniccia. ""Adventures of Auto-Eroticism": Economies of Traveling Masculinity in *On the Road* and *The First Third*." *What's Your Road, Man?: Critical Essays on Jack Kerouac's On the Road*. Eds. Hilary Holladay and Robert Holton. Carbondale: Southern Illinois University Press, 2009. 77–98. Print.

Dickstein, Morris. "On and Off the Road: the Outsider as Young Rebel." *The Cambridge History of American Literature*. Vol. 7. Ed. Sacvan Bercovitch. Cambridge: Cambridge Univ. Press, 1999. Print.

Foxe, Gladys. ""And Nobody Knows What's Going to Happen to Anybody": Fear and Futility in Jack Kerouac's on the Road and Why It Is Important." The Psychoanalytic Review. 95.1 (2008): 45–60. Print.

Giamo, Benedict. *Kerouac, the Word and the Way: Prose Artist As Spiritual Quester*. Carbondale: Southern Illinois University Press, 2000. Print.

Holladay, Hilary. "Preface." *What's Your Road, Man?: Critical Essays on Jack Kerouac's On the Road*. Eds. Hilary Holladay and Robert Holton. Carbondale: Southern Illinois University Press, 2009. ix-xiii. Print.

Holton, Robert. "Jack Kerouac's Duluoz Legend: the Mythic Form of an Autobiographical Fiction (review)." *Biography*. 24.2 (2001): 499–501. Print.

Hrebeniak, Michael. *Action Writing: Jack Kerouac's Wild Form*. Carbondale: Southern Illinois University Press, 2006. Print.

Hunt, Tim. *Kerouac's Crooked Road: The Development of a Fiction*. Carbondale: Southern Illinois University Press, 2010. Print.

Jones, James T. *Jack Kerouac's Duluoz Legend: The Mythic Form of an Autobiographical Fiction*. Carbondale: Southern Illinois University Press, 1999. Print.

Jones, James T. "Sharing a Shadow: The Image of the Shrouded Stranger in the Works of Jack Kerouac and Allen Ginsberg." *Post-Jungian Criticism: Theory and Practice*. Ed. James S. Baumlin, Tita French Baumlin, and George H. Jensen. Albany: State University of New York Press, 2004. 223–241. Print.

Maffina, Stefano. *The Role of Jack Kerouac's Identity in the Development of His Poetics. Morrisville: Lulu*, 2012. Print.

Maher, Paul., David Amram. *Kerouac: The Definitive Biography*. Lanham: Taylor Trade Pub, 2007. Print.

Melehy, Hassan. "Kerouac's Quest for Identity: Satori in Paris." *Studies in American Fiction*. 41.1 (2014): 49–76. Print.

Nicholls, Brendan. "Melting Pot That Boiled Over: Racial Fetishism and the Lingua Franca of Jack Kerouac." *MFS Modern Fiction Studies* 49.3 (2003): 524–549. Print.

Nicosia, Gerald. *Memory Babe: A Critical Biography of Jack Kerouac*. London: Penguin Books, 1986.

Skau, Michael. "The Makings of Paradise." *What's Your Road, Man?: Critical Essays on Jack Kerouac's On the Road*. Eds. Hilary Holladay and Robert Holton. Carbondale: Southern Illinois University Press, 2009. 155–168. Print.

Stephenson, Gregory. *The Daybreak Boys: Essays on the Literature of the Beat Generation*. Carbondale: Southern Illinois University Press, 2009. Print.

Sterritt, David. *Mad to Be Saved: The Beats, the '50s, and Film*. Carbondale: Southern Illinois University Press, 1998. Print.

Swartz, Omar. *The View from on the Road: The Rhetorical Vision of Jack Kerouac*. Carbondale: Southern Illinois University Press, 1999. Print.

Theado, Matt. *Understanding Jack Kerouac*. Columbia: University of South Carolina Press, 2000. Print.

Trudeau, Justin T. "Specters in the Rear-View: Haunting Whiteness in Jack Kerouac's On the Road." *Text and Performance Quarterly*. 31.2 (2011): 149–168. Print.

Vopat, Carole Gottlieb. "Jack Kerouac's *On the Road*: A Re-Evaluation." *Jack Kerouac's On The Road: Bloom's Modern Critical Interpretations*. Ed. Harold Bloom. Philadelphia: Chelsea House Publishers, 2004. 3–18. Print.

Weinreich, Regina. *The Spontaneous Poetics of Jack Kerouac: A Study of the Fiction*. Carbondale: Southern Illinois University Press, 1987. Print.

Jacques Lacan

André, Serge. "Otherness of the Body." *Lacanian Theory of Discourse: Subject, Structure, and Society*. Ed. Mark Bracher, et al. New York: New York University Press, 1994. 88–104. Print.

Apollon, Willy, et al. *After Lacan: Clinical Practice and the Subject of the Unconscious*. Albany: State University of New York Press, 2002. Print.

Azari, Ehsan. *Lacan and the Destiny of Literature: Desire, Jouissance and the Sinthome in Shakespeare, Donne, Joyce and Ashbery*. London: Continuum, 2008. Print.

Berressem, Hanjo. *Lines of Desire: Reading Gombrowicz's Fiction with Lacan*. Evanston: Northwestern University Press, 1998. Print.

Biswas, Santanu. "Have We Exhausted Lacan in the Field of Literary Criticism?" Journal of Moving Image 3 (2004): n. pag. Web. 10 August 2014.

Borch-Jacobsen, Mikkel. *Lacan: The Absolute Master*. Stanford: Stanford University Press, 1991. Print.

Braunstein, Néstor. "Desire and Jouissance in the Teachings of Lacan." *Cambridge Companion to Lacan*. Ed. Jean-Michel Rabaté. Cambridge: Cambridge University Press, 2003. 102–115. Print.

Brockelman, Thomas. "Lacan and Modernism: Representation and its Vicissitudes." *Disseminating Lacan*. Eds. David Pettigrew and François Raffoul. Albany: State University of New York Press, 1996. Print.

Bryant, Levi. R. "Sexuation 2 – The Logic of *Jouissance*." *Larval Subjects*. Ed. Levi R. Bryant. Web. 24 May 2014.

Burgoyne, Bernard. "From the Letter to the Matheme: Lacan's Scientific Methods." *Cambridge Companion to Lacan*. Ed. Jean-Michel Rabaté. Cambridge: Cambridge University Press, 2003. 69–85. Print.

Cruz, Anne J. "Mirroring Others: A Lacanian Reading of the *Letrados* in *Don Quixote*." *Quixotic Desire: Psychoanalytic Perspectives on Cervantes*. Eds. Ruth S. El Saffar and Diana A. Wilson. Ithaca: Cornell University Press, 1993. Print.

Davis, Robert Con. "Critical Introduction: The Discourse of the Father." *The Fictional Father: Lacanian Readings of the Text*. Ed. Robert Con Davis. Amherst: University of Massachusetts Press, 1981. 1–26. Print.

Dean, Tim. "Lacan and Queer Theory." *Cambridge Companion to Lacan*. Ed. Jean-Michel Rabaté. Cambridge: Cambridge University Press, 2003. 238–252. Print.

Durand, Régis. ""The Captive King": The Absent Father in Melville's Text." *The Fictional Father: Lacanian Readings of the Text*. Ed. Robert Con Davis. Amherst: University of Massachusetts Press, 1981. 48–72. Print.

Evans, Dylan. *An Introductory Dictionary of Lacanian Psychoanalysis*. London: Routledge, 2006. Print.

Eyers, Tom. *Lacan and the Concept of the 'Real.'* Basingstoke: Palgrave Macmillan, 2012. Print.

Fink, Bruce. "The Real Cause of Repetition." *Reading Seminar XI: Lacan's Four Fundamental Concepts of Psychoanalysis*. Ed. Richard Feldstein, Bruce Fink, and Maire Jaanus. Albany: State University of New York Press, 1995. 223–232. Print.

Friedlander, Jennifer. *Feminine Look: Sexuation, Spectatorship, Subversion*. Albany: State University of New York Press, 2008. Print.

Maire Jaanus. *The Lacanian Subject: Between Language and Jouissance*. Princeton: Princeton University Press, 1997. Print.

Gherovici, Patricia. "Psychoanalysis: Resistible and Irresistible." *Lacan in America*. Ed. Jean-Michel Rabaté. New York: Other Press, 2000. 93–105. Print.

Glowinski, Huguette. "Ideal Ego." *A Compendium of Lacanian Terms*. Eds. Huguette Glowinski, Zita M. Marks, and Sara Murphy. London: Free Association Books, 2001. 83–86. Print.

Glowinski, Zita M. "Jouissance." *A Compendium of Lacanian Terms*. Eds. Huguette Glowinski, Zita M. Marks, and Sara Murphy. London: Free Association Books, 2001. 101–109. Print.

Grigg, Russell. "Signifier." *A Compendium of Lacanian Terms*. Eds. Huguette Glowinski, Zita M. Marks, and Sara Murphy. London: Free Association Books, 2001. 185–191. Print.

Gurewich, Judith Feher. "The Lacanian Clinical Field: Series Overview." *Lacan in America*. Ed. Jean-Michel Rabaté. New York: Other Press, 2000. ix-xv. Print.

Hyldgaard, Kirsten. "The Conformity of Perversion." Lacan Dot Com. N.p, n.d. Web. 3 May 2016.

Iversen, Margaret. *Beyond Pleasure: Freud, Lacan, Barthes*. University Park: Pennsylvania State University Press, 2007. Print.

Johnston, Adrian. "Jacques Lacan." *The Stanford Encyclopedia of Philosophy*. Ed. Edward N. Zalta. Stanford: Stanford University, 2013. Web. 5 Feb 2014.

Kaltenbeck, Franz. "Sublimation and Symptom." *Art: Sublimation or Symptom*. Ed. Parveen Adams. London: Karnac, 2003.

King, Robert. "The Mirror Stage." *A Compendium of Lacanian Terms*. Eds. Huguette Glowinski, Zita M. Marks, and Sara Murphy. London: Free Association Books, 2001. 114–118. Print.

Lee, Jonathan Scott. *Jacques Lacan*. Boston: Twayne Publishers, 1990. Print.

Levy-Stokes, Carmela. "Castration." *A Compendium of Lacanian Terms*. Eds. Huguette Glowinski, Zita M. Marks, and Sara Murphy. London: Free Association Books, 2001. 42–50. Print.

Liu, Catherine. “Lacanian Reception.” *Lacan in America*. Ed. Jean-Michel Rabaté. New York: Other Press, 2000. 107–137. Print.

Liu, Catherine. “Lacan's Afterlife: Jacques Lacan Meets Andy Warhol.” *Cambridge Companion to Lacan*. Ed. Jean-Michel Rabaté. Cambridge: Cambridge University Press, 2003. 253–271. Print.

Luepnitz, Deborah. “Beyond the Phallus: Lacan and Feminism.” *Cambridge Companion to Lacan*. Ed. Jean-Michel Rabaté. Cambridge: Cambridge University Press, 2003. 221–237. Print.

Malone, Kareen Ror. “The Place of Lacanian Psychoanalysis in North American Psychology.” *Lacan in America*. Ed. Jean-Michel Rabaté. New York: Other Press, 2000. 3–24. Print.

McQuillan, Martin. “Departures: The American Future of Psychoanalysis.” *Performatives After Deconstruction*. Ed. Mauro Senatore. New York: Bloomsbury Publishing Plc, 2013. 207–222. Print.

Mellard, James M. *Using Lacan, Reading Fiction*. Urbana: University of Illinois Press, 1991. Print.

Moore, Gerald. *Politics of the Gift: Exchanges in Poststructuralism*. Edinburgh: Edinburgh University Press, 2011. Print.

Nobus, Dany. “Lacan's Science of the Subject: Between Linguistics and Topology.” *Cambridge Companion to Lacan*. Ed. Jean-Michel Rabaté. Cambridge: Cambridge University Press, 2003. 50–68. Print.

Nobus, Dany, and Malcolm Quinn. *Knowing Nothing, Staying Stupid: Elements for a Psychoanalytic Epistemology*. London: Routledge, 2005. Print.

Rabaté, Jean-Michel. *Jacques Lacan: Psychoanalysis and the Subject of Literature*. Basingstoke: Palgrave, 2001. Print.

Rabaté, Jean-Michel. “Lacan's Turn to Freud.” *Cambridge Companion to Lacan*. Ed. Jean-Michel Rabaté. Cambridge: Cambridge University Press, 2003. 1–24. Print.

Rabinovich, Diana. “What Is a Lacanian Clinic?” *Cambridge Companion to Lacan*. Ed. Jean-Michel Rabaté. Cambridge: Cambridge University Press, 2003. 208–220. Print.

Roazen, Paul. “What is Wrong with French Psychoanalysis? Observations on Lacan's First Seminar.” *Lacan in America*. Ed. Jean-Michel Rabaté. New York: Other Press, 2000. 41–60. Print.

Robins, C. Edward. “Please Read Lacan!” *Lacan in America*. Ed. Jean-Michel Rabaté New York: Other Press, 2000. 61–70. Print.

Roudinesco, Elisabeth. “The Mirror Stage: An Obliterated Archive.” *Cambridge Companion to Lacan*. Ed. Jean-Michel Rabaté. Cambridge: Cambridge University Press, 2003. 25–34. Print.

Schreiber, Evelyn Jaffe. *Subversive Voices: Eroticizing the Other in William Faulkner and Toni Morrison*. Knoxville: University of Tennessee Press, 2001. Print.

Schreiber, Evelyn Jaffe. "Reader, Text, and Subjectivity: Toni Morrison's 'Beloved' as Lacan's Gaze qua Object." *Style* 30 (1996): 445-461. *The Free Library*. n.pag. Web. 3 January 2015.

Sharpe, Matthew. "Lacan, Jacques." *The Internet Encyclopedia of Philosophy*. Eds. James Fieser and Bradley Dowden. The Internet Encyclopedia of Philosophy and its Authors, 1995. Web. 15 May 2014.

Shepherdson, Charles. *Lacan and the Limits of Language*. New York: Fordham University Press, 2008. Print.

Smith, Joseph S. "Lacan in America." Ed. Jean-Michel Rabaté. New York: Other Press, 2000. 15–39. Print.

Soler, Colette. "Hysteria and Obsession." *Reading Seminars I and II: Lacan's Return to Freud*. Eds. Richard Feldstein, Bruce Fink, and Maire Jaanus. Albany: State University of New York Press, 1996. 248–282. Print.

Stoltzfus, Ben. *Lacan and Literature: Purloined Pretexts*. Albany: State University of New York Press, 1996. Print.

Swales, Stephanie S. *Perversion: A Lacanian Psychoanalytic Approach to the Subject*. New York: Routledge, 2012. Print.

Verhaeghe, Paul. "Causation and Destitution of a Pre-ontological Non-entity: On the Lacanian Subject." *Key Concepts of Lacanian Psychoanalysis*. Ed. Dany Nobus. London: Rebus Press, 1998. 1–25. Print.

Zupančič, Alenka. "Ethics and Tragedy in Lacan." *Cambridge Companion to Lacan*. Ed. Jean-Michel Rabaté. Cambridge: Cambridge University Press, 2003. 173–190. Print.

Žižek, Slavoj. "Rossellini: Woman As Symptom of Man." October. 54 (1990): 18–44. Print.

Žižek, Slavoj. *Looking Awry: An Introduction to Jacques Lacan Through Popular Culture*. Cambridge,: MIT Press, 1992. Print.

Žižek, Slavoj. *For They Know Not What They Do: Enjoyment as a Political Factor*. London: Verso, 2008. Print.

Other Sources

Agnew, Jean-Christophe. "The Walking Man and the Talking Cure." *After Freud Left: A Century of Psychoanalysis in America*. Ed. John C. Burnham. Chicago: The University of Chicago Press, 2012. 233–245. Print.

Barton, Walter E. *The History and Influence of the American Psychiatric Association*. Washington, D.C: American Psychiatric Press, 1987. Print.

Baudrillard, Jean. *America*. Trans. Chris Turner. London and New York: Verso, 1988. Print.

Bennett, David. "Sexual Revolutions: Towards a Brief History, from the Fall of the Man to the Present." *Sexual Revolutions: Psychoanalysis, History, and the Father*. Ed. Gottfried Heuer. New York: Routledge, 2011. 35–52. Print.

Boskin, Joseph. *Rebellious Laughter: People's Humor in American Culture*. Syracuse: Syracuse University Press, 1997. Print.

Boym, Svetlana. *The Future of Nostalgia*. New York: Basic Books, 2001. Print.

Breitenberg, Mark. *Anxious Masculinity in Early Modern England*. Cambridge: Cambridge University Press, 1996. Print.

Buccino, Daniel L. "Book Review: Gary Snyder and the American Unconscious: Inhabiting the Ground." MLN. 107.5 (1992): 1061–1063. Print.

Burnham, John C. "Conclusion." *After Freud Left: A Century of Psychoanalysis in America*. Ed. John C. Burnham. Chicago: The University of Chicago Press, 2012. 247–253. Print.

Burnham, John C. "Introduction." *After Freud Left: A Century of Psychoanalysis in America*. Ed. John C. Burnham. Chicago: The University of Chicago Press, 2012. 1–21. Print.

Burnham. John C. "Introduction to Part II: A Shift in Perspective." *After Freud Left: A Century of Psychoanalysis in America*. Ed. John C. Burnham. Chicago: The University of Chicago Press, 2012. 157–162. Print.

Burroughs, William S. "The Cut-up Method of Brion Gysin." *The Beat Book: Poems and Fiction of the Beat Generation*. Ed. Anne Waldman. Boston: Shambhala, 1996. 182–185. Print.

Caraman-Pasca, Lorelei. "From the Text-As-Symptom to the Critic-As-Analysand: New Approaches in Psychoanalytic Criticism." *Analele Universitatii Ovidius Constanta, Seria Filologie*. 24.1 (2013): 86–94. Print.

Culler, Jonathan D. "The Genius of Barbara Johnson." *Diacritics*. 34.1 (2006): 74–76. Print.

Dalzell, Thomas. *Freud's Schreber between Psychiatry and Psychoanalysis: On Subjective Disposition to Psychosis*. London: Karnac Books, 2011. Print.

Eagleton, Terry. *Literary Theory: An Introduction*. Minneapolis: University of Minnesota Press, 1996. Print.

Eagleton, Terry. *Trouble with Strangers: A Study of Ethics*. Chichester: Wiley-Blackwell Pub, 2009. Print.

Eburne, Jonathan Paul. *Surrealism and the Art of Crime*. Ithaca: Cornell University Press, 2008. Print.

Falzeder, Ernst. "*A Fat Wad of Dirty Pieces of Paper*: Freud on America, Freud in America, Freud and America." *After Freud Left: A Century of Psychoanalysis in America*. Ed. John C. Burnham. Chicago: The University of Chicago Press, 2012. 87–109. Print.

Ginsberg, Allen. *Collected Poems, 1947–1997*. New York: HarperCollins Publishers, 2006. Print.

Harris, Oliver. *William Burroughs and the Secret of Fascination*. Carbondale: Southern Illinois University Press, 2003. Print.

Jarniewicz, Jerzy. *Od pieśni do skowytu: szkice o poetach amerykańskich*. Wrocław: Biuro Literackie, 2008. Print.

Kernberg, Otto. "Psychoanalysis in America." *European Journal of Psychoanalysis (JEP)* 5 (1997): n. pag. Web. 15 May 2012.

Lunbeck, Elizabeth. "Heinz Kohut's Americanization of Freud." *After Freud Left: A Century of Psychoanalysis in America*. Ed. John C. Burnham. Chicago: The University of Chicago Press, 2012. 209–231. Print.

Lusty, Natalya. *Surrealism, Feminism, Psychoanalysis*. Aldershot: Ashgate, 2007. Print.

Makari, George. "Mitteleuropa on the Hudson: On the Struggle for American Psychoanalysis after the Anschluß." *After Freud Left: A Century of Psychoanalysis in America*. Ed. John C. Burnham. Chicago: The University of Chicago Press, 2012. 111–124. Print.

Markowski, Michał Paweł. *Czarny Nurt. Gombrowicz, świat, literatura*. Kraków: Wydawnictwo Literackie, 2004. Print.

Menand, Louis. "Freud, Anxiety, and the Cold War." *After Freud Left: A Century of Psychoanalysis in America*. Ed. John C. Burnham. Chicago: The University of Chicago Press, 2012. 189–207. Print.

Myers, Tony. *Slavoj Žižek*. London: Routledge, 2003. Print.

Nitzschke, Bernd. "Psychoanalysis and National Socialism. Banned or Brought into Conformity? Break or Continuity?" Trans. Channing Bates. *International Forum of Psychoanalysis*. 12 (2003): n. pag. Web. 15 May 2012.

Pessoa, Fernando. *Book of Disquiet*. Trans. and Ed. Richard Zenith. London: Penguin Classics, 2002. Print.

Porter, Carolyn. "Symbolic Fathers and Dead Mothers: A Feminist Approach to Faulkner." *Faulkner and Psychology*. Eds. Donald M Kartiganer and Ann J. Abadie. Jackson: University Press of Mississippi, 1994. 78–122. Print.

Reinhard, Kenneth. "Disgrace and the Neighbor." *Encountering Disgrace: Reading and Teaching Coetzee's Novel*. Ed. William E. McDonald. Rochester: Camden House, 2009. 93–105. Print.

Rinon, Yoav. *Sadian Reflections*. Madison: Fairleigh Dickinson University Presses, 2005. Print.

Robinson, Edward S. *Shift Linguals: Cut-up Narratives from William S. Burroughs to the Present*. Amsterdam: Rodopi, 2011. Print.

Ronen, Ruth. *Aesthetics of Anxiety*. Albany: SUNY Press, 2009. Print.

Ross, Dorothy. "Freud and the Vicissitudes of Modernism in the United States, 1940–1980." *After Freud Left: A Century of Psychoanalysis in America. Ed. John C. Burnham*. Chicago: The University of Chicago Press, 2012. 163–188. Print.

Shamdasini, Sonu. "Psychotherapy, 1909: Notes on a Vintage." *After Freud Left: A Century of Psychoanalysis in America*. Ed. John C. Burnham. Chicago: The University of Chicago Press, 2012. 31–47. Print.

Shorter, Edward. *A Historical Dictionary of Psychiatry*. New York: Oxford University Press, 2005. Print.

Skau, Michael. *A Clown in a Grave: Complexities and Tensions in the Works of Gregory Corso*. Carbondale: Southern Illinois University Press, 1999. Print.

Skues, Richard. "Clark Revisited: Reappraising Freud in America." *After Freud Left: A Century of Psychoanalysis in America*. Ed. John C. Burnham. Chicago: The University of Chicago Press, 2012. 49–84. Print.

Vice, Sue. *Psychoanalytic Criticism: A Reader*. Cambridge: Polity press, 1996. Print.

Vidler, Anthony. *The Architectural Uncanny: Essays in the Modern Unhomely*. Cambridge: MIT Press, 1992. Print.

Vintiadis, Elly. "Why Certainty Is Not a Mansion." *Journal of Philosophical Research*. 31 (2006): 143–152. Print.

Wagner, Tilman Otto. *Beat Generation in a Scholastic Analysis*. Munich: Grin Verlag, 2011. Print.

Wright, Elizabeth. *Psychoanalytic Criticism: A Reappraisal*. Cambridge: Polity press, 1998. Print.

Zweig, Stefan,. *Mental Healers: Mesmer, Eddy, Freud*. Trans. Eden Paul and Cedar Paul London: Pushkin Press, 2012. Print.

Index

New Americanists in Poland

Edited by Tomasz Basiuk

Vol. 1 Tomasz Basiuk / Sylwia Kuźma-Markowska / Krystyna Mazur (eds.): the American Uses of History. Essays on Public Memory. 2011.

Vol. 2 Bohdan Szklarski (ed.): Quo vadis America? Conceptualizing Change in American Democracy. 2011.

Vol. 3 Irena Ksiezopolska: The Web of Sense. Patterns of Involution in Selected Works of Virginia Woolf and Vladimir Nabokov. 2012.

Vol. 4 Ewa Alicja Antoszek: Out of the Margins. Identity Formation in Contemporary Chicana Writings. 2012.

Vol. 5 Izabella Kimak: Bicultural Bodies. A Study of South Asian American Women's Literature. 2013.

Vol. 6 Jerzy Kamionowski / Jacek Partyka (eds.): American Wild Zones. Space, Experience, Consciousness. 2016.

Vol. 7 Małgorzata Ziółek- Sowińska: Images of The Apocalypse in African American Blues and Spirituals. Destruction in this Land. 2017.

Vol. 8 Agnieszka Łobodziec / Blossom N.Fondo (eds.): The Timeless Toni Morrison. The Past and The Present in Toni Morrison's Fiction. A Tribute to Toni Morrison on Occasion of Her 85th Birthday. 2017.

Vol. 9 Izabella Kimak / Julia Nikiel (eds.): Spaces of Expression and Repression in Post-Millennial North-American Literature and Visual Culture. 2017.

Vol. 10 Tomasz Sawczuk: On the Road to Lost Fathers: Jack Kerouac in a Lacanian Perspective. 2019.

www.peterlang.com